Paul Auster's Writing Machine

Paul Auster's Writing Machine

A Thing to Write With

Evija Trofimova

Bloomsbury Academic
An imprint of Bloomsbury Publishing Inc

B L O O M S B U R Y
NEW YORK · LONDON · OXFORD · NEW DELHI · SYDNEY

Bloomsbury Academic

An imprint of Bloomsbury Publishing Inc

1385 Broadway	50 Bedford Square
New York	London
NY 10018	WC1B 3DP
USA	UK

www.bloomsbury.com

Bloomsbury is a registered trade mark of Bloomsbury Publishing Plc

First published 2014
Paperback edition first published 2016

This edition contains minor corrections to the original edition.

Library of Congress Cataloging-in-Publication Data

A catalog record for this book is available from the Library of Congress

ISBN:	HB:	978-1-6235-6986-0
	PB:	978-1-5013-1825-2
	ePub:	978-1-6235-6854-2
	ePDF:	978-1-6235-6081-2

Typeset by Fakenham Prepress Solutions, Fakenham, Norfolk NR21 8NN
Printed and bound in the United States of America

Contents

Acknowledgments

This book was assembled over a couple of years and amongst a variety of places—Auckland (where I was inspired to write it), New York (where I wrote and lived through other books), and Riga (my home city, where I returned to put an end to writing).

There were also institutions whose academic and financial support allowed this project to mature into a book, chiefly the University of Auckland and Education New Zealand. I am thankful for their support.

I am very grateful to the one who inspired this project—Paul Auster himself, for his kindness and generosity, and for that afternoon we spent in Brooklyn's Park Slope sharing stories and cigars.

My colleagues, friends, and collaborators at the University of Auckland gave me guidance, encouragement, and examples of inspirational scholarship. Most of all, I owe my gratitude to Stephen Turner, my mentor extraordinaire, who taught me to be brave. Without him, I would have been lost.

I am thankful to Alex Calder, who provided a very useful lead; Jan Cronin, who diligently read everything I wrote; Lee Wallace, who was my first guide; and Emily Perkins, who was the kindest, most inspiring of writers. Kirby-Jane Hallum, Emma Willis, David Stillaman, Francisc Szekely, Keyvan Allahyari, Maria Prozesky and Dominic Griffiths were some of my great companions on the road, and each in their own way has left their footprints in this book.

I want to thank Barry Lewis, Dennis Barone and Scott Wilson, who all gave invaluable feedback on my work. Richard Klein and Darren Wershler-Henry let me quote abundantly from their influential books on smoking and typewriting. Editors Haaris Naqvi, Laura Murray, and Mary Al-Sayed believed in this project, made it happen, and looked after me in the process.

I am grateful to artists Sam Messer, Paul Karasik, David Mazzucchelli, and Jacques de Loustal, who were happy to let their art loose in this book, helping to evoke Auster's "writing machine." Readers of this book are lucky to have Alena Kavka's amazing sketches to add another dimension to it. My thanks also to Silja Pogule, who helped prepare these drawings for publication.

There were other people who have in their own special way been integral to the project. Jesús Ángel González helped me on my detective quest. Anne Garner guided me through Auster's manuscripts. Janet McAllister and Michael Onslow-Osborne helped me find my way through some entangled thoughts and eventually refine sections of the book. At the end, Misha Kavka graciously took upon herself the task of editing – an act of kindness that left me touched and ever so thankful.

I am happy to thank Ērika Zariņa, who welcomed me to Aotearoa. Līna Leitāne,

Ingus Jakstiņš, and little Jēkabs welcomed me to the best writing retreat, where I experienced months of bliss and inspiration, and not much writing. At the other end of the world, Elita Zante's intelligent heart gave me encouragement.

Later, Lee Baker gave me his writer's desk and never-ending support. This book is a testimony to his immense generosity and patience while I was writing. To him I am endlessly grateful.

Above all, I want to thank my family and good friends on both sides of the globe for bringing so much joy and purpose to my life and writing. I am particularly indebted to my parents, Maija and Gunārs. My gratitude for their support of all kinds goes beyond words.

And so I am reminded—even though things are inspiring, the world's true splendor is its people. For that, too, I am very grateful.

List of Illustrations

Preface

Introduction: Paul Auster's Intratext

Chapter 1: Smoke that Means the Entire World

Chapter 2: The Story of the Typewriter

Chapter 3: Doubles and Disappearances

Chapter 4: New York, Where All Quests Fail

Inconclusion

Preface

For Paul Auster, a story can grow out of a tin of cigars, or the pages of a blank notebook. For me, this book grew out of a particular image of a writer, the chain-smoking, typewriting New York writer so emblematic of Auster's life and work that it sums up my idea of both "Paul Auster" and his fictional surrogates. For me, Auster's work condenses into this single image, which painter Sam Messer so intensely explores and exploits in his portraits of the writer. This study largely originated from contemplating the significance of what I believed to be Auster's nostalgic attachment to this particular image of a writer.

But it all started much earlier. As a reader my interest in Auster's work was also marked by my fascination with this image, which I associated with proper, "real" writing, and with the nostalgia-infused things, objects and spaces required to assemble this archetypal idea: an old, rattling, manual typewriter, cigarettes and cigars, spiral notebooks and fountain pens, and the writer's solitude at his desk in a studio somewhere in New York, where his solipsistic mind generates captivating stories that gradually fill up the bare room. Back then, I never thought to question the value, functions and meaning of each of the elements in this peculiar "collaboration" between the writer and his writing tools that ultimately makes writing possible and creates our idea of "a writer." Back then, I could not see that the things we use to tell stories also tell stories.

Auster's earlier texts in particular often portray an isolated character writing about the process of writing and reflecting on the writing self, or writing about someone else's writing, or someone else as a writer. And although I never thought about myself in those terms, I nevertheless could not help but identify with this character and his existential and literary quests. I remember wanting to be a writer, too, and hoping to find myself in the sort of universe that this writer inhabited.

In his introduction to *The Writer's Desk*, a collection of black-and-white photographs depicting acclaimed writers at their desks amidst the tools and paraphernalia of their trade, John Updike states that "[h]ere, the intimacy of the literary act is caught *in flagrante delicto*: at these desks characters are spawned, plots are spun, imaginative distances are spanned."[1] One sees there typewriters, computers, notebooks, pens, pencils and ashtrays on these desks, the different tools described by the writers as having their own values, algorithms, rhythms and functions that are all set to work during the writing process. Yet, Auster's "writing machine"—the construct of the chain-smoking, typewriting New York writer figure—beats them all. This is because, as I will show, this writer-figure is not only the source of an Auster text but also the tool that writes it, and, likewise, its own end-result, as new texts about writer-characters are generated by the same "machine."

* * *

What if the writer were actually unaware of the effects his tools produced on his writing, I wondered? What if the tools wrote through the writer, as much as the writer wrote through them? When I think about Auster's oeuvre, I cannot not think about this correlation—between his highly self-referential and interconnected work, and the work of this writing machine that collaborates with the author's existential mind.

It started with the realization that Auster's work is porous and uncontainable: each of his texts leaks out into his other texts, creating a cross-spillage that knows no generic boundaries. Auster, of course, is mainly known as a novelist. But his films and other collaborative projects, located on the margins of traditional scholarship, are so closely entwined with the writer's canon that, far from being mere extensions of it, I could elevate them to the status of safe "entrance points" into his entire life-work. And so I started reading his oeuvre from its margins, and my long-harbored suspicion was confirmed: all his texts are one, and one, in turn, is many.

I named this bizarre interconnected structure "rhizomatic intratext." It echoes with the French philosophers Gilles Deleuze and Félix Guattari's concept of the rhizome, which is a sort of enmeshed and a-centered system of false roots, criss-crossing lines and interstitial spaces that resist genealogical readings. It challenges the arborescent (traditional Western) thought that is based on binary oppositions, genealogy and stable interpretation. And I realized that, in such a textual maze, the reader has only one option: to traverse the network of texts and read them "horizontally," tracing associations and connections established between them, observing how a plurality of meanings is simultaneously created and scattered through their shifting relationships.

And as I was doing so, I kept stumbling across the same node, a sort of "drifting" center, that seemed to hold the writer's work together. It was that epitomous writer-figure—which I saw as a type, a template, that Auster consistently puts in use to create his literary and filmic texts. That was when I first started to suspect the involvement of this writer-character in the process of writing. Its frequent appearance and re-enactment of the same set of values and functions suggested a sort of machinery at work.

The thought at first seemed preposterous—Auster, after all, is seen as an existential writer with a postmodern twist (or the other way round). But the old-fashioned image of the writer and his nostalgic writing tools, which seemed to speak of a simple and straightforward approach to writing, turned out to be more deceptive. I discovered there indeed was a "machinic" side to Auster's writing, which I thought to be co-responsible for the rhizomatic nature of his work.

To see this machine at work—to notice it, perhaps, for the first time—one has to pay closer attention to the writer's tools: typewriters, notebooks, fountain pens, cigarettes, New York cityscapes, and other "things" used in writing. For, in peculiar ways, as I found out, they actively participate in the creative processes, their power much greater than their ability to inspire. Like some sort of semi-automata, these prosthetic writing tools work to produce textual "copies," *mises en abyme*, narrative splits and alternative storylines. But all of this can only become visible, if one dares to turn away, for a moment, from the centered intent of the human author, and to look more closely at the work of "things."

I saw their acting happen through associations, which, unlike the intratextual connections established within the writer's own body of work, had a "source" beyond these texts and affected them from "outside." For each thing, when seen up close, opened up an entire discourse of its cultural history that contained layers and layers of narratives that all added to its shifting signification. I gave this cultural context the name "extratext" to separate it from my interest in Auster's oeuvre, which I called the "intratext." Things, I discovered, tend to be ambiguous semantic multiplicities and bundles of sometimes contradictory associations, so that, in the end, it is quite difficult for us to say what a thing means, what it functions as, or what exactly its effects are. And if a single thing (such as a cigarette, or a typewriter) can be semantically uncontainable, how much more so the story in which it "acts."

*   *   *

As I started work on this book, I thought it would be possible to maintain a required scholarly distance from the subject of my research in order to carry out and present an academic and objective study of his texts. But that was a naïve supposition. I quickly discovered that, when tracing associations in a rhizomatic formation, where the fictional is suffused with the real and *vice versa*, personal involvement on the scholar's part is impossible to avoid. The whole world was contained in Auster's "book," and that book spilled out into the world.

Very soon, I found myself smoking while exploring the "metaphorical potencies" of the cigar and cigarette smoke, the meaning of the process of smoking for the writer, and its agency in the creation of a story. And, while smoking, I was thinking about the ambiguous, fluid relationship between the author, his critic and the reader in producing meanings for texts, and I kept asking myself whether one could be a critic without being a reader, or a reader without being a critic? Where did they all come from, those associations evoked in my mind by the things I was reading about? Could a non-smoking reader ever understand why a cigarette meant no less than "the entire world" to Jean-Paul Sartre? Or, that it was, in fact, no less than another writing tool, like the writer's typewriter, the pen, the notebook, and the book, among other things?

And a "thing" such as New York, where Auster's writer-character is customarily situated and where he acts and writes, seemed not just a place or an event, but an experience that demanded to be lived through. And so, from my quiet study and my writer's desk, crammed with stacks of materials by and on the subject of my research, I suddenly found myself rambling through the noisy streets of New York, consumed not only by the city, but also by Auster's facto-fictional ("impossible") worlds that were even more treacherous, full of paradox. Strange things happened to me there, which are all faithfully documented in this book to give an account of my extraordinary quest, which started with some innocent questions about the ways of reading and writing, and the role that one writer's tools played in these acts.

Tracing the associations of Auster's facto-fictional New York meant reading his texts on location, yet as I followed the footsteps of his characters, and gradually found myself inhabiting "Austeralia," new questions arose that problematized my interpretative work. Was it Auster's New York that I was reconstructing from his texts, or was I, perhaps, constructing something new? I felt my presence in New York was somehow changing it, extending it, in the same way that this book hopes to add to my reader's sense of Auster's books. And so, along with the discoveries made, the implications of this study for Auster's intratextual writing machine—the questions of what and how much is being reflected, recreated or created in the process—remain open, resisting simple explanations.

Introduction: Paul Auster's Intratext

There is an oil painting by Sam Messer that depicts Auster as some kind of a seven-armed spider or a multi-limbed Hindu god of writing. The hands are busy and animated. One is holding a pencil, another holding a pen, its fingers also clasping what looks like a glass of whiskey. Ten fingers are dancing on the keys of a white typewriter; another hand is dialing a number on an old-fashioned analogue telephone. The sixth hand is tipping ash off a lighted cigarette (or rather, cigarillo), while the seventh is majestically supporting the writer's head on its palm. These hyperactive semi-automatic hands seem to be carrying out their tasks quite independently from the mind, which appears deceptively still, exhibiting a blank stare, completely lost in thought.

The typewriter is typing up *The Story of My Typewriter*, which is the name of the book where this painting appears. There is also a red spiral notebook lying next to the typewriter on its right; the writer's right-side hands in general are the pencil-pen-notebook-and-paper-holding hands. Yet it does not mean they are doing more writing than that left hand that holds the cigarillo. In the background, there is a horizontal line of shelved books that goes all the way from the one side of the picture to the other, and I can see that those are not only Paul Auster's books but also books by other writers, such as Cervantes' *Don Quixote*, with which Auster's work forms a subterranean lineage. The row of books separates the writer's figure and its paraphernalia from the background against which it is set—a cityscape of New York.

The frantic work of hands and the objects they are tied to are no less intriguing to me than the dazed stillness of the writer's mind behind those blank eyes. Things seem to have come alive in this painting, whereas the mind remains a mystery, a silent puzzle, a locked room. Perhaps that solipsistic mind is exploding from activity, and is as loud, and fast, and hectic as the streets of the big city in its background. Perhaps it is, as we speak, traversing those same streets, walking down those alleyways, taking unexpected turns, finding itself in dead-ends, and running into strange encounters, as one so often does in Auster's work.

I think that everything by Paul Auster that you have read, watched, observed and listened to over the past thirty years is the result of the work of that mysterious mind in collaboration with its many hands and tools. It may be that the only way to speak about this process of writing is by using metaphors, although even they fall short of describing what I am trying to convey here. A cobweb-weaving spider is not so much a metaphor for the author, or the writer, as it is an abstraction used to relate the complexity of this part-machinic collaboration and the ways it functions. The spider-machine weaves an elaborate and extensive web of texts that is so complex and uncontainable that it cannot be adequately depicted in any way. Its cobweb spreads in all directions, its strands intersecting at the most unusual

Figure 0.1 The "writing machine" at work. A portrait by Sam Messer, "The Wizard of Brooklyn", from *The Story of My Typewriter*.

places, weaving back into themselves, cloning each other and canceling each other out, multiplying and disappearing. The spider weaves itself into the web where it appears in a multitude of transfigurations, filling it with miniature replicas of the self. It is multiplying itself.

Such metaphors are, of course, banal, even if helpful. How could I show you this writing machine at work? At this point, I have no choice but to commit a slightly sinister and violent act. It needs to be done for this book to work. In order to expose the creative agency of writing tools, such as cigarettes, notebooks or New York cityscapes, we need to silence what we conventionally believe to be the main source of expression and meaning: the human author with his realms of emotion and thought. I am afraid it means no less than killing, in a literary sense, the empirical author Paul Auster, who, in spite of his zeal for postmodern literary games, is equally (increasingly?) being recognized as an existential-humanist writer. It might be that only through such removal of authorial authority can we distance ourselves from the assumed natural order of things that prescribes how something is read and what something means. Only when "the author is dead" can we freely roam through his work and pick out neglected strands of texts or notice their less apparent aspects (accidental connections, unwanted meanings, alternative truths).

One such neglect is related to our perception of the body of this author's creative work. Of course, here we must presuppose that there exists a certain assortment of texts whose authorship, regardless of their genre and media, or the number of people involved in production, can be at least partly ascribed to Auster—all this while keeping in mind that, as Michel Foucault reminds us, the idea of a complete oeuvre itself is an illusory one.[1] But if we wanted to list all the published work by Auster so far, this is more or less what we would get: 17 novels, including one under a pseudonym and three shorter "novellas"; nine collections of essays and memoirs; six collections of poetry; one work of prose poetry; two edited collections (of French poetry and of American stories); one collection of correspondence with another writer; four films, independently or collaboratively directed; five screenplays; a number of translations of French prose and poetry; and around a dozen other miscellaneous collaborative projects with painters, photographers, conceptual artists, comic artists, radio listeners and jazz musicians.

We mainly recognize Auster as a novelist, while his other projects tend to remain marginalized by readers and critics. Perhaps, it is easier to "recognize" a novel than a prose poem such as *White Spaces*, which more than 30 years ago marked Auster's shift from writing poetry to writing in other forms, to being "a writer." There is also the question of adaptations. Something like the graphic novel *City of Glass*, adapted by artists Paul Karasik and David Mazzucchelli in 2004 to great critical acclaim, exists in its own right, and yet is also firmly tied to Auster's oeuvre. It contains less text than the original novel, yet not a single word there has been changed ("adapted"). We associate the book with Auster and read it as a companion to his *City of Glass*. After all, there is also a clear statement on the copyright page that the rights to the material belong to Paul Auster as much as they do to the two artists. These are tricky questions, of course, and I cannot claim to be able to provide satisfactory answers to them all. But this book, which studies his marginal projects (films and collaborations), aims to discuss a "Paul Auster, writer" whose creative output goes well beyond the novelistic genre.

In a way, this is a very simplified outlook, and my reduction of the author's creative work of more than 30 years to one abstract image (a web) might seem heretical. And yet, Franco Moretti once similarly justified his "distant," diagram-based reading as a valid form of literary knowledge: "fewer elements, hence a sharper sense of their overall interconnection"[2] and of their "[s]hapes, relations, structures. Forms. Models…"[3] Those textual interconnections, structures and relations are exactly what I am interested in because I think they are directly related to the writer's "writing machine" and the way it "writes."

And so I want to start this book by sketching out those territories that are occupied both by Auster's texts and by critical responses to them. Think of this introductory chapter as a preliminary investigation before embarking on the actual quest. As in traditional detective work, we will start with the discovery of "the body" and "the crime." What is it that we have here, and how to explain this mystery? After which we can ask, what made a thing like this possible, how was the act done? In our case, of course, we suspect that answers to the mystery of Auster's "text" lie in the work of a writing machine that we will look at in parts in the following chapters. Indeed, think of this introduction as the necessary preparation stage at which evidence is gathered, scrutinized and compared, and conclusions are drawn about its nature. There certainly is a lot of challenging and contradictory material to inspect.

The interpretive work on Paul Auster's work itself has a history of some 30 years. The discourse surrounding his name conjures up a variety of claims, facts, questions, opinions and exegeses. What is this Paul Auster like? If we followed some of the associations established with his name, we might, for example, notice that the critical path often leads to a certain split in his scholarship. The two main critical approaches to Auster's works, which are roughly described as the humanist and the postmodernist, result from a schizophrenic reading experience: the humanist themes of loss, fate, chance, identity and creativity appear at odds with the postmodern intertextuality, self-reflexivity and open semiosis. "Are there ... two writers, humanist and postmodernist, co-existing in Paul Auster?" asks one reviewer.[4] Many scholars note this difficulty of critical placement ("The mystery is this—how to best classify Auster's works?" asks Barry Lewis; "His oeuvre is difficult to categorize," states Rüdiger Heinze).[5] A taxonomy of Auster's work proves to be a never-ending struggle.

We might also notice that reading Auster often means not really knowing your whereabouts, or whether you stand on sure ground at all. In the end, perhaps, to be an Auster critic means to always be slightly lost. But for those who, in the hope of new discoveries, want to take the risk of wandering through yet unknown territories, the important thing is to grow comfortable with the feeling of slight discomfort at times.

I want to begin my exploration from where I started—the portrait of the chain-smoking, typewriting writer, which I will use as my point of entrance into Auster's body of work. This figure of the writer is both a motif that proliferates in his work and an image associated with the empirical author himself. One encounters that same writer (who lives and works in Brooklyn and smokes little Dutch cigars while contemplating chance and coincidence and the nature and meaning of identity and language, and who drafts his stories in spiral notebooks and then types them up on a manual typewriter) not only in Auster's novels but also in his films and various collaborative projects, and interviews published in popular media.

Assembled from a conspicuously similar set of elements and placed in similar narrative situations, his characters on the surface level all appear alike. So whenever I think of a writer like Quinn (*City of Glass*), I also think of August Brill (*Man in the Dark*), Paul Benjamin (*Smoke*), Peter Aaron (*Leviathan*), Paul Auster and "Paul Auster," the A. ("The Book of Memory") and even the "you" (*Winter Journal*), who all smoke and typewrite, and live in New York, and struggle with crises of sorts.[6] That immediately raises questions about the differences between the real author and the implied author of Auster's work, Paul Auster the character (as in *City of Glass*), and Auster's many other fictional stand-ins.

The majority of critics in the past, among them Dennis Barone, Aliki Varvogli, and Markus Rheindorf, have commented on Auster's tendency to inscribe himself in his texts by obliterating the borders between fact and fiction.[7] In Auster's pseudo-autobiographical text *The Invention of Solitude*, a character whom A. knew, a composer named S., had "made the equation between his life and his work," so that he "was no longer able to distinguish between the two."[8] The Auster reader, too, is confronted with a similar equation that erases the boundaries between fact and fiction, and problematizes the search for any fixed authorial intent. The life of Auster's writer-characters is like their work, and the life and work of Auster are like those of his characters, and *vice versa*. Here is one conclusion, then: a more accurate way of describing Auster's oeuvre would be to call it his "life-work."

What are the interpretative consequences of the critical reader's realization that numerous details and facts related to the characters, names, events, situations and entire stories resonate with Auster's "real" life? I see one apparent consequence. Because it is only possible to speak of Auster's life-work (in which his fiction is inseparable from his life, and the other way round) and because, on the surface level, the empirical author, the writer Paul Auster, and the writer-characters of his works appear to be the same (assembled by the same set of associations), I have to attribute to Auster's own commentary on his work the same significance as to his creative works—no less, no more than that. This is slightly different from ascribing critical authority to "the author." If the factual is equated to the fictional, both have equal value: the significance of personal commentary is the same as of that which gets expressed through fictional work. In other words, I have to approach Auster's own explanation of his texts as expressed through public interviews the same way as I would approach his novels or films. It is in this sense that Auster with his own commentary will be allowed to participate in the interpretation of his work.

Paul Auster, "Paul Auster," his many doppelgängers, and the texts authored by any of these identities, however heterogeneous, seem to evoke almost the same set of associations: Brooklyn, Manhattan, detective, anti-detective, quest, the double, the city streets, an empty study room, baseball, urban labyrinths, Edgar Allan Poe, Nathaniel Hawthorne, Herman Melville, Jewishness, the figure of the absent father, storytelling, smoking, typewriting, coincidence, Franz Kafka, Samuel Beckett, loss, identity, failure, existentialism. Some of these recurring motifs, as Rheindorf points out, are suggested by the titles of Auster's texts themselves—solitude, hunger, chance, illusion, invention, disappearance.[9] Other themes derive from tangible things and biographical facts from Auster's own life, such as manual typewriters, spiral notebooks, Schimmelpenninck cigars, years spent in Paris, translations of French poetry, and undergraduate studies at Columbia University.

Critic Michelle Banks has noted that recurring motifs for which Auster is "certainly known"—that is, "artist-characters, the Fall, Brooklyn settings, story-telling, and so on"—have produced over time certain expectations in Auster's readers, who "now may approach a new Auster novel as a kind of ludic game of recognition."[10] Indeed, this important question will re-emerge whenever we stumble across familiar patterns in Auster texts. What happens to the process of interpretation when the reader realizes he or she is traversing the same terrain again, finding him- or herself walking through the same door, entering the same spaces and encountering the same plots, characters, situations?[11]

But readers and critics of Auster's work are by no means abandoned on their own to deal with the task of disentangling the web of repetitive, intermingled texts, identities and authorships. They have the reassuring company of Auster's characters themselves. Protagonists of various Auster texts (*The Locked Room*, *Leviathan*, "Portrait of an Invisible Man," *The Book of Illusions* ...) undertake similar interpretive activities, and their attempts to understand (or rather, reconstruct) the identity and life-work of someone else are so scrupulously investigative that they resemble detective work.

Some of Auster's texts suggest that, in the words of the protagonist of *The Locked Room*, a human life (a life-work?) can be read as "no more than the sum of contingent facts."[12] "Contingent facts as opposed to necessary facts," adds the narrator of *Winter Journal*.[13] Or, to use the almost identical words expressed by Anne Blume from *In the Country of Last Things*, human life is "no more than the sum of manifold contingencies."[14] (It is exactly in moments like this that I feel I am re-entering the same door.) Yet Auster's writer-turned-detective characters, like Auster himself in the memoir devoted to his deceased father ("Portrait of an Invisible Man"), constantly have to face failure when trying to read the other's life as a sum, or assemblage, of certain events, objects, texts, *contingencies*. We are told that to attempt to uncover the essence of someone else's life and work means "to recognize, right from the start, that the essence of [such a] project is failure."[15]

Why is that failure, and why does mathematics not work? Because of the limitation that this book also exhibits: the attempt to understand always leads to an attempt to find a structure, an order, some sort of a center, some sort of core elements, but such reduction can only work for methodological purposes. "Writing isn't mathematics, after all," states Auster.[16] Any reduction is superimposed on something that is essentially irreducible ("a book is composed of irreducible elements," he adds).[17] The structure of Auster's body of work cannot be adequately presented in the form of a diagram or map. I, for instance, think of Auster's texts as forming clusters and assemblages—in fact, each text is an assemblage itself—but it is impossible to draw exact borderlines around those, or ascribe any exclusive meaning to them.

In their work *A Thousand Plateaus: Capitalism and Schizophrenia*, French philosophers Gilles Deleuze and Félix Guattari ask questions about the boundaries of a book and, indeed, "literature" in its entirety, among other entities. They call a book "a multiplicity," which refuses unity. Both philosophers, in their anti-humanist approach, deny the book a subject, an object and a singular or pre-existing point of origin, such as an author. In this way, they uproot the classical Western arborescent model of thought and perception, which emphasizes origin and unidirectional evolution, and replace it with the freely-moving rhizome.[18] "A book is an assemblage," they conclude, "and as such is unattributable. It is a multiplicity—but we don't know yet what the multiple entails when it is no longer attributed, that is, after it has been elevated to the status of the substantive ... Literature is an assemblage."[19]

In a similar vein, Michel Foucault talks in *The Archaeology of Knowledge* about the impossibility of a unity of discourse and of the idea of a finite oeuvre with one identifiable author: "The frontiers of a book are never clear-cut: beyond the title, the first lines, and the last full stop, beyond its internal configuration and its autonomous form, it is caught up in a system of references to other books, other texts, other sentences: it is a node within a network."[20] An obvious statement of intertextuality, this also reminds us of Roland Barthes' postulate of the death of the author, which perceives reading practice as a collaboration between the text, the reader and the presumed author, while the book itself becomes a site for connections with other readings, texts and experiences. Or I could say this: a book, rather than being a clearly structured, well-defined unity that generates a singular reading, is itself a network, an assemblage of discrete parts set in a dynamic relationship with other assemblages. It is, therefore, capable of producing an infinite number of "effects."

This thought is easily applicable to my object of inquiry. In fact, in one of his early texts, *The Invention of Solitude*, Auster elaborates on the same implicit idea of reading the world (and the text) in terms of networks of assemblages. The following lines are not just a statement about the forceful relationship that exists among semantic textual bundles. It is no less than Auster's statement about his life-work:

> [T]he world is not just the sum of things that are in it. It is *the infinitely complex network of connections* among them. As in the meanings of words, *things take on meaning only in relationship to each other* … it is possible for events in one's life to rhyme as well … *The rhyme they create when looked at together alters the reality of each.* Just as two physical objects, when brought into proximity of each other, give off electromagnetic forces that not only effect the molecular structure of each but the space between them as well, altering, as it were, the very environment, so it is that two (or more) rhyming events set up a connection in the world, adding one more synapse to be routed through the vast plenum of experience.[21] (my emphasis)

Auster's work rhymes with many things, and many other texts. It is highly intertextual, as suggested by the number of essays and a monograph published on his literary affiliation with Franz Kafka, Samuel Beckett, Nathaniel Hawthorne, Herman Melville, Edgar Allan Poe and Knut Hamsun, among others.[22] However, what I am interested in more are those spaces in-between, which open up when we consider Auster's work taken all together. I am interested in the intricate relationships woven among his texts themselves.

Many Auster scholars have noted the self-referencing, cross-referencing, repetition and replication in his work, but the implications of these traits across his work of all genres and media seem to ask for more critical attention. It has become quite common for Auster critics to say that his texts deal with a limited set of themes, or that they are all pseudo-autobiographical. Yet the effects of the reader's recognition of this "limitedness" on the perception of the text(s) and production of meaning(s) should be investigated more. Perhaps it is criticism's gray area that is customarily being avoided. It takes the focus away from what is considered unique, idiosyncratic and human in an author's work in favor of abstract repetitions, patterns and machines. Does it appear blasphemous?

Michelle Banks is among the minority of critics who recognize that Auster's works have "consistently pursued these very multiple dynamics of connections."[23] And I agree with her that there are "phenomenological and material issues inevitably brought about by this particular type of multi-textual connectivity," or interpretive issues complicated by intratextuality ("auto-intertextuality").[24] Throughout Auster's intratext, there are texts that "rhyme," look the same, or appear to know each other. These *intra*textual spaces where connections get set up, meanings altered and new synapses routed are the no man's land that Auster talks about in the excerpt above. Invisible but invasive, they destabilize the ontological grounds of the already marked territories, of what the reader takes to be singular texts produced by a particular author. But within Auster's web-like intratext, any text not only refers to another text, but in many cases also becomes a source for a new project and a new offshoot.[25] It is impossible to talk about the interpretation of a single Auster book because, strictly speaking, there is no such thing as a single, self-contained Auster text. Let me show you exactly what I mean.

Uncontainable assemblages

Perhaps this delusion that a text can be "contained" is partly the fault of the medium through which it gets channeled. As I am writing these lines, I am suspiciously eyeing that pile of hard-bound Auster novels that are sitting neatly on the desk in front of me. A printed book (which is a reading machine no less than a typewriter is a writing machine) prescribes a certain way of reading because of its inherent nature, or its "affordances," as semiotician and media theorist Gunther Kress calls it. This way of thinking about the book suggests that a text has an identifiable starting point (the first sentence on the first page), a linear development (which in Western societies flows from the top left corner of a page to the bottom right), and a clear closure (the final punctuation mark used in the book). The materiality of the printed book attempts to persuade us that a text can be enclosed within its two covers. In such a way, the medium of the printed book makes us forget about that infinite openness of a text that Deleuze and Foucault, among other thinkers, reiterate.

Auster—perhaps unknowingly—warns us against this false sense of security in his early work *White Spaces*, which itself is an ambiguous amalgamation of philosophical poetry and elliptical prose, and as such cannot be "contained" within any given genre:

> In the realm of the naked eye nothing happens that does not have its beginning and its end. And yet nowhere can we find the place or the moment at which we can say, beyond a shadow of a doubt, that this is where it begins, or this is where it ends ... Whoever tries to find refuge in any one place, in any one moment, will never be where he thinks he is.[26]

And I am thinking: Auster's books are almost anti-books because they are remarkably "open." And it is not that this invisible openness has passed unnoticed by Auster scholars. The fact that Auster's narratives do not want to comfortably sit between the covers of their books, and that they prefer circularity and embranchment over linearity, is a feature that has constantly both excited and frustrated his critics, resulting in its own tradition of reading this author's written work.

It seems to me that there is a particular way of thinking about the openness of Auster's texts. Such texts are generally seen as practicing tenets of postmodern theory, accounting not only for their destabilized authorship and self-referentiality, but also their lack of closure and somewhat elliptical quality.[27] Since this criticism emerged in the mid-1990s, it has mainly focused on separate early and late novels by Auster, such as *The New York Trilogy*, *In the Country of Last Things*, *Moon Palace*, *Travels in the Scriptorium* and *Man in the Dark*, which we tend to think of as paradigmatic of Auster's postmodernism.

But this points to a slightly curious tendency. Although we seem to recognize the openness of the narrative structures in Auster books, and even their embeddedness in or connection with his other texts (as in the case of *The New York Trilogy*), we still seem to insist on treating them as separate entities. We are reluctant to consider seriously what Auster himself implicitly states in one interview—that all his books are in fact the same book. This type of criticism may note the connections between Auster's texts, but does not fully acknowledge the extent to which all his texts are inter-connected—inseparable from, and becoming, one another. Not just one or two related books, but his entire oeuvre. And, I think, once the reader recognizes the connection, there is no other way but to follow it.

This is how it works. In her essay on Auster's "postmodernist fiction," Dragana Nikolic points out that the randomness and complexity of his narrative structure, and his reliance on "chance," gives the writer freedom for "endless possibilities and combi-nations."[28] No matter how hard the reader tries to interpret the text—and Nikolic points in particular to the "detective" novels of *The New York Trilogy*—"the emaciated story always escapes him, until the reader is left with the feeling that nothing is sure and nothing adds up."[29] This overwhelming uncertainty, and the lack of a visible solution at the end, prompts the reader to consider alternative versions of it, and to "look for" answers elsewhere.

At the same time, Auster's deliberate inclusion in the text of intertextual references to his other works makes it almost certain that the reader will take them as clues. Towards the end of *The Locked Room* (the last book of *The New York Trilogy*), the anonymous narrator and protagonist suddenly directs the reader's attention to the previous two novellas and announces, unexpectedly, that all three stories "are finally the same story."[30] That suggests that the key to understanding each of them is their relationship to the other two texts. The situation becomes even more complicated: the diegesis of one story is no longer limited to one book, but encompasses the writer's other works as well, leaking from one text into another.[31]

It has, of course, become a commonplace to view the three pseudo-detective novels (or "novellas") of *The New York Trilogy*—*City of Glass*, *Ghosts* and *The Locked Room*—as one super-novel. Republished under the name of a trilogy, the three texts, although different in terms of style, story-worlds and narrative voice, show similarities in the development of the plot, themes and characters. All three protagonists—Quinn, Blue and the anonymous "I"—are isolated writers turned into self-proclaimed detectives who undertake cases that require them to construct false identities for themselves and to search for and spy on other people. Their investigations at the end turn inwards, becoming an introspective exploration of their own fragile, shifting selves. There is, as Robert Briggs has noted, "a certain persistence of duplicitous identities."[32]

And there are more clues. Not only characters with duplicitous identities but also things surrounding them establish such affiliations. The sense of apparent interconnectedness is further enhanced by other shared items—such as the notorious (red) notebook. In *City of Glass*, Quinn as well as his suspect, Peter Stillman Sr., both make notes in a red notebook; in the novel *Ghosts*, the character named Black writes in a notebook of unspecified color; and in the last part of the trilogy, a red notebook is owned by the mysterious Fanshawe. Early on in each of the texts we are told that the notebook might be crucial in deciphering the story—that it is more than just a prop—which seems like an encouragement to consider all three texts together because a notebook appears in all of them.[33] But instead of a solution, clarity and sense of completeness, the credulous reader feels even greater confusion, because the words which promise a larger singular meaning—"these three stories are finally the same story"—are as mysterious as each of the three novels.

But *The New York Trilogy* with its red notebook is even more deceptive than this. It is not even a trilogy (and I am not the only one to claim that). Briggs has torn out a piece of Auster's intratext to show, under close inspection, that it is a tissue made out of possibly countless texts.[34] He set out to decipher the "mystery" of the red notebook (what exactly is the red notebook and who, after all, is its author?) to find its origin and follow its journey through different hands. This initially led Briggs to a collection of essays that Auster published eight years after the trilogy and which the writer entitled *The Red Notebook: True Stories, Prefaces and Interviews by the Author of The New York Trilogy and Mr. Vertigo*. This volume consists of two parts, one of which has the title *The Red Notebook*, and three sub-parts (a trilogy!). That already problematizes the issue of the "original" red notebook. A statement that Auster makes in one of the interviews published in this collection, that "the *Trilogy* grows directly out of *The Invention of Solitude*,"[35] throws Briggs back to that work, which Auster published in 1982 and which is traditionally read as autobiographical.[36] In the course of this investigation, Briggs not only encounters nine (or eleven, according to another way of calculating) texts that are related to a/the red notebook, but he also draws attention to the impossibility of setting borders between the end of one story and the beginning of another, and between what is fiction and what is autobiography.[37]

We know that Auster admits in *The Red Notebook* that *City of Glass* could be read as "a kind of fictitious subterranean autobiography," an alternative history of himself, which would have happened, had he not met his wife Siri.[38] Briggs concludes: "Consequently, or according to Auster at least, *City of Glass* (and perhaps the entire *Trilogy*) is not the work of detective fiction that it always seems to be taken for, but rather is a work of autobiography, albeit a fictitious one."[39] At the same time, he also doubts the claim made by *The Red Notebook* to tell "true stories," also calling this book "a sort of 'fictitious autobiography'."[40] In an early interview (the same interview in which he claims that the trilogy grew out of *Invention of Solitude*), Auster admits: "I don't think of it as an autobiography so much as a meditation about certain questions, using myself as the central character." And so we realize: every text is a part or fragment of another text, and not what it initially appears. *The New York Trilogy* is not a trilogy any longer, but something else altogether, while the boundaries of this "else" are quite impossible to locate.

What does this mean for the reader, the critic? Texts which duplicate or reflect each other and which leak and spill over their own boundaries open up possibilities for ever new readings. The conclusion that Briggs reaches at the end of his dissection of *The New York Trilogy* points to the impossibility of a singular reading, given each work's openness to infinity—to infinite interpretations. Briggs calls that "the endless fiction of Paul Auster," because each text is "always simultaneously more than one (a multiplicity) and less than one (a part)."[41] And "so we come back to where we started," he concludes towards the end of the essay.[42] A certain circularity marks the textual relationships within Auster's intratext. As his texts endlessly point to each other, they turn from over-determined signifiers into emptied-out signs that are trapped in cyclical cross-referencing.[43]

Perhaps *The New York Trilogy* was too obvious an example to illustrate this point. We should find more supportive evidence. So, think of *Leviathan*, which was published in 1992 and which critics tend to view as the most political of Auster's novels. Because of the conspicuous similarities in the plot, motifs and set-up of the relationships between the main characters with the above-mentioned novella *The Locked Room*, to some extent this novel wants to be read—so both Aliki Varvogli and Ilana Shiloh note—as an alternative version of the latter.[44] Here is Varvogli explaining it:

> If, as Paul Auster has remarked, all his novels are really the same book, *Leviathan* is another version of *The Locked Room*. Both narratives involve a quest for a missing writer in the course of which the narrator, a writer himself, confronts the problem of gaining access to another person's self and trying to turn the events of another man's life into a coherent narrative.[45]

And if that is the case, why should we not assume that both novels could well be read as "other versions" of *The Invention of Solitude*, Auster's first published prose book? After all, it too deals with Auster's futile struggles as a young author to make sense of the life and character of his father (who has suddenly passed away and is "missing") by arranging his memories of him in a meaningful "biography." And so we have arrived at yet another potentially infinite (auto)fiction.

One encounters many paradoxes when reading Auster's work. I think, for example, that his texts want to be read together while resisting any ontological coherence. When you notice the many striking connections and similarities between these texts, you feel compelled to view them together, as if they were part of the same diegetic world. You want, in Banks' words, "[these fictional] worlds to make sense *together*"[46] (her emphasis). Yet any "togetherness" of Auster's intratext is a problematic notion, or so Banks concluded after her attempt to disentangle the conflicting biographies of recurrent Auster characters that reappear in different texts. When the "life stories" of certain recurring Auster characters (Quinn, Peter Stillman, Anna Blume, David Zimmer, etc.) are considered together, they fail to make sense and are, in fact, "impossible." Although there is a certain Auster intratext constantly at work, we will never be able to perceive it as a coherent "sum of particulars."

Intratextual interpretation, where one text would help explain another, does not lead very far—or, rather, it leads to infinity. That same warning also applies to any text containing *mises en abyme*, or texts-within-texts (think of *The Book of Illusions*, think of *Lulu on the Bridge*), which further enhance the sense of interpretive abyss. It seems that the meaning of such books is and is not significantly tied to their own embedded texts. One closes such books with a strong sense that they have a multitude of possible readings, all of which simultaneously co-exist.

I think of Auster's texts as polyhedric, where the surface they reveal depends on your viewing angle. Each text can be read in at least several ways, but none is fully sustainable. This interpretive multiplicity largely results from the relationship between the texts themselves. That is one conclusion we can make. It is a structural issue and a question that pertains to the entire oeuvre, rather than to separate texts and their peculiar hermeneutics. The interpretative challenges of Auster's life-work occur not only because he exercises the postmodern sensibility of reflexivity, as suggested by many of his critics (Stephen Bernstein, Madeleine Sorapure and Brendan Martin, among others). The essence of the problem does not lie in the unsolvability of textual puzzles like Auster's early "meta-anti-detective stories" (as Sorapure calls them); it lies in the inherent dynamic multiplicity of every Auster text and its constituent parts—each is an assemblage, made of assemblages, which are part of other larger assemblages, and so on *ad infinitum*.

No wonder that in such a network of *mises en abyme* any attempts to "detect" narrative closure, stable authorship, traceable origins, or one interpretative solution, regardless of the text's medium or genre, are necessarily bound to fail. We witnessed earlier that Banks and Briggs both fail in their tongue-in-cheek genealogical tracings. It is simply a futile task. The quests that Auster's writer-detective characters undertake, and what the reader wants to follow, are genealogical in their nature, but genealogy, which implies traceable origins, beginnings and ends, is an illusory construct. I will return to this question of genealogy later on in the book.

For now, a genuine question comes up: so what is there left for the reader to do? Perhaps, if genealogy fails, one has to learn to read non-genealogically—horizon-tally. Instead of "detecting" a meaning, an Auster reader could follow the given leads without the false expectation of ever arriving at one final destination. One could trace the dynamic connections and associations formed within the writer's intratext, and explore how their meanings are assembled and simultaneously scattered.[47] That would be an invitation to read not just the lines, or between the lines—but to read across the lines, traversing across the no-man's lands that lie between what we take to be boundaries of books and films.

In his study of the connections of interior and exterior landscapes in Auster's work, Rheindorf suggests an approach that is vaguely reminiscent of such tracing, saying that "[i]n the world(s) of Auster's writing, the only alternative to an enumeration of parts is to read the world as made up of connections."[48] "If one accepts ... that every-thing is connected to everything else," he writes,

> ... then it must be possible for the reader to choose a given element in Auster's
> work and trace its development over thirty or so years of writing, through poetry,

essays and fiction. Not only should it be possible to pick such an element from his first or last works and follow it to its respective conclusion or beginning, but also to start somewhere in the middle, and uncover that particular strand extending in both directions across time.[49]

And that is what Rheindorf has done by picking from the canon of Auster's texts a dozen or so "elements" that he believes to be the main features of the writer's work. The result is a sort of catalogue of a number of characteristics conventionally attributed to Auster's texts that Rheindorf also identifies as symptomatic of the author's work. His list of "given elements" includes thematic continuities (the road/street metaphor, holism, solipsism, the language of innocence, and so on), narrative strategies (intertextuality, self-referentiality, meta-fictionality, *mises en abyme*, unreliable narration, etc.), and cultural and ideological critique (gender and class issues, political commentary, the politics of money, etc.).

Thematic continuities? There is another customary way of thinking about Paul Auster and his work. Continuity suggests unity and sameness, not poststructural fragmentedness. It connotes a flow, a movement along already-marked tracks and riverbeds. It also connotes repetition, which has a cyclical (or, perhaps, spiral) nature, as in *The Inner Life of Martin Frost*, where Auster uses the metaphor of a spiral to talk about the growth of stories.

Auster's texts show a certain (spiraling?) sameness—a sort of recognizable "Austerness." So it can be understood why critics find it difficult to avoid focusing on a very limited set of motifs in his work.[50] In fact, as Aliki Varvogli has noted, if Auster claims that "all his books are really the same book," a study of his oeuvre "needs to take into account how the author gives a different treatment each time to a limited set of questions or themes."[51] And so the studies of Auster's work published over the last decade mainly focus on the common and shared elements of his writing: patterns of themes, characters, plots or narrative forms that are seen as repeatedly being rehearsed anew. This kind of criticism takes a more "humanistic" view of Auster—it focuses on the representation of certain motifs that are recognized as belonging to the great commonplaces of human existence.

Here are three examples, monographs on Auster's work, by Carsten Springer (*Crises: The Works of Paul Auster*, 2001), Ilana Shiloh (*Paul Auster and Postmodern Quest: On the Road to Nowhere*, 2002) and Mark Brown (*Paul Auster*, 2007), which all argue for the thematic unity of Auster's oeuvre.[52] An existential crisis, says Springer, is what, regardless of the work's genre, always serves as the initial catalyst for an Auster story that then becomes a story of redemption. That continuity indeed is difficult to miss.[53] For Springer, other hallmark themes—loss, solitude and isolation, quest and challenge, literature and writing, chance and fate, annihilation and emptiness—are also to be read in relation to identity crises. Shiloh picks out another type of sameness: the narrative form of quest or journey, which seems to hold Auster's novels together. For her, as for Springer, Auster's texts revolve around identity and selfhood, and place the protagonists "on the quest ... for the mystery of the self,"[54] which is both a physical and inner journey. The third example of sameness is the continuity of space. What unites Auster's various textual assemblages is the urban space (mainly New York) that they all gravitate towards, says Brown in his monograph. He picks on the same motifs as identified by Springer and Shiloh (self, journey). But, for him, identity is intangibly tied to the environment in which the character is placed. Other continuous Auster themes, "loss and disconnection, language and storytelling, and illusion," are also all "affected by place."[55] Auster's life-work is an answer to the question of "how the individual locates her or himself in the world."[56]

This little review suggests that crisis, quest and space constitute three different yet related concepts that are seen by scholars as consistently questioned and explored in Auster's work. It seems to acknowledge that there are explicit or implicit thematic patterns that unite all of his texts. In fact, regardless of their chosen focus, the scholars suggest that, essentially, Auster's stories are variations on one and the same theme: human identity. The related concepts of crisis, quest and urban space are all made subservient to it.

Such a suggestion adds some human pulse to Auster's work, which becomes audible to his readers who seek in it some resonance with their own existential struggles. That is a reason why Auster's work keeps speaking to us and why we keep responding by reading it. Its appeal is deeply existential. Yet I am more interested in those things that allow a book to come into being, even before it becomes "a human being."[57] The view that only notes the writer's human impulse to write misses all the other reasons why, and ways how, one's life-work gets written, spread, connected, read and re-written. It takes away the credit that other organic and non-organic entities, things and concepts should receive for their (co)participation in the creative process. The presence of these non-human agents, the writer's "tools," is not merely a precondition for writing. These things do more than create "a story." They account, I think, for the machinic side of Auster's life-work—the intratext—itself.

For example, to the question "Why is it so difficult for the writer to let his story end with the final full stop?" a common critical commentary might be this: Auster is aware that there are no satisfactory solutions to his existential (or linguistic) quests. They are often left unsolved, the stories collapsing upon themselves at the end. Since a solution to the narrative predicament is difficult (if not impossible) at the end of an Auster story, the same scenario gets explored and rehearsed in different variations, reiterating the same concerns.[58] That is one way of looking at it.

But here is what I think. There is a machinic side to Paul Auster's writing that places little interest in reaching any epistemological goals, in bringing a story to a closure. In fact, it does the opposite. It is directly related to his writing tools (typewriters, cigarettes, doppelgängers), and finds its expression through his use of the "machine" (through smoking, through typewriting, through introducing doubles in his texts). A kind of *perpetuum mobile*, it never ceases to replicate, emulate, transform, and pursue connections and associations in and among his texts.

The combination of these two elements (the human writer and his writing machine) creates an unusual synthesis. There is a seemingly autonomous and machinic process of writing that is constantly multiplying and transforming the text, but at the center of this writing—one author's existential journey, a genuine philosophical question which gets expressed by the mind lost in thought that we see in Sam Messer's apt portrait of Auster. This paradox is not easy to explain via the traditional categories (humanist-postmodern), which is why his exegetes have always struggled to classify his work. But I think that there is a way that allows us to see Auster's life-work in a more encompassing way, dismissing any concerns about this apparent "dichotomy."

Let me explain what I mean. The idea, for example, that this book proposes about the prosthetic machinery of writing as the driving mechanism behind Auster's text-generation is in its essence a dehumanizing notion. Deleuze and Guattari's philosophy is anti-humanist, and so is the philosophy surrounding Bruno Latour's actor-network theory (ANT) that we will use to investigate the work done by Auster's writing tools. Latour's theory attributes equal agency to human and non-human actants. It removes the analytical divide between humans and objects, and the priority of human intent over the agency of non-human things. Very much like this book, which is primarily interested in exploring the machinery of copying and multiplying textual assemblages through prosthetic tools of writing, that eternal motion machine. And yet it never excludes the simultaneous co-existence of a certain humanistic dimension in Auster's work.

There is no doubt that Auster's texts operate and can be read at multiple levels. Theoretically, it is possible to read even a heavily intratextual, cross-referential work like *Travels in the Scriptorium* as an autonomous entity in its own terms. But it becomes more than what it first appears as soon as we recognize its embedded place in Auster's intricate network of texts. Or else: a story by itself, such as the quest for identity in an ambiguous, absurd and chance-ridden universe, may appear existentialist/humanist, but the moment one notices the same story being reproduced, copied and reflected in other related texts in a myriad of ways, it becomes merely a pattern in Auster's infinite recycling of texts.

Through the idea of rhizomatics, borrowed from Deleuze and Guattari, we can come to terms with such ontological open-mindedness and interpretive tolerance. In a rhizomatic (net-like) model, arborescent (tree-like) structures are allowed to co-exist alongside rhizomes, and, in fact, often intersect with them—"[t]here are knots of arborescence in rhizomes," the same way as there are always "rhizomatic offshoots in roots."[59] Rhizomes themselves, as Deleuze and Guattari warn, can have "their own, even more rigid, despotism and hierarchy," that is, arborescent traits.[60] As they remind us, "the important point is that the root-tree and canal-rhizome are not two opposed models."[61] It is not a question of "either-or":

> No, this is not a new or different dualism … We invoke one dualism [of arborescent versus rhizomatic structures] only in order to challenge another. We employ a dualism of models only in order to arrive at a process that challenges all models. Each time, mental correctives are necessary to undo the dualisms we had no wish to construct but through which we pass. Arrive at the magic formula we all seek—PLURALISM = MONISM—via all the dualisms that are the enemy, an entirely necessary enemy, the furniture we are forever rearranging.[62]

Rhizomatics is not so much a binary opposition to an arborescent model of thought as it is a method of challenging a dominant discourse (and its focus on dominant texts). It is a way of creating plurality of thought. And I think this sort of dynamics and pluralism is required to understand Auster's oeuvre. What I am suggesting is not a model that invalidates existing interpretations. It merely points to their fragility and limitations, and flips them over to reveal another side.

Let me give you another example of this interpretive pluralism that allows arborescent ("humanist") and rhizomatic ("postmodernist") ways of thought to co-exist. Here, we have to return to the writer-figure and his "writing machine" assembled from a set of "things" (cigarettes, doppelgängers, typewriters …). Think of Auster's films *Smoke* and *Blue in the Face*, of smoking cigars and cigarettes. It is possible to read these films through a cigarette, a small and particular thing, which itself can be read in a variety of ways (which is yet another reason for existing interpretive plurality). The cigarette has something of the nature of a prosthetic writing machine that works in certain ways to facilitate production of a text. Smoking assists the writer in the process of writing, as any smoking writer (Martin Amis, William Faulkner, Dennis Potter, Mark Twain …) would tell you. Blame the metaphorical power invested in this thought for the fact that, at this exact moment, I too feel compelled to smoke as I am typing these lines. So, it becomes a tool, necessary for writing. To some extent, it is the cigarette that does the writing, and its way of writing is peculiar, as we will see.

But it is likewise possible to see the cigarette as a thing invested with human moral values and so to read the entire text in which it plays its symbolic role as no less than a moral tale. My smoking can become a statement about personal liberty or tolerance of human flaws. And so the image of a lit cigarette also encapsulates the moral dimension of both *Smoke* and *Blue in the Face*. But I am moving forward too fast.

For now, notice this: there is also present in Auster's intratext what I call the "extratext," the cultural histories of the things and concepts that constitute each text, each story situation, each narrative space, and the very image of "the writer" that is constantly set in productive motion in Auster's life-work. The discourse of social history, with its many layers of signification, that is attached to each "thing" (such as the typewriter and typewriting, the cigarette and smoking, the notebook and notebook-writing, etc.) affects the way that associations are formed and the connections established within the texts. That should be apparent to you as you contemplate the given portrait of our writer—what do you think of when you think of an old typewriter, or a fountain pen? Which direction does your mind go, what connections does it build up?

"Thinging" things

Because of its interest in the writing machine, this book "opens up" Auster's self-referential intratext to read his texts through a set of objects, concepts, and things as much as through their own rhizomatic relationships. In a sense, it means moving beyond the supposed boundaries of a text, an author, his oeuvre, a particular genre and medium. It means reading Auster's stories internally (through themselves, through their own relationships) as much as externally (through the long social and cultural histories of objects, spaces and concepts that are all evoked by and communicated to us through his life-work).

The intratext-extratext approach illustrates this principle of interpretative dynamics, which can start with a small shift in the way one views a single element in a larger assemblage. It is for that reason that assemblages are never "fixed" but always fluid, always changing. For Deleuze, this heterogeneity of components is an important characteristic of assemblages, while Manuel de Landa, in his theory on social assemblages (himself borrowing from Deleuze), sees heterogeneity "as a variable that may take different values."[63] "Things" in general fail to fall into "this or that category of thought" because they themselves are bundles of varied associations and act out different values and functions.[64] Indeed, it may be that the hermeneutic plurality of Auster's texts is also the consequence of the polysemy of his tools of trade, and their unsettled ways of "thinging."

If you combined the Deleuzian ideas of the rhizome and the social assemblage with object theory, you would arrive at something that resonates with Bruno Latour's actor-network theory. The latter brings a whole new dimension to our discussion of Auster's work, which allows us to shift our attention away from the pensive writer-figure as the author that sits in the center of the image to those things and their "invisible forces" that not only surround and comprise him, but that incessantly "act" through him. For Latour, as for Deleuze and Guattari, all entities are to be understood in terms of assemblages. Any kind of social situation or network is an assemblage of certain human and non-human actors, or actants.

Latour in particular is interested in the role of objects in forming social networks or assemblages. For him objects are as "active" as humans, an idea he derived from Martin Heidegger's "things that thing" or "gather." But if objects and "things" equally participate in forming an assemblage alongside the presumed human "author," and if they have equal power to dissolve it, then, by implication, such an assemblage has shared authority and authorship. Assembling a text, an idea, a situation or a character becomes collaboration. Such an assemblage can never be stable, fixed, or finished, but, according to Latour, should be seen as a "type of connection." It is a practice of relations that is always in flux, since "things accelerate, innovations proliferate, and entities are multiplied."[65] Objects and things that we encounter in texts are not static units invested with fixed meaning, but dynamic sites of "intensities" and associations, and active agents in the text-generating process.

In our case, the agents that constitute Auster's smoking, typewriting New York writer become prosthetic tools of text-production, resulting in what we could call "prosthetic writing" (I borrowed this idea from Brian McHale, and we will get back to it).[66] It shows how narrative functions are assumed by objects as much as they are by human characters, or "the author." To see how a thing inscribes particular narrative formulas in the texts it co-produces, we need to pay attention to the thing's metaphorical strength. What sorts of forces does this smoking machine run on, what is its fuel, what are its capacities? If we want to understand how one writes books with a cigarette, we should look at the historical discourse of cigarettes and smoking. It is there, through rich and versatile cultural contexts, that the "thing" (the otherwise "empty" cigarette) gets filled with meanings and potencies to act. Yet we hardly notice the overwhelming potency of "cigaretteness," its "thingness" in writing—for we are captivated by the gaze of the author.

Michelle Banks has said that the characters from Auster's "*auto*-intertextual project" have through repetition become empty, self- (or rather, cross-) referential signifiers that exist in "an elastic environment" and whose meaning is constituted by their "*ongoing* interrelationships"[67] (her emphasis). They are known, she says, "in and through the complexity of their mutual existences, at times merging with previous versions of themselves, at other times recoiling from these past constitutions."[68] Her description points to one more reason why we tend to think of some of Auster's characters (Quinn, Blue …) as "empty". Or else we perceive them as mere narrative functions (a "postmodern" feature). They are empty like mathematical variables, ready to take on any value.

But there is another way of reading such characters, which acknowledges that there are, in fact, meanings that pass through them, or pour into them, marking them and filling them up as they do so. The apparently empty shells that give form to these characters are vessels with their own semiotic weight, laden with contents from the vast cultural history. So we could likewise read these "character constitutions" through more arborescent interpretations of the things that work to assemble them and operate within them. How else? After all, the world and the text, and the things inhabiting both, are imbricated with one other. We should ask questions like: What are these characters "made of"? And then, what associations are they made of? And we will notice that seemingly flat, self-referential characters are constituted by elements that themselves are so abundant in meaning that they tell their own stories. It is thus, by the way, that "Auggie Wren's Christmas Story" for Auster "literally comes out" of a tin of Schimmelpenninck cigars.

Figure 0.2 The empty shell of "Paul Auster"—naked Quinn in his study. A frame from *City of Glass: The Graphic Novel*.

But at first we only notice mere patterns of things. The many literary, visual and audiovisual representations of the Auster character-template depict him as made up of a few repetitive components. The writer becomes "a sort of bundling," "a gathering of symptoms" tied to a limited set of signifiers.[69] Among these components are certain locations (a bare and empty room, the streets of New York, and, very occasionally, also vast open spaces), objects (a manual typewriter, a notebook and a pen/pencil, Schimmelpenninck cigars or cigarettes, jazz records, baseball paraphernalia), and emotions or experiences (loss, crisis, chance, journey, transformation). These elements, together with other themes and tropes favored by Auster, constantly reappear in his works, becoming a kind of connective tissue for his texts. They hold the "intratext" together.

The components making up the machinic body of the writer, in their own paradoxical way, are both writing tools *and* the thing produced or "written" (as is the rhizome itself, which is both the way of writing and the written text). It is not unlike sociologist Anthony Giddens' attempt to "transcend the duality of agency and structure by arguing for their mutual constitution," an example which Manuel de Landa uses to characterize the dynamic assemblage.[70] De Landa puts it in the following way: "[a]gency is constituted by its involvement in practice which, in turn, reproduces structure."[71]

In other words—Auster's writer-character assemblage is also his own "writing machine," producing other writing-characters that keep operating as writing machines, and so on *ad infinitum*. Unable to resist the temptation of diagramming, my mind produces the following image: countless miniature typewriting Paul Austers dispersed across an ever-changing network of texts, which all write while being written. They are all interconnected: a hand writing a book that contains a character that is smoking a story about a typewriting writer who is producing stories, in which the characters write, smoke and typewrite…

In order to illustrate such heterogeneous connections between Auster's texts, Briggs uses the following metaphor: a book is "not a container" but rather something that is "full of holes," through which connections can be made to other books.[72] (Which reminds me: even if we insist on thinking of the book's medium as a container, it has to be a container full of holes.) Briggs sees Deleuze and Guattari's rhizomatic book as "both an assemblage of multiple components and a part within other assemblages."[73] Connections are made not only between "books," but any kind of text, not only fictional but also biographical, and not only texts as representations of the world, but also reality itself.

Here is an example of a straightforward, linear connection: the red car that takes away the protagonist Marco Stanley Fogg toward the end of *Moon Palace* (1989) also opens the journey for the main character of the following book, *The Music Of Chance* (1990). It is a simple vehicle that brings together two consequent books, emphasizing their continuity.

Most connections in a rhizome, on the other hand, are non-linear and non-hierarchical. They are kinetic, and respect no boundaries. For example, the manual typewriter—the writer's main attribute, and one node for such connections—appears

Figure 0.3 *The Story of My Typewriter* is a *mise en abyme*—alongside Auster's text, the book contains Sam Messer's images that themselves include Auster's text. This image shows Auster's Olympia typing up *The Story of My Typewriter*, which is the writer's account of his manual typewriter, depicted here in this "portrait." In this way, the typewriter writes itself, along with Auster's life-work. "The Player," by Sam Messer, from *The Story of My Typewriter*.

in *The New York Trilogy*; in the novels *Oracle Night, Travels in the Scriptorium, Man in the Dark*; in the films *Smoke* and *The Inner Life of Martin Frost*; in the pseudo-autobiographical collaborative project *The Story of My Typewriter* (in which Auster's story about his relationship with his typewriter alternates with dozens of Sam Messer's colorful paintings of the typing machine); and in Auster's New York home, where it is also replicated as a small bronze figurine. And, somewhere in Brooklyn's Park Slope studio, there is, of course, also the "real" Olympia whose mouth has rolled out everything Auster has produced so far, including ideas for books and films featuring typewriters. The typewriter is both "a thing to write with," and the thing written about. It diffuses the borderlines surrounding authorship, reality, and fiction. It produces a multiplicity of texts in which all these are woven together.

As Deleuze and Guattari explain,

> [t]here is no longer a tripartite division between a field of reality (the world) and a field of representation (the book) and a field of subjectivity (the author). Rather, an assemblage establishes connections between certain multiplicities drawn from each of these orders, so that a book has no sequel nor the world as its object nor one or several authors as its subject.[74]

For both philosophers, contrary to the current "deeply rooted belief," the book "is not an image of the world." Instead, "[the book] forms a rhizome with the world," complicating, and yet liberating, the relationships between fiction (the text) and "reality" (the world). To form the rhizome, the book, the world and the author interact. Fact fuses with fiction not only through the personal names and biographical data that often "fill up" the otherwise empty Auster characters.[75] Through meta-fiction, these writer-characters constantly contemplate this borderline between reality and imagination, as David Zimmer does in the book *The Book of Illusions*, or Martin Frost in the film *The Inner Life of Martin Frost*. For Auster, life is as strange as fiction, and fiction must become as strange as the world Auster believes he lives in. Adrian Gargett sums this up in a metaphor that could just as well be used to describe the humano-machinic nature of Auster's life-work:

> The comprehensive worlds constructed in Paul Auster's fiction function like a Möbius strip. The Möbius strip that results from joining the two ends of a strip of twisted surface is unexpected and ambiguous. It is a surface with only one side, which may be called either the top or the bottom.[76]

Yet the writer himself insists that, "in the strictest sense of the word," he is still "a realist."[77] If so, there is a way for us to understand and accept Auster's "realism."[78] All we need to do is take into account his own conviction that "there's no single reality … There are many realities."[79] The protagonist of the novel *Man in the Dark* (2008), a writer called August Brill, has his fictional creation Lou Frisk explain it in more detail: "There's no single world. There are many worlds, and they all run parallel to one another, worlds and anti-worlds, worlds and shadow-worlds, and each world is dreamed or imagined or written by someone in another world."[80] The result is purely rhizomatic as Auster's texts start to unfold like "a universe of Russian dolls, in which everybody seems to be someone else's puppet" (as Antoine Traisnel puts it).[81]

Essentially, it does not really matter what kind of metaphors we choose to talk about Auster's life-work. We can say that his texts resemble amorphous rhizomatic formations that run in all directions, entwining his life and work into one giant tangle. Or that it looks like a Möbius strip, where reality and fiction turn out to inhabit one and the same plane and where a sense of paradox is always present. Auster's works exhibit amazing resistance to contained explanations and canonical interpretations, and cannot indeed be reduced to any conventional schema. The "clues" are easy to identify in Auster's work (tropes and patterns, self-references and cross-references), but difficult to interpret.

That happens because, as Deleuze and Guattari insist, "[t]he rhizome is altogether different" from the genealogical tree.[82] It is "a map" and not "a tracing." Here, Deleuze and Guattari do not mean tracing in the Latourian sense of following the flight of connections or associations made—quite the opposite. They warn against a kind of tracing that seeks genealogy, linear progression, original meaning, the beginning and the end. Because the rhizome is in constant flux, transforming and proliferating, it is virtually impossible to represent its structure fully, or to "map" it out, in the traditional sense. In the rhizome, there is "an undecided (undecidable?) flux of connective signification."[83]

Investigation, then, leads nowhere. In the novel *City of Glass*, Quinn tries for weeks to literally follow Peter Stillman Sr., writing down in a notebook everything his suspect does. Although Quinn "could … see with his own eyes what happened," and "dutifully recorded" all these things in his red notebook, "the meaning of these things continued to elude him."[84] "What Stillman did on these walks remained something of a mystery to Quinn," making him wonder "if he had not embarked on a meaningless project." When Quinn finally comes up with the idea of tracing the route of his suspect's walks and making schematic depictions of them, he realizes, to his astonishment, that they form an expression, "THE TOWER OF BABEL," a concept that the mad Stillman explored in his writing before he was put in jail. Quinn thinks he has found the key to the mystery of the Stillman case, but this clue leads to no understanding or solution. The whole thing was "so oblique, so fiendish" that Quinn soon starts to doubt it: "He had imagined the whole thing," and seen it only because he wanted to see it.[85] Or, "even if the diagrams did form letters, it was only a fluke. Stillman had nothing to do with it. It was all an accident, a hoax he had perpetrated on himself."[86]

Yet, despite this obvious warning, it is difficult not to follow in Quinn's footsteps. And how could one resist? The human desire to reduce uncertainty is as fundamental as the desire to obtain pleasure. And what better image for the deluded scholar who feels invited (obliged!) to uncover, interpret, elucidate, and always increase understanding and order, than a triumphant sleuth. There are also maps, diagrams and notes, which are likewise tempting tools of literary navigation, even if one rightly suspects that they often might be more than inaccurate. These reading tools give the illusion of a structured and measurable world. After all, that is what I have been doing since we began this discussion—attempting to map out what is essentially unmappable, a rhizomatic intratext that is more like a beguiling labyrinth than a reliable map. I do this in spite of my knowledge that traversing across the intratext leads nowhere in particular—there is no center to reach, no destination. There are certainly tensions and contradictions sprawling in my own work. What to do?

Perhaps it is still possible for us to embark on what philosopher Igors Šuvajevs would call "a venture of interpretation, a detective-like adventure," given that we constantly remind ourselves that all such art, as well as its interpretation, is but a game.[87] Umberto Eco, like Jorge Luis Borges, another master of deception, believes in the life-affirming force of the act of meandering through such ontological labyrinths. As Šuvajevs points out, for Eco the rhizomatic labyrinth is not "an epitome of delusion" but "the source of a game," and there are valuable discoveries that can be made along the way.[88] It cannot be taken too seriously. The rhizomatic labyrinth persistently reminds us of "the initial groundlessness and existence without grounds."[89] This is a similar observation to what Eco's detective William of Baskerville once had to make: "the world in which [he] realizes he is living already has a rhizome structure: that is, it can be structured but it is never structured definitively."[90] For the detective (scholar), the only alternative to playing leads to madness (Quinn's fate).

So this is what I am going to do. I am going to investigate the connection between Auster's writing tools and his life-work's rhizomatic nature. I am going to follow the work of our main suspect, Auster's "writer" (as someone who writes, as well as *something*—a thing—writing). So I will have to inspect the values and functions of its elements (the cigar/-ette, the typewriter, the New York cityscape ...) and trace their "thinging" across his oeuvre. To uncover how Auster's texts acquire their pluralistic meanings, I will engage in some interpretative processes and trace the associations generated by these "things" throughout the discourse of their histories. While such genealogical tracing suggests an arborescent approach, "it is plausible that one could even enter [the rhizome] through tracings or the root-tree, assuming the necessary precautions are taken," as Deleuze and Guattari instruct us.[91]

It is inescapable that following the work of non-human actors will lead us across Auster's entire life-work. Still, we need to set limits to the scope of our work (so that this might become a book that fits between two covers). And I have decided we should focus on those routes in particular that lead through the territories marked by Auster's films and collaborations. These are all marginal projects that, very much like the work of non-human agents themselves, have suffered from lack of critical attention.[92]

What I ultimately hope for is that Auster's machinery of the book can reveal to us something about the process of writing, about writing as an assemblage, and about the kinds of relationships that exist between authors, texts, and writing technologies, and our understanding and reading of all of the above. If, for a moment, we turned our attention away from the human-writer, books could even open themselves up in an entirely new light. We might notice that the composition of a text is an assemblage or gathering, where implicated in the process of text-generation is also the work of non-human actants, objects and things, each with certain values and functions.

What if that is what books are—little machinic assemblages made up of and written by heterogeneous "things" (like cigarettes, and typewriters, and Brooklyn, and storytelling, and …)? And what if these books are dynamic and uncontainable because the things that write them are themselves bundles of different functions and associations—"multiplicit[ies] that var[y] according to the dimensions considered"?[93] With such questions in mind, perhaps this book is not even about the writer Paul Auster and the texts he writes. Indeed, perhaps, this is a book about his writing machine: the things to write with, and the texts they produce.

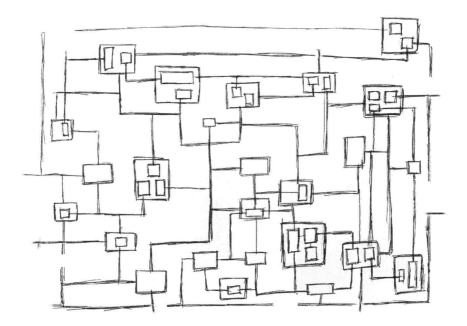

Smoke that Means the Entire World

How to start? That is an agonizing question that often occupies the mind of a struggling writer. There are different kinds of starts. One of them is the first sentence in a printed book. An Auster book can start with a misleading phone call, as in *City of Glass*: "It was a wrong number that started it, the telephone ringing three times in the dead of night ..." The first sight might be more dramatic: a man blowing himself to pieces (*Leviathan*), a man walking on the water (*Mr. Vertigo*). That opening sentence can affirm life ("One day there is life," *The Invention of Solitude*), suspect death ("Everyone thought he was dead," *The Book of Illusions*), or acknowledge the presence of both ("I had been sick for a long time," *Oracle Night*). The book can start with the end: "These are the last things, she wrote. One by one they disappear and never come back" (*In the Country of Last Things*).[1]

But where does an author's oeuvre start? There are no such first sentences. The first sentence of a published book? Paul Auster published his first book, *Squeeze Play*, back in 1982 under a pseudonym (Paul Benjamin). Does it necessarily have to start with a book? What about a published article, an essay, a poem or a translation? "How can we enter into Kafka's work?", Deleuze and Guattari ask rhetorically as they embark on their study of Franz Kafka, a writer to whom Auster has often been compared. "The castle has multiple entrances whose rules of usage and whose locations aren't very well known," they write, referring to Kafka's novel *The Castle*.[2] After all, in such textual rhizomes, every entrance point has the same value: "none matters more than another," and "no entrance is more privileged."[3] Eco, too, has said that "[t]he main feature of a net is that every point can be connected with every other point, and, where connections are not yet designed, they are, however, conceivable and designable. A net is an unlimited territory ... The abstract model of a net has neither a center nor an outside."[4] Or else (and this is Auster speaking): "the center is everywhere. Every sentence of the book is the center of the book."[5]

There can be many starts—we know that—and no finite end points. But some of the starts are false, illusory. Some entrances are too narrow, and their gates quickly lead to a dead-end. An Auster intratext cannot be entered through an image of withering flowers on a balcony in a Tuscany villa, or the song of cranes gathering in wetlands before their autumn migration. These elements (flowers, cranes) are like foreign molecules that, when colliding with Auster's body of work, instead of interacting with it merely bounce off. This collision does not result in a chemical reaction. Some doors simply do not lead anywhere.

Others, however, open up worlds of possible trajectories. That is suggested by the piles of research material that I have gathered on my desk as evidence: entire collections of textual particles that, within this particular author's body of work, seem to always interact with one another, transform, connect, multiply, flourish. Nouns dominate there—things, and spaces and ideas—and there are only very few adjectives, such as "lost" or "empty." If all these elements were written down, we would get an infinite book, a never-ending scroll. But this list would be more than a glossary of Paul Auster. It would conjure up an entire diegetic universe that is open and overlapping with other universes, and yet also so uniquely Austeresque that you would unmistakably recognize it as inhabited by this writer. Together, these particles work to form Auster texts, from small *mises en scène* to entire plots.

What things are most Auster-like? Things that are both concrete and abstruse—like the meta-mind of Auster's writer-character that always wants to ponder the relationship between the external (the physical body, the world) and the internal (the mind, the imaginary) in an eternal loop of the Möbius Strip. Or, like a cigarette, this tiny harmful object whose pungent fumes nevertheless contain creative forces so powerful that I can confidently say: Paul Auster's texts are written by cigarettes—first written, and then obscured by the accompanying clouds of smoke. And, as I am sitting here in my study, smoking, and contemplating the numerous portraits of Auster's smoking characters that I have pinned up to the wall in front of me, it seems to me that cigarettes and smoke make a good starting point for entering his work. It is not only because they are ever-present tools of writing that are intrinsically linked with the process of artistic creation. It is also because of the inherent contradiction they exhibit. It seems to "rhyme" with the paradoxical nature of Auster's life-work itself.

"Smoke is something that is never fixed, that is constantly changing shape."[6] Paul Auster used these words to comment on the title of his film *Smoke* and to describe the kind of relationships between the characters, who "keep changing as their lives intersect."[7] Yet these words are more than an allegorical comment on the intangible and dynamic quality of human relationships. The metaphor of tobacco smoke is one of the central elements in Auster's meta-story, and its changing symbolism reveals the multilayered and inconsistent texture of both his characters and texts. And, as I recall the pleasure that Quinn from *City of Glass* takes in smoking as he blows the smoke into the room and watches it "leave his mouth in gusts, disperse, and take on new definition as the light caught it,"[8] I sense that the ritual of smoking is not unlike Auster's text-creating ritual, where the same ideas, the same substances, leave the author's mind to take on a new form and definition.

In some contexts, the significance of tobacco expands beyond its purely metaphorical dimensions, becoming an active agent in the process of constituting Auster's universe. Rather than a passive and inanimate object, tobacco appears as a living element, which, like the manual typewriter, is always present in his work, although with changing moods and meanings. Like the typewriter (which I suspect to be haunted), cigarettes, too, are capable of talking to the writer and channeling inspiration. The cigarette is that thing that opens up the space where the interior of the book (or the writer's mind) merges with and leaks out into the exterior of the world. It is the door

Figure 1.1 Cigarette fumes that engulf the smoking person open up the imaginary space in which he can simultaneously be truthful and pretending. Oil painting of Auster by Sam Messer, "My name is Paul Auster, that is not my real name," from *The Story of My Typewriter.*

that opens up the realm of the imaginary. Its function as such is not unlike that of the writer's bare room in which he produces his often solipsistic texts.

In the Heideggerian sense, tobacco in Auster's texts is the thing that "things." In order to understand how exactly tobacco and smoking "acts" in Auster's polyphonic texts, one has to "follow the actors themselves," as Latour would say, to see what kind of associations they establish, and how they work to make these textual networks fit together.[9] We have to look into the "metaphorical potencies"[10] of tobacco, and the work they do in assembling certain concepts, ideas and relationships. If there is an interpretive plurality characterizing Auster's films *Smoke* and *Blue in the Face* (two texts literally wrapped in clouds of tobacco smoke), that is also because of the different possible ways in which we can read "smoking." Because the cigarette has what Eco calls a "plurifilmic personality," the texts which it helps to assemble and within which it acts also acquire a "plurifilmic" quality.[11] This potential for parallel, multilayered readings of the metaphor of smoke and of Auster's texts reminds us that, rather than having one fixed meaning, "the fabric of the rhizome is the conjunction, 'and … and … and …'."

How can I introduce this small cylindrical object, this thing—the cigarette—which in Richard Klein's words turns out to be "bigger than life"?[12] For Klein, cigarettes are especially ambiguous signs which are difficult to read, and the difficulty is related to "the multiplicity of meanings and intentions that cigarettes bespeak and betray" as they "speak in volumes."[13] The cigarette is itself "a volume, a book or scroll" that "unfolds its multiple, heterogeneous, disparate associations around the central governing line of a generally murderous intrigue."[14] This thing is a multilayered text that wants to be read and decoded. One wants to disperse that smoke that surrounds it and that appears to be hiding a hermeneutical secret.

The following passages from *Cigarettes are Sublime*, Klein's book that itself has a dual function as both an elegy and an ode to smoking, sums up the impossibility of capturing the contradictory essence and trickster-like nature of the cigarette. Its laconic form, visual simplicity and "whiteness" deceptively hide complexities of meaning:

> One has difficulty asking the question, the Aristotelian philosophical question, 'Ti estin [What is] a cigarette?' The cigarette seems, by nature, to be so ancillary, so insignificant and inessential, so trifling and disparaged, that it hardly has any proper identity or nature, any function or role of its own—it is at most a vanishing being, one least likely to acquire the status of a cultural artifact, of a poised, positioned thing in the world, deserving of being interrogated, philo-sophically, as to its being. The cigarette not only has little being of its own, it is hardly ever singular, rather always myriad, multiple, proliferating. Every single cigarette numerically implies all the other cigarettes, exactly alike, that the smoker consumes in series; each cigarette immediately calls forth its inevitable successor and rejoins the preceding one in a chain of smoking more fervently forged than that of any other form of tobacco.
>
> Cigarettes, in fact, may never be what they appear to be, may always have their identity and their function elsewhere than where they appear—always requiring interpretation. In that respect they are like all signs, whose intelligible meanings are elsewhere than their sensible, material embodiment: the path through the forest is signaled by the cross on the tree.[15]

Yet nothing perhaps sums up its nature better than the statement that the cigarette and smoking always imply a certain paradox that Klein sees epitomized by Zeno Cosino's life-long attempt to quit smoking in Italo Svevo's 1923 masterpiece *La coscienza di Zeno*, or *Zeno's Conscience*.[16] The determination to give up cigarettes and the never-ending succession of repetitions of the same resolution to stop smoking become not only a lifestyle for Zeno but also what defines him as a smoker. Not wanting cigarettes becomes a major pretext for continuously smoking the "last" cigarette, a paradox encapsulated by Klein in the sentences below and illustrated by Jim Jarmusch's smoking character in an episode in Auster's film *Blue in the Face*. (There, Jarmusch's "Bob" is sharing the moment of smoking his "last" cigarette with Harvey Keitel's character Auggie.) Klein on the paradox:

> To stop, one *first* has to smoke the *last* cigarette, but the last one is yet another one. Stopping therefore means continuing to smoke. The whole paradox is here: Cigarettes are bad for me, therefore I will stop. Promising to stop creates enormous unease. I smoke the last cigarette as if I were fulfilling a vow. The vow is therefore fulfilled and the uneasiness it causes vanishes; hence the last cigarette allows me to smoke many others after that.[17] (his emphasis)

This unsolvable contradiction is inherent in the double nature of the cigarettes, which makes them appear so desirable because they are so deathly. You would agree with me that the pleasure itself that the cigarettes offer, strictly speaking, is not really pleasure. Cigarettes stink, they burn your throat, and you surely would not smoke them for the taste. Of all the "pleasure goods" that were introduced to the European society at the dawn of the modern age—coffee, or chocolate, or sweet spices—tobacco, as Wolfgang Schivelbusch writes, is "undoubtedly the most bizarre."[18] Cigarettes are simultaneously bad and good, beautiful and ugly, tasty and repulsive, adored and hated, associated with the sacred and the demonic. The dual nature of the cigarette expresses itself also in terms of the physiological and psychological effects of smoking that vary according to the different conditions in which cigarettes are consumed: to calm and to excite, to numb the senses and to intensify them, to remember and to forget, to celebrate and to mourn, to pull yourself together and to let go of yourself.

Nick Tosches' description of the city of Las Vegas as "a religion, a disease, a nightmare, a paradise for the misbegotten" could be equally attributed to smoking.[19] Klein concludes that "[n]othing ... is simple where cigarettes are concerned" because "they are in multiple respects contradictorily double."[20] Cigarettes are like doppel-gängers, which also proliferate in the work of Auster, for whom, I think, both become "a way to express [his] contradictions" via "paradoxical shuttling" between two opposite ends.[21] This tolerance of inner contradiction that characterizes the cigarette is one of the reasons why Paul Auster's life-work, which has the same inherently "incon-sistent" quality, is full of characters who are essentially smokers. To light a cigarette means to embrace a paradox.

It is difficult for me to visualize the Brooklyn writer Paul Auster without his low, smoky voice and the always-there Dutch mini-cigars, which he passionately smokes 10 to 12 of a day and which have become a special trademark of his personal style. Auster's enthusiasm for the particular Schimmelpenninck brand's "Media" cigarillos (dry-cured and machine-made in Holland, and sold in 20s in metal tins) is so remarkably strong that it is passed over to his fictional characters Peter Aaron (*Leviathan*), Paul Benjamin (*Smoke*) and James Freeman (from the recent novel *Invisible*). "What are you smoking these days?" someone asks *Leviathan*'s protagonist Peter at one point, and he replies: "*Schimmelpennincks*. The same thing I've always smoked."[22]

It does not even matter whether at this point one is thinking of the empirical Paul Auster, or the figure of the writer "Paul Auster" that one has constructed through a collage of bits and fragments gathered from his interviews and book reviews, or the implied author of his books, or even his fictional characters. As Brendan Martin points out, "Auster inhabits both factual and fictional universes,"[23] and this "Auster" is a passionate smoker. Moreover, tobacco not only appears throughout his works, but it is clear that every writer-character must smoke, as if without cigarettes and cigarillos the writer-figure would be inadequate—at least the image of the writer as seen and shared by Auster.

Yes, imagine for a moment Auster's writer-character. Certain signifiers mark his space as an urban writer—a bare study room in the city of New York, a desk, a chair, an old manual typewriter, a (red) notebook and a fountain pen, a pack of cigarettes, maybe a few books here and there. In amongst all this, the writer is struggling with his inability to write. Different kinds of elements work to build up this image: the human actor/the author/the protagonist, the non-human objects, such as desks or cigarettes, but also intangible and abstract notions, such as the lack of creativity or sense of emotional comfort, or the ever-felt absence of the father figure, or other references extracted from his past. Take as an example the assemblage of Marco Stanley Fogg from Auster's novel *Moon Palace*. Towards the end of this *Bildungsroman/ Künstlerroman*, when Marco returns to writing after years of wandering the Wild West, what defines him is but a string of actions and objects, all expressed in one sentence: "I took up smoking again, I read books, I wandered around the streets of Manhattan, I kept a journal."[24] Why is it crucial that the writer smokes?

The writer's prosthetic cigarette

I sometimes think of the writer-figure as a result of the gathering of certain things and ideas about what a writer is and what writing means. It is a cluster of elements with both material and semiotic value, one that is constantly in the process of being made and that in Auster's oeuvre gains significance through rearrangement and reiteration of its basic components. It is almost impossible to read an Auster book or watch a film without encountering this image. When we realize that, the true function of these objects and spaces becomes apparent: they are not only there to set up the *mise en scène* of the work but in fact are defining parts of the character himself, acting almost as surrogates for his flattened physical and emotional body that is so often defined by an absence or lack. A cigarette, then, is a writer's prosthesis as much as his typewriter or notebook is. These elements in their own paradoxical way serve as writing tools, while they are also the source and the end-product of writing. The Paul Auster writer-character assemblage is also his own "writing machine."

The image of an often flat, two-dimensional character of a lonesome male writer who is confined to creative agony in his bare room constantly re-emerges with slight variations in Auster's facto-fiction, from the early *City of Glass*, *Ghosts*, *The Locked Room*, *Moon Palace*, and *Oracle Night* to the later novels *Travels in the Scriptorium* and *Man in the Dark*. Perhaps he is thinking about the mystery of someone else, since this "other," whose life he must uncover and document, is present in almost every Auster text as the writer's reflection and double. (We will return to this set-up later on in the book.) The process of investigation always at some point gets turned against the detective-writer himself, revealing his fragmented and unknowable identity and the impossibility of not only chronicling someone else's life but also of writing an emotionally accurate and meaningful story of his own life. In his bare study room, "[h]e smoke[s] a cigarette, and then another, and then another."[25] The ascetic space is dominated by emptiness, isolation and the absence of other objects and (often) any emotional satisfaction.

In her essay on smoking in French culture, Dawn Marlan compares it to the pleasure of emptiness, "a pleasure that involves an experience of emptiness," where a cigarette stands as an emblem for unfulfilled satisfactions and cravings, and concretizes the emptiness of the interiority of one's self and body by filling them with the inhaled smoke.[26] It also concretizes any anxiety that might result from such emptiness of thought or feeling. Every smoked cigarette reminds the smoker about the possible deathly consequences of smoking, so that the fear of suffering or dying from a smoking-induced illness replaces the fear of the unknown (which is at the basis of anxiety), making this new fear more concrete and therefore more tolerable, more manageable.

That may seem like a very grim view. But, for Auster, this emptiness is predominant in the blank page in front of the writer, or the blankness in his mind (the "white spaces"), or the bareness of the room in which this mind is situated, the subjective interior exteriorized through objects as the writer struggles to start from point zero, always reinventing himself anew. This ever-present emptiness expresses the burden of insatiable craving that every writer must endure. What matters for Auster in art is ideas whose "compelling force is identical with that of hunger."[27] Auster's writer-figure needs to be, in his own words, "rootless, without friends, denuded of objects," so that he can become "both the subject and object of his own experiment."[28] Nicotine in the cigarette induces hunger-like craving for smoking. It is the hunger itself. And hunger, in turn, is "the means by which this split [of the writing self] takes place, the catalyst, so to speak, of altered consciousness" (says Auster on Knut Hamsun's *The Hunger*).[29] Emptiness is this separation, hunger perpetuated.[30]

But the cigarette also helps to ease the burden of emptiness that the writer feels, and the angst evoked by it. Here is a common assumption: tobacco increases brain activity, as it calms the rest of the body by reducing its motoricity to a minimum.[31] All one requires to smoke is a hand to hold a cigarette and lift it up to the mouth. But, if needed, it also works the other way round—the physical act of smoking a cigarette briefly postpones or replaces the process of writing. It soothes the writer's uneasy mind because, to paraphrase Schivelbusch, "[i]n the act of smoking the nervously restless hand [of the writer] fixes on a purpose [that is, holding the cigarette]."[32] The cigarette becomes the substitute for the writer's disobedient pen. It gives an illusion that, unlike the pen, it can be mastered.

And it does its thinging very faithfully: it always burns, shrinks and eventually finishes (dies), or else it falls apart. In the unlikely case that it refuses to work, it can be easily destroyed: snapped in half like a broken pencil, or shredded into pieces like a wasted sheet of writing paper. So, unlike writing, smoking is almost always a productive process that is visibly traceable and results in the consumption of the cigarette. It is easier for a smoker to smoke a cigarette than for a writer to write. I can vouch for that. Through a series of repetitive movements, the cigarette is being gradually smoked, its ash tapped off its end into an ashtray, its size shrinking until it is finished and gets extinguished. For a struggling writer, this process grants a momentary satisfaction of "having done something." The act of smoking, after all, can also be a creative act (as I will show you shortly).

The cigarette has a very peculiar relationship with the emptiness that the writer feels and that precedes the creative process. Apart from being a thing that gradually vanishes as it is being used, the cigarette itself is "empty." The cigarette's attributes are not inherent in it. Rather, it is a door, or a keyhole in the door, which leads to another place altogether that is otherwise inaccessible because it belongs to the realm of the imaginary.

Klein notes that, too, in the introductory passage I quoted earlier. He describes the cigarette as "analogous to what linguists call a shifter"—like the personal pronoun "I."[33] That pronoun is a device we use to express "the irreducible particularity of [our] innermost self," but, universally available to every speaker, it is also "the least particular thing in the world."[34] The cigarette, for Klein, is a similar shifter—the smoker manipulates it, like the word "I," to tell stories about himself to himself, or to someone else.[35] Hence, the importance of holding a lit cigarette in hand for all the writers, actors, painters, musicians … all the storytellers. The action of putting a cigarette to one's mouth resembles the gesture of pointing to one's chest, pointing to one's self. It is a reminder of the self of the artist that gets expressed through the act of (artistic) creation. Smoking draws attention to "the self" that is being transformed, transported, enacted, iterated. As one smokes, one loses oneself and becomes the "I," which at the time the shift occurs could be anyone and yet is no one in particular.

Smoking helps perform this dual action: lose oneself to become someone else, either someone particular or simply not-oneself (the other). It is illustrated by the words borrowed from Quinn (who in the novel impersonates "Paul Auster, the detective") and written above that portrait of the smoking Auster that I presented to you earlier: "My name is Paul Auster. That is not my real name." This echoes the schizophrenic splitting of the self that occurs as a writer sits down at his desk to write, losing himself to become the performing "I" that gets inscribed in the text. And Auster is only too aware of that:

> Rimbaud: "Je est un autre." It opened a door for me, and after that I worked in a kind of fever, as though my brain had caught fire. What it came down to was creating a distance between myself and myself. If you're too close to the thing you're trying to write about, the perspective vanishes, and you begin to smother. I had to objectify myself in order to explore my own subjectivity—which gets us

back to what we were talking about before: the multiplicity of the singular. The moment I think about the fact that I'm saying "I," I'm actually saying "he." It's the mirror of self-consciousness, a way of watching yourself think.[36]

The act of pulling the self apart is encouraged and obscured by clouds of tobacco smoke. Smoking "engenders the gauzy pleasure of ephemera" and "promotes the dissolving of the I, the movement of depersonalization that is the condition of the Mallarméan poetic experience"[37] (which Auster, having translated Stéphane Mallarmé's work from French, easily relates to). As that happens, the writer's mind is able to fill the cigarette's inherent "emptiness" with substance that in its size and scope is no less than the entire world—many worlds, in fact, both imagined and remembered. Cigarettes, after all, are not smoked for their taste but for this quality, which could potentially create anything. Cigarettes, as Luc Sante writes, "fill the room with a screen of smoke on which anything can be projected,"[38] and it is our desire to "surrender to, to be transported by," to be "kidnapped by" what is "on the screen"—words that Susan Sontag attributes to the movies—that to a large extent fuels one's wish to always light another cigarette. (Always another cigarette? Perhaps the pleasure that the smoker gets through the formal repetition of beginnings by lighting yet another cigarette also works to negate ends, very much like good stories or movies do, leaving the audience always wanting more.)

Cigarettes and movies, then, have certain things in common. Both are gates to and vehicles of the imaginary. But there is a whole set of other cigarette-related associations that have emerged predominantly from the movie screen. Here, I have in mind film noir and the trope of the private detective in particular. The combination of the cigarette and the detective figure evokes a new set of meanings and functions for smoking, many of which we can also trace throughout Auster's work.

The image of Paul Auster's writer-detective in his bare room is often as gloomy as it is clinical, and in his early texts it is supplied with qualities and icons derived from the standard repertoire of American film noir from the 1940s to early 1950s. Among these, one always finds cigarettes, which play a dual role as *mise en scène* decorations and signs that "allegoriz[e] abstract qualities, virtues and, perhaps, most aptly, states of things."[39] Fittingly, in the noir-like *City of Glass*, the writer-turned-detective Quinn lies in bed during a sleepless night "smoking a cigarette, listening to the rain beat against the window."[40] His desk is covered with debris—"dead matches, cigarette butts, eddies of ash, spent ink cartridges, a few coins, ticket stubs, doodles, a dirty handkerchief."[41] This is not unlike what Quinn is greeted with when he visits the hotel room of his suspect, Stillman Sr., which "stank of cockroach repellant and dead cigarettes."[42] Altogether this scene conjures up the Austeresque vision of a world in which things are falling apart, like the urban wastelands in *City of Glass* or *In the Country of the Last Things*. When constructing their identities based on hard-boiled detective heroes (whether invented or borrowed), Auster's writers take elements from iconic figures of the genre in an attempt to gain closer proximity to them. Because the noir attitude associates smoking with glamour, masculinity, and intrinsic sexual connotations, Auster's wannabe detectives are also required to smoke. When Quinn, the insecure and doomed faux detective, visits the house of the *femme fatale* Virginia Stillman and, overwhelmed by her sexuality and perfume, starts imagining her with no clothes on, his thoughts immediately turn to his idol, the fictional private eye and alter ego Max Work. He wonders "[w]hat Max Work might have been thinking, had he been there," he wonders, and impulsively "decide[s] to light a cigarette," in an attempt to merge with his fictional idol.[43]

Alongside other key elements of Auster's writer-character assemblage, smoking is visually emphasized in *City of Glass'* graphic adaptation, which its editor, Art Spiegelman, calls "a strange *doppelgänger* of the original book," itself a schizoid offshoot of the work that deals with the doppelgänger theme. The visual treatment given to Auster's text by artists Paul Karasik and David Mazzucchelli, who use black-and-white graphics, rough brush strokes, light and shadow plays, as well as shifting focus between close-ups and wide shots, makes this project resemble noir cinema-tography. In the deliberately evoked noir chronotope, close-up "shots" of objects (a burning cigarette in an ashtray, a telephone, a typewriter, a book, a record player) play a crucial role in defining Quinn as a writer and detective, as well as marking the space he inhabits. Besides its active role as a "thinging thing," the cigarette is, quite plainly, also an irreplaceable prop setting up a noir *mise en scène*.

Yet such constructed identities as Quinn's detective persona are essentially flat and fake, empty of any deeper content. Quinn remains a struggling writer and miserable impersonation of a detective, a symbol of emptiness and loss who never manages to solve the task assigned to him and who at the end of the novel vanishes into thin air like smoke. Did Virginia really kiss him and offer herself as a reward? Did she exist at all? After all, she too disappears from the story unexpectedly and without explanation. Perhaps it all happened in the imagination of Quinn-the-failed-writer? This pattern of externalized subjectivity is a trope in Auster's narratives, and is consciously thema-tized in such works as *The Inner Life of Martin Frost* and *Lulu on the Bridge*. Dennis Barone notes that Auster knows how to exercise "one of the most basic methods of art"—selection—and what he selects he then "turns into a metaphor that merges an external object and the mind's interior."[44] And so the cigarette becomes a metaphor for expressing a struggling writer's mind. Here is one possible, if slightly pessimistic, reading of the cigarette: it is the condition of creative agony and failure, the emptiness and hunger that fail to get fulfilled.

But wait. There is also another, very different writer-character portrayed in *City of Glass*. His name, somewhat unsurprisingly, is "Paul Auster," who earlier in the text had been mistakenly taken for a private investigator, and whose identity Quinn had stolen. When Quinn meets him for the first time, this Auster radiates an aura of authority and self-satisfaction: "Auster leaned back on the sofa, smiled with a certain ironic pleasure, and lit a cigarette. The man was obviously enjoying himself, but the precise nature of that pleasure eluded Quinn."[45] At the end of the story this Paul Auster feels guilty about having treated Quinn badly, as if he, as someone who is a writer by trade, in some inexplicable way could indeed be blamed for Quinn's erasure from the pages of the book at the end of the novel. This Auster is everything that Quinn is not, and above all he is a successful and prolific writer, which is reflected in the way he smokes.

For him, smoking is not an emblem of emptiness, but becomes an embodiment of reward for productivity. The characters of Quinn and Paul Auster are revealed as two sides of the same figure, the creatively empty and unfulfilled one, and the fulfilled and productive one.[46] One is always also its own opposite—"[n]ight and day were no more than relative terms" as "[a]t any given moment, it was always both," we are told.[47]

Either way, in both cases, smoking becomes an inseparable part of the writer, who appears dehumanized, reduced to an assemblage of tangible and intangible elements, such as the objects or spaces within which he is located. When watching the film *The Inner Life of Martin Frost*, I may not know much about what kind of a person the protagonist Martin Frost is, but I immediately know that he is a writer because the camera shows him tapping away at the keys of his typewriter, next to which stands an ashtray with a lit cigarette.

If, for an Auster character, elements like cigarettes assume a prosthetic function, augmenting his capacities and efficiency, then they become what Elizabeth Grosz calls "instruments that the body must learn to accommodate, instruments that transform both the thingness of things, and the body itself."[48] Such an observation implies that, in order to appreciate the thing's thingness and potential, one needs to engage with it in a bodily experience. As Richard Polt comments on the phenomenology of things: "It is through the body that the form of the [thing] and the form of [its 'thinging'] get generated, actualized, incorporated. The body allows the eidos [or the 'thingness'] to be instantiated ..."[49] So, naturally, we are also clicking away at typewriters here, while puffing out little smoke rings: to experience the cigaretteness and typewriterness of these things—the only way to follow the work of Auster's writer-machine. At times, a very contemplative way ...

In his essay on the meaning of smoking in art, Benno Tempel describes eighteenth- and nineteenth-century artists, writers and philosophers as always being "lost ... in thought amid colors of smoke curling into the air." Like Auster's writer-character who is recognized by his cigarette and typewriter, the "contemplative gaze" of the artist of that time "was recognizable by the fact that he smoked."[50] Tempel gives an example: Édouard Manet's 1876 portrait of the French poet and Auster's inspiration, Stéphane Mallarmé. In it, the poet's right hand, holding a cigar, rests on the pages of a notebook, as if suggesting that the actual agent through which the lines of the poems are written is a cigar and not a fountain pen. There, the cigar/cigarette almost literally works as a writing tool. Tempel suggests that smoking not only brought about inspiration—it was in fact "the rising clouds of smoke" that "wrote a 'poem.'"[51] So, there is a stronger connection between the wordsmith and his cigarette than the supposed reflection of his thoughts in smoke patterns. The ghostly patterns of rising, fleeting tobacco smoke appear to form letters or words in the air. There is the text itself—smoke-written.

The same "trinity" of values and functions that characterize a thing like a typewriter (which we must likewise inspect) can also be seen at work here: the cigarette is not just a writing tool and the written text, but, simultaneously, also the source of the writing (an inspiration, a muse). It is often also its subject (as in Auster's films *Smoke* and *Blue in the Face*, two tributes to tobacco).[52] As Klein notes, the cigarette is "not just an object one holds in one's hand," but something that must be considered a subject, a creature alive with a body and spirit of its own. Not merely a poem, the cigarette is a poet, -esse or -ette: the fiery cinder ash is the heart of a living being, and effemin-ette, perhaps even a feminine being, endowed with abundant resources of seduction and diverse powers to focus the mind.[53]

Two thoughts can be extracted from this passage. First, the cigarette, like the typewriter, talks to the smoking writer. The thoughts are traveling from the cigarette, held in one hand, to the pen in the other hand via the writer's body and mind. Thoughts that get written up into the air by the rising smoke also get written down on paper, immortalized in concrete form. The cigarette is the writer's mentor and guide, the more abstract and authoritative poet, who is looking over the young writer's shoulder. It is his encourager (smoking boosts confidence). Second, it is also the seductress, the muse, which tantalizes the smoker/writer with the promise of granting what essentially cannot be obtained—"the right word" (Gustave Flaubert's "*le mot juste*"), the absolute satisfaction of craving. Again, that is what makes it so desirable. Yet the image of the desired and inspiring female muse is not the only image that the cigarette evokes. That is only part of its evocative power. Although throughout the discourse of its history the cigarette has always been associated with feminine seduction, its main attraction lies in the fact that it acts as an empty shifter and as such can be filled with any desired content (including the female figure).

Here, we arrive at another paradox of the cigarette, which has been noted by most chroniclers of its history—it is a thing that cannot be appropriated. An object of intangible essence, a cigarette/cigarillo literally vanishes as one smokes it and, unlike a pipe, it cannot be possessed and called "mine." At the same time, the cigarette facilitates the appropriation of anything imaginable in the world precisely because it itself is "empty" and depersonalized. The power of cigarettes lies not in the "things-in-themselves" but in their capacity as things to move "towards something other than themselves; fleeting, they are always signs or mediators for something else that unveils itself in the moment they vanish…"[54] The cigarette that itself cannot be possessed allows one to symbolically appropriate anything outside it. It acts to create an illusion, an invention—and Auster is a master of both.

That appropriation happens through the cigarette's ability to "gather" thoughts through associations. I mentioned this already when drawing your attention to the portrait of the smoking writer. We see his head wrapped in a translucent cloud of what could be either his thoughts or transformative cigarillo smoke. This detail is unclear from the painting, yet we sense the connection. And so the cigarillo becomes associated with contemplation. We find this coupling of smoking and contemplation in all the literary and artistic representations of smoking that are not hostile to tobacco.[55] Schivelbusch, discussing the portraits by the seventeenth- and eighteenth-century artists Martin Engelbrecht and Johann Kupetzky, points out that in these paintings "smokers always appeared as relaxed, meditative contemporary figures seated often at writing desks, as lost in wreaths of pipe smoke as they were in their own thoughts."[56] Here, the connection between smoke and thoughts gets reinstated. Schivelbusch cites an eighteenth-century text: "There is nothing better for contemplation than tobacco smoking, for here *straying thoughts are recollected*, this being most beneficial for students [one could say—writers], in that while smoking they can grow accustomed to pondering everything well"[57] (my emphasis). Smoking "gathers" any straying thoughts, pulls together images, assembles ideas.

Images and ideas of what? Of no less than "the entire world," of course, through an act of symbolic appropriation. And so I can understand why the existentialist philosopher Jean-Paul Sartre struggled to quit smoking:

> Through the tobacco I was smoking it was the world that was burning, that was being smoked, that reabsorbed itself in steam to reenter in me. To maintain my decision to stop, I had to achieve a sort of decrystallization—that is, without exactly realizing it, I reduced tobacco to being only itself: a leaf that burns; I cut the symbolic links with the world, I persuaded myself that I would take nothing away from the theatre, from the landscape, from the book I was reading, if I considered them without my pipe, that is, it finally came down to my having other modes of possessing these objects than that sacrificial ceremony.[58]

For Sartre, tobacco becomes, in Klein's words,

> "the symbol of the appropriated object" because, as it is smoked, the solid thing is gradually turned into smoke which enters my body. Smoking mimes the desired transformation of an object into myself through an act of appropriative possession; the object becomes "mine" by a process of "continuous destruction," "the transformation of the consumed solid into smoke," whereby it passes into me and becomes (part of) myself.[59]

Yet if Sartre talks about inhaling tobacco smoke as a means of appropriating the world, and sums up the whole world in smoking a cigarette or a pipe, then Mallarmé, as Klein also notes, describes the reverse act in one of his poems—the externalization of what was held within by exhaling smoke—and sums up the whole "soul" in the process of smoking a cigar:

> *Toute l'âme résumée*
> *Quand lente nous l'expirons*
> *Dans plusieurs ronds de fumée*
> *Abolis en autres ronds …*

> The whole soul summed up
> When slowly we exhale it
> In several rings of smoke
> Abolished in other rings …[60]

The act of smoking tobacco, then, works in two directions, allowing the writer first to take in the whole world through association, and then to respond to it with his or her soul—a response externalized and manifested in the created text, either spoken or written. And Auster, who has translated work by both Sartre and Mallarmé, and with whom he certainly shares some poetic affinity, would have surely experienced these same connections. The cigarette opens up that space, which for Auster is accessible also through the blank pages of a notebook or through his bare study, a space that *has room* to fit "the entire world," which then gets projected back as the text inscribed onto the pages of the notebook, the typescript, the book.

As an actant the cigarette wants to substitute its own emptiness with meaningful contents, which are so close to the creator's thoughts that the cigarette that is being smoked becomes the created text itself, transformed and externalized. The smoke that fills the air as the artist or the writer smokes a cigarette represents symbolically an expression of his or her mind or soul that consequently gets externalized in the form of the created artwork or text. Reflecting upon the French intelligentsia's passion for smoking, Richard Corliss remarks that in the 1960s film director Jean-Luc Godard, for example, "blew smoke rings as profligately as he exhaled movie ideas; that cloud of smoke was a thought-balloon in the comic strip of French aesthetic life."[61] The cigarette is the text-to-become.

There seems to be a "peculiar ambivalence" that surrounds the act of writing (that starts with contemplation) and the "curiously intimate relation" it bears to the act of smoking cigarettes.[62] We keep coming back to the same association between the writer's mind and his cigarette, between his thoughts and smoke. Are those the writer's thoughts reflected in the dancing smoke, in its swirls and spirals and curls that fill the air? Or is it that the rising tobacco smoke affects the writer's mind and transforms it in such a way that what comes out of that mind and finds its expression in ink on paper is no longer what it would have been, had there been no tobacco? It is both, of course.

Smoking propels the creation of text in ways that are difficult to replicate without the cigarette. The cigarette's extraordinary assistance in the processes of thinking and writing is the reason why Auster and his fictional characters smoke along with almost the entire Western canon of male writers, philosophers, thinkers and artists of the previous two centuries (Jean-Paul Sartre, Antonin Artaud, Samuel Beckett, Julio Cortázar, Jean Cocteau, Bertolt Brecht, Knut Hamsun, John Steinbeck, to name but a few). For those who see this connection, an image of a smoker lost in the clouds of smoke (thought) suggests the anticipated act of creation. And so it is understandable why, in Auster's intratext, smoking signposts, above all, the presence of the writer-figure on the verge of creation, which in turn subtly shapes the way each particular text wants to be read.

In Auster's oeuvre, the presence of elements that constitute the dehumanized and as-if-objectified figure of the writer always seems to point back to the same meta-story that is constantly repeated and recycled in a different variation. For example, in Auster's film *Smoke*, as soon as the iconic writer-character is introduced (and that happens in the opening scene), the spectator feels compelled to read the story in one particular, already familiar way. A man, a writer, as one learns, walks into a cigar store to buy a tin of Schimmelpennincks. What follows confirms the spectator's recognition of not only a familiar character but also a well-known story pattern. After the writer leaves the store, we are told about a tragedy that struck his life years before, robbing him of the ability to write. Which is of course a classic set-up for an Auster story.

On the narrative level, Auster's meta-story is always the same symptomatic story of an existential and artistic recovery from a crisis after the loss or death of an intimate, which has resulted in the character also losing his ability to write (or perform music, as in the case of *Lulu on the Bridge*, where the traditional writer-protagonist is substituted by a jazz musician). Unsurprisingly, this story repeats itself again in *Smoke* in the life of Paul Benjamin, who experiences writer's block after the loss of his pregnant wife, who was killed by a robber's stray bullet outside Auggie's tobacco store a few years earlier. After this personal tragedy the writer "hasn't been the same since."[63] At this point, it becomes clear that *Smoke* organically fits alongside Auster's novels as a slightly different version of the story that deals with the same themes that have preoccupied the writer throughout his creative career. Stripped down to his bare essence, Paul Benjamin becomes indistinguishable from his doubles Martin Frost, Sidney Orr, Peter Aaron or any other of Auster's fictional stand-ins. The re-emergence of the same writer-figure that faces the same problems across a number of novels and films does seem to suggest that to a large extent Auster's works are—with slight variations—an infinite repetition of the same existential story, over and over again.

That the embedded story of the blocked writer is actually the principal story of *Smoke* is implied by the place that has been structurally allotted in the film's narrative to the story of Paul Benjamin. The film opens with Paul's problem—his inability to recover and write following the family tragedy—and closes with its solution. The culmination takes place at the end of the film, when Paul "retells" Auggie's Christmas story by typing it on his typewriter. That story has brought him back to writing. The summary of the plot printed on the back cover of the published film script confirms this: "*Smoke* tells the story of Paul Benjamin, a novelist suffering from writer's block—as well as the death of his wife—who comes into contact with a young black kid who shakes Benjamin out of his lethargy and inspires him to begin writing again."[64]

Yet when in Auster's intratext I come across this kind of master narrative about a writer's creative block and its eventual positive resolution I begin to suspect the narrator because I have encountered this story before. It evokes a sense of *déjà vu* and suspicion that what the protagonist tells and shows us (that is, all other characters and stories) is the fruit of his imagination. Critic Timothy Bewes suggests a similar interpretation to the story of Paul. He connects the appearance and role of Claire, "the muse" from *The Inner Life of Martin Frost*,[65] with the figure of Rashid in *Smoke*:

> The scenario is not dissimilar to a subplot of a film Auster himself scripted, *Smoke* …, in which a writer named Paul Benjamin … accepts an apparently homeless boy as a guest in his Brooklyn apartment after the boy saves his life. Both films—the real and the fictional—include relatively conventional uses of montage, in which cinematographic shots of the writer banging away on a typewriter (Martin Frost and Paul Benjamin respectively) are juxtaposed with actions *which may or may not be anything more than a scenario being played out in the writer's head and on his page.*[66] (my emphasis)

This view is further enforced by the words expressed by Rashid (who may or may not be an imaginary character) to Paul when he tells him: "The material world is an illusion … The world is in my head."[67] The entire world … Unsurprisingly, the adolescent Rashid smokes, too.

I think Paul Auster enjoys puffing away on his cigarillos because smoke blurs the boundaries. His passion for smoking is not unlike that of Sartre, who, through the act of smoking, succeeds in bringing together the external physical world and the interior world of the mind, turning them inside out. It works, because tobacco smoke acts to create a space in-between. Smoking is what brings the two realms together into the Möbius Strip, which itself resembles a twisted smoke ring. Smoke fills the writer's bare room, turning it from an empty space into a sort of a "mysterious locale, poised between fiction and reality," and "between dreaming and writing."[68]

French poet and writer Pierre Louÿs notes the ability of cigarette smoke to erase the "hard edges" between here and there, now and then, me and the other, the exterior and interior, and fact and fiction—boundaries that must collapse as a writer sits down to write:

> The important thing is always to have a cigarette in hand; one must envelop the surrounding objects with a fine celestial cloud which bathes the light and shadows, erases hard edges, and, by means of a perfumed spell, imposes on the agitations of the mind a variable equilibrium from which it can fall into daydreaming.[69]

The result is the space of "I am Paul Auster … not my real name" that is depicted in Messer's painting of the writer engulfed by cigarillo smoke. That smoke is not only the mask that the writer puts on in order to become someone else, somewhere else. It essentially sets up a stage for performance—writing—by shielding and covering up what is real to make way for the imaginary that can only be sensed through the fog of smoke, and can never be clearly seen. We can grasp the connection with the use of theatrical smoke in stage performances for atmospheric effect. (Meanwhile, actual cigarettes used on stage are deemed too "real" and clichéd to depict certain character prototypes. Setting up a "stage situation" on stage would be an excess in itself.)

What is the result of the cigarette putting a story up "on stage"? It generates *mises en abyme*, narratives opening within one another, as a seemingly "truthful" story turns out to have existed solely in the writer's imagination. Yet, in Auster's case, it is not only the boundaries between the interior and exterior that get erased in such a way, making one question the credibility of the story. It is also, as I said before, the distinction between fact and fiction that is in a haze. In Auster's work, these border-marking lines between real life and fantasy are deliberately and skillfully interwoven so that it is no longer possible to unentwine them. Particular characters, episodes and nuances in Auster's work simultaneously are and are not perceivable as autobiographical references. In a tongue-in-cheek manner, for example, Auster has christened the writer-character of *Smoke* with his own name (Auster's full name is Paul Benjamin Auster) in order to "add to the confusion," to "bring reality and fiction as close together as possible" and to "leave some doubt in the reader's mind as to whether the story was true or not."[70]

Paul Benjamin Auster resides neither solely in the real (the world), nor the fictional (the book), but in both universes entwined together. He can be found in "the world that is the book." This title, which Aliki Varvogli has given to her study of intertextuality in

Auster's work, seems fully appropriate for describing the point of intersection between the two worlds where Auster has located himself, always between the real world and the imaginary, in the space between the physical room and the writer's mind, a room filled with and obscured by smoke. And so, semi-fictionalized and semi-biographical characters (like Paul Auster from *City of Glass* with his wife Siri, or Peter Aaron from *Leviathan* with his wife Iris, or all the Schimmelpenninck-smoking men) who inhabit the much-exploited and fictionalized spaces of New York (*The New York Trilogy*, *In the City of the Last Things*, *Moon Palace*, *The Brooklyn Follies*, etc.) appear to belong to the same universe we recognize as our physical reality, and where the "real" Paul Auster with his family inhabits Brooklyn's Park Slope neighborhood, writing his novels and smoking his cigarillos. That is what *Smoke* is also about—the blurred boundaries.

And yet, like the idea of smoking itself, the film *Smoke* seems to insist on several parallel readings. Auster's description of the image of smoke as something that is intangible yet present, "never fixed" and "constantly changing shape," illustrates the kind of dreamlike texture and shifting surfaces of his own narratives. He equates the way that dreams operate through *"a kind of repetition of objects*, or just putting one thing next to another," with the collage-like multi-layered structure of his texts where "several stories [are] going on at once"[71] (my emphasis). There is "story one, story two, and story three all on the same canvas," which creates a new kind of interesting "energy" between them.[72] Several contrastive interpretations appear to coexist. Here is another one.

The gathering of the tobacco shop

Smoking fills, smoking gathers—as it does within an isolated smoker's mind. Think of a cigarette that helps a soldier in the trenches "pull himself together" before a battle. This gathering also has a physical side that shows in its capacity to hold together the smoker's body, which has grown accustomed to tobacco over time. Auster notes this in his meditation on the writer's body, the recent *Winter Journal*:

> … the older you become the less likely it seems that you will ever have the will or the courage to abandon your beloved little cigars and frequent glasses of wine, which have given you so much pleasure over the years, and you sometimes think that if you were to cut these things out of your life at this late date, your body would simply fall apart, your system would cease to function.[73]

Tobacco holds and embraces the smoker; it works like braces. Cigarettes are no less than crutches (a permissible cliché here, I think). And a soldier post-battle is the epitome of a person wounded, if not physically, then emotionally. He is in need of some support, of something to lean on, in order to be able to keep on marching. And so the cigarette becomes a crutch, or a prosthetic limb—a defining part of Auster's crippled "soldiers." Paul Auster:

> No doubt you are a flawed and wounded person, a man who has carried a wound in him from the very beginning (why else would you have spent the whole of your

adult life bleeding words onto a page?), and the benefits you derive from alcohol and tobacco serve as crutches to keep your crippled self upright and moving through the world.[74]

Yet this same prosthetic function of holding something or someone in place—holding it together—happens also at a larger scale because smoking is an act as communal as it is intimate. Through its social, moral, and spiritual associations, smoking can assemble and "hold together" not just an individual but an entire group of people. Luc Sante agrees: "If a cigarette is a stalwart companion in solitude, in company it is an ally."[75] A lit cigarette, like a bonfire, has that peculiar force to draw people around itself, quite literally, as in the episode in Erich Maria Remarque's World War I novel *Im Westen nichts Neues* (or *All Quiet on the Western Front*), where, towards the end of the book, "[t]he munificent cloud of smoke," as Klein calls it, "draws a ring around the battle-hardened comrades and circles them in its embrace, drawing them closer together."[76] The novel's protagonist, Paul Bäumer, describes the gathering: "We drink and I look them in the face, one after the other. Albert sits next to me and smokes, and slowly we all gather together ... Over our heads a cloud of smoke spreads out. What would a soldier be without tobacco?"[77]

The function and meaning assigned to tobacco in Remarque's novel echoes Heidegger's concept of "the thing," where objects are transformed from their inanimate passivity into the more active role of "thinging." Drawing on the etymology of the word from the Old German "*das Ding*" (which denotes a certain type of archaic assembly as well as the matter of concern to those that have assembled), Heidegger prefers to describe things as "gatherings." When "the thing things," its "thinging gathers."[78] A thinging thing has the capacity to assemble humans and non-humans around it, physical entities as well as abstract concepts. In Auster's *Smoke*, and its sequel *Blue in the Face*, the perfect examples of "a thing thinging" are embodied in a number of smoke-related concepts—smoking, tobacco, cigars, cigarettes, and also The Brooklyn Cigar Co. tobacco store—which, like many other "things" in the film, assemble "a sheaf of relations that come together then go again their separate ways."[79] Instead of mobilizing an isolated concept—like that of the lonesome writer-protagonist—tobacco works here to connect ("associate") and hold together an entire Brooklyn neighborhood.

Notice that Auggie's tobacco shop is one such spatial and social network, assembled from things, objects, people, ideas, actions, and the dynamic relationships between them all. It is itself a "thinging" thing. It contains the double meaning of Heidegger's "thing"/*das Ding*, which designates both an assemblage of people as well as what causes their concerns. The tobacco shop not only assembles in itself the neighborhood's people, who are all associated with it one way or another, but it also becomes a matter of concern for the gathering when plans for its closing become obvious. When Vinnie, the owner of The Brooklyn Cigar Co., announces to Auggie, its manager and salesperson, his plans to sell it to a health food company (here a threatening concept in contrast to a shop dealing in tobacco), the shop starts to act as Heidegger's "thing," and also becomes its own "thingstead" (the place where the archaic Germanic assembly met).

Auggie makes an appeal to Vinnie's conscience: "Sure," he says, "it's just a dinky little nothing store, but everybody comes in here. Not just the smokers … The whole neighborhood lives in this store. It's a hangout, and *it helps hold the place together*"[80] (my emphasis). Like the object-turned-thing discussed in a "Reflections on a Table" essay,[81] a thing like a shop becomes an assembly, a gathering, not only of the objects contained and exchanged within it, but also of human beings, their emotions, opinions, ideas, actions, and stories that emerge with every person who enters the store.

Some of the cigarette's acting is informed by the symbolic link established over the last few centuries between tobacco and fundamental human values and rights, especially one's personal liberty. Nowadays, of course, the association is reversed—I can claim it is my basic right to health not to be forced to breathe second-hand smoke. Either way, such associations can still be easily evoked as the presence of smoking in Auster's texts unavoidably triggers moral questions. It forces me to read these texts in more humanistic terms. When I think about this connection, I feel like correcting myself to tell you that the film is not at all about the isolated writer-character and his existential crises. No, it is more about basic values and experiences shared by all of humankind. *Smoke* is a "communal" story and a story about community.

It is entirely possible to read the film from this perspective. *Smoke* does not have a single protagonist but multiple main characters, which contrasts with Auster's solo/ novelistic works, especially from his early period, where the narrative deals with an isolated protagonist's subjective perception of the world and the self. Partly because of this widened focus and partly because of its collaborative nature, *Smoke*, along with its sequel, is among the most optimistic of his works and in its lightness of mode can only rival his novel *The Brooklyn Follies*, which has been tagged as Auster's most humane and most positive book.[82] This idea of multiple protagonists is supported by the film's structural division into five segments, each of which has been named after one character (Paul, Rashid, Ruby, Cyrus and Auggie), as if suggesting to the viewer that this part of the film will be about this particular person. Cut into little episodes, the film focuses on each of the characters in turn, while keeping in balance the overarching narrative about the ways that people interact and influence each other's lives.

Set in a Brooklyn tobacconist shop, which becomes the film's epicenter, *Smoke* emphasizes the bond between people united by either their smoking habit or their ties with the particular neighborhood. The modest-sized space embodies the spirit of the big city, accented by cigars, cigarettes and other combustibles, and by the black-and-white photographs hanging on the walls, with portraits of smoking celebrities—mainly actors and comedians from the golden age of Hollywood—as well as by its ability to attract through these objects all kinds of colorful characters and unpredictable events.

The majority of character interactions take place within this space, which is both intimate and domesticated, and yet so public, open, and unprotected. Although the film contains only a few shots of street life, the surrounding hustle and bustle can be sensed in the background noises. Or it might sneak into the shop in a form of a thief (played by Auster's son Daniel). The elements establishing all connections ("associations") in the film are both human and non-human actants, such as the diverse Park

Slope residents, the tobacco shop, and the habit of smoking, as well as the street corners and thieves. All these elements are necessary to set up the scene so that "things" and exchanges can happen and the plot can be driven forward.

When Bruno Latour, who with Michel Callon and John Law pioneered the idea of actor-network theory, examines "the social," he speaks of particular networks formed by humans and non-humans together rather than the abstract notions of "the social sphere" of traditional sociologists. Since the words "social" and "association" evolved from the same Latin root "*socius*," which means both "to share" and "to associate," then the social could likewise be acceptably defined as "a trail of *associations* between heterogeneous elements"[83] (his emphasis). Auggie's tobacco shop in *Smoke* is the epitome of such an assemblage—it is not merely a spatial construct but an entire social network built by objects, people, "things," and ideas, all of which participate and interact to incessantly reconstitute and reassemble itself.

Auster's films highlight this role of non-human actors in forming "social" assemblages. In *Smoke*'s sequel, *Blue in the Face*, objects and things are constantly the focus of attention. There is Waffle Man in pursuit of a $4.95 Belgian waffle; the man whose hobby is to remove plastic bags from the Prospect Park trees; Man With Strange Glasses (played by Lou Reed), who wants to receive a patent for his invention; and, of course, tobacco and cigarettes themselves, the center of the discussions of Auggie, Jim Jarmusch's character Bob, and Man With Strange Glasses. The film does feature a few sustained narratives that get developed in its course (the relationship between the couples Auggie and Violet, and Vinnie and Dot; the story surrounding the sale of the tobacco shop). But it also constantly steps away from these narratives to expand horizontally and reveal more about Brooklyn as a rhizomatic assemblage of multifarious elements and their crisscrossing relationships.

In pseudo-documentary style, the film attempts to literally show the things that Brooklyn is "made of," while Brooklyn "residents" stand in front of the camera to recite additional facts and statistics about Chinatown, street corners, underage thieves, Tahitian music, salsa dances, Belgian waffles, baseball and the Dodgers, little convenience and specialty shops, as well as Brooklyn's 90 different ethnic groups, 32,000 businesses, 1,500 churches, synagogues and mosques, 3,268,121 potholes (as registered in 1995), 1,600 miles of streets, 4,513 fire boxes, 50 miles of shoreline, 30,973 robberies, 14,596 felonious assaults, and so on and so forth. Each chain of associations, and every assemblage built on it, is, of course, potentially infinite and semantically uncontainable.

Such chains of "things" make me think of chain-smoking, and the rhythm of this habit. As one lights up one cigarette after another, one's mind establishes new connections with smoking or traverses the already-established domains. There is something list-like about chain-smoking. This may be because it resembles the thought of the cigarette itself. A smoker does not think of a particular cigarette, but thinks of the cigarette in general—one that includes all the other cigarettes that precede and follow it. Donald Hall shows such signs of list-smoking when he presents in his article "No Smoking" a long catalog of spaces that, for him, were once all transformed by the very act of smoking:

… bars, restaurants, hardware stores, hotel lobbies, cabins, business offices, factory floors, sedans, hospital rooms, pizzerias, sweatshops, town meetings, laboratories, palaces, department stores, supermarkets, barbershops, McDonald's, beauty parlors, art galleries, bookstores, pharmacies, men's rooms, corner groceries, women's rooms, barns except for my grandfather's, movie houses, dairies, airports, offices of thoracic surgeons, depots, tearooms, Automats, cafeterias, town halls, Macy's, gymnasiums, igloos, waiting rooms, museums, newsrooms, class-rooms, steel mills, libraries, lecture halls, emergency rooms, auditoriums, parks, Mongolian yurts and beaches—not to mention funeral parlors.[84]

Auster's chain-smoking evokes a similar chain of positive associations between cigarettes and spaces, which he, in turn, lists in his *Winter Journal*:

[T]here is nothing you miss more than the world as it was before smoking was banned in public places. From your first cigarette at age sixteen (in Washington with your friends at Kennedy's funeral) until the end of the previous millennium, you were free—with just a few exceptions—to smoke anywhere you liked. Restaurants and bars to begin with, but also college classrooms, movie theatre balconies, bookstores and record stores, doctors' waiting rooms, taxicabs, ballparks and indoor arenas, elevators, hotel rooms, trains, long-distance buses, airports, airplanes, and the shuttle buses at airports that took you to the planes.[85]

There is no surprise that the narratives of the two films, marked by so much tobacco smoke, likewise have a slightly sequential—in fact, causal—feel to them. In *Smoke*, one thing leads to another, which leads to another, which leads to another, and this situational causality gets constantly emphasized in the text.

Smoke, too, consists of assemblages of human and non-human actants, which all work together to form situations that make a variety of exchanges and interactions possible. The film has minimal plot in terms of action as people simply disappear or unexpectedly appear in one another's lives. Ruby, Auggie's lifelong love, storms into his cigar shop one day after 18 years of absence from his life. Auggie suddenly learns that he might be a father to a grown-up daughter and travels to the slums of Brooklyn to meet her. Writer Paul Benjamin mourns the death of his wife and unborn child until Rashid suddenly appears in his life, saving him from a serious traffic-related injury or perhaps even death. Paul then becomes a father figure for the young and troubled Rashid, while the boy himself goes off to find his real father, who, having left Rashid after a family tragedy 17 years ago, has started a new life with his new wife and child, and a modest gas-station business in Peekskill, where the last person he expects to see is his long-lost offspring. The kind of connections these characters form is to a large extent based on the exchange of objects that circulate among them, the quintessence of which is the tobacco shop itself, which "holds together" the whole neighborhood.

I could use another actant—money—to better illustrate this point about human and non-human interactions in *Smoke*. As the ultimate token of exchange, money is in many ways related to tobacco. A paper bag with $5,814 in cash in *Smoke* becomes a kind of a relay baton, which the characters in turn pass on to one another (bank clerks—bank robbers—Rashid—Paul—Auggie—Ruby—Ruby's daughter?), so that their personal narratives can be developed. In *Smoke*, the work of the money-thing that questions each character's moral actions is concealed behind another trademark feature of Auster's novels, that of chance and coincidence, which makes the plot appear to be relying on strange incidents and unbelievable coincidences.

Is it not strange that the nearly $6,000 that Rashid picks up off the street during a gang robbery is the same sum which Auggie would have earned by selling his contraband Cuban cigars, if Rashid had not accidentally messed the deal up? Is it not a strange coincidence that—as it is implied—this is the sum that was also needed to cure Ruby and Auggie's (possibly) common daughter from drug addiction? And, after all, is it not interesting that, after telling his story about Bakhtin's "smoking manuscript" to Rashid, Paul approaches the large bookshelf in his room and stretches his arm towards exactly that one book (a study of Bakhtin), behind which Rashid has hidden the paper-bag with all the cash? We will yet come back to this story. But this use of a limited and homogenous set of chance encounters suggests that the notion of chance includes for Auster something predetermined rather than arbitrary. Because Auster's characters always experience the same kind of "unexpected" events and coincidences, their fates are likewise similar (and not very unexpected).

So money, this hazardous thing that is always surrounded by moral culture, not only connects and assembles people around it but also makes them expose their personal lives, strengths and weaknesses to each other. Money strips the characters bare. It confronts them with moral dilemmas that affect their own lives and the lives of those around them. A paper bag containing pieces of green paper turns out to be exactly what is needed to make up with one's boss after ruining his business deal; to save a tobacco shop from bankruptcy; and to cure one's daughter from drug addiction.

The thing, as Elizabeth Grosz writes, "poses questions to us, questions about our needs and desires, questions above all of action: the thing is our provocation to action and is itself the result of our action."[86] Or, to repeat Latour's point: material objects play a certain role in prompting moral actions from humans exactly because social networks, such as the one that the Brooklynites in *Smoke* belong to, are always built by non-human and human actants ("actors") together. Invested with certain moral values, these things, such as money or cigarettes, actively participate in building and changing social relationships and/or assembling new social structures. What does that tell us as readers? It means we can simultaneously read Auster's films in Latourian terms (a postmodern, dehumanizing way of reading that prioritizes the agency of objects) and humanistic terms (where the text is a story with a moral value).

A little thing like a cigarette has the power to hold a whole neighborhood together because it is a concentrate of some of the most fundamental moral values. As a social activity that affects both smokers and non-smokers (who are often exposed to the burning presence of the thing), it has always been accompanied by strong moral convictions that have changed from idolizing the cigarette at the beginning of the previous century, to demonizing and renouncing it at the start of the present one. As Sante writes in his photo-essay compilation *No Smoking*, "[b]orn in the late 19th century, the cigarette's history coincides with a century of glamour and industry."[87]

Then the twentieth century, which "created, promoted, and glorified the cigarette" all of a sudden "declared war on it," and, nowadays, in most Western countries, "smoking is considered a provocation, a shameful urge—almost uncool."[88] So the cigarette has always been a statement not only about the smoking individual but about the entire society via its attitude towards it. A small but telling sign of the prevailing Zeitgeist— no less than its burning torch.

In the twenty-first century, which prioritizes longevity and health over the sublime pleasures of the cigarette, smoking has acquired a stigmatized social status—it is shameful, condemnable, increasingly "antisocial," and almost taboo. In his article on what he calls the increasing "tobaccophobic vigilantism" in contemporary society, Richard Corliss laments: "what was once a seductive pleasure is now an endangered cult, subject to demonization by the fuming, non-smoking majority."[89] Very soon, perhaps, the cigarette will disappear altogether. Hence the significance of books such as Sante's *No Smoking* (2004) and Richard Klein's *Cigarettes are Sublime* (1993), and of Auster's films *Smoke/Blue in the Face* (released around the same time as Klein's book). They are all social histories of smoking—visual, textual, and audio-visual. They function simultaneously as elegies to smoking *and* the authors' protests against the growing "anti tabagisme" that could ultimately mark the end of the values smoking signifies.

You might want to object here. Values of tobacco? Perhaps you are right. The age of innocence (ignorance) is over, and it may be challenging today to think about smoking as having any value, never mind an honorable one. The only value we might think of is the profits made by global tobacco companies at the expense of public health (something that these texts remain silent about). They show no interest in exploring the dangers of smoking to public health (deaths due to heart disease and cancer, the effects of exposure to second-hand smoke on kids …). Neither do they feel like saying anything about the stained history of commercial tobacco production, which, like all plantation economies, has historical associations with slavery. No, instead, these texts insist on associating smoking with one of the highest human values—liberty.

The cigarette's dual nature, no doubt, is to be blamed here. And yet I get a sense that these nostalgia-imbued texts are aware that they are being written at their subject's deathbed. They are reassuring final attempts to revive the reputation of tobacco before it disappears from the world (or at least, the developed world) in the next half-century. There is also present a tender thought that those on the deathbed must be forgiven. Smoking and tolerance, after all, are bound in another strong connection (as I am about to show you). "It is time for us to take leave of tobacco," agrees V. G. Kiernan in his *Tobacco: A History*, "but it should not be an ungrateful farewell."[90]

And, yet, I find it increasingly difficult to think about the cigarette in a grateful way. The current world does not value the transcendental ideals of smoking but instead desires health and longevity and, as such, reduces the cigarette to its earthly qualities. This goes against the logic of smoking, whose positive effects are as fleeting and elusive as the substance itself. The strength of tobacco lies in the imaginary. Its acting is not as easily visible and measurable as the effects of nicotine (itself another actant) on the human body. The fact is, over the past few decades, the cigarette-as-nicotine has started to dominate over the artist's sublime cigarette, and I, too, am gradually failing to retain my faith in its powers. That is also why I am quitting. But not yet—for now, the task is to try to grasp the hidden strength and values of the cigarette that Auster's texts so enthusiastically endorse.

Smoking encapsulates the writer's moral views, which he expresses not only through his work or public commentary but, of course, also through his habit of smoking. If one stopped regarding smoking as "one of most grievous examples of destructive behavior in the history of humankind"[91] (the words of a former president of the American Cancer Society) and instead thought about the associations of tobacco established through Auster's life-work, it would be possible to read these texts as "moral tales" (the words of critic Jesús Ángel González).[92] Auster's cigarette, it seems, wants to teach us some lessons in morality.

It is impossible to capture one single "moral value" ascribed to tobacco and, in particular, the cigarette. Rather than evoking one "thing," its meaning and significance are disclosed as a long chain of related connotations, so that one can only move from one association to another, and observe how each acts out its "thinging" in particular contexts. Tobacco, for example, inspires generosity. Klein draws attention to the opening scene of Molière's version of *Don Giovanni* (the play *Dom Juan ou le Festin de pierre/Don Juan or The Feast with the Statue*), which begins with an extended monologue "praising tobacco for the generosity with which it inspires felicitous human exchange."[93]

Part of the pleasure of smoking cigarettes comes from the pleasure of sharing and giving that the cigarettes themselves facilitate. There is something inexplicable about the cigarette's ability to encourage generosity. The cigarette is a thing best enjoyed when shared, like a gift. It is the "*socius*" itself, social and shared. This "gift of giving"[94] that smoking inspires manifests itself throughout both Auster films (but *Smoke* in particular) as its characters, puffing away on their cigarettes and cigars, pass on to one another object-things such as money or books, but also their time, attention, affection, and stories. This sharing of gifts, in turn, is what brings people closer to each other. The cigarette becomes, above all, "a bond, a token of the camaraderie that rivets soldiers to one another."[95] That is how Auster's "wounded soldiers" gather.

Within both smaller and larger communities, smoking as a communal "thing" seems to have a highly social function. But smoking is more than just socializing. In a sense, the act of smoking, even when shared by two strangers, is like a conversation about the weather between strangers who meet in the street. And, for Auster, the act of conversing about weather with a stranger (or, alternatively—sharing a cigarette) becomes "a sign of good will, an acknowledgement of your common humanity with the person you are talking to."[96] Smoking, after all, is a distinctive sign of humankind (animals do not smoke by choice). Weather (or tobacco) is "the great equalizer," one of "the things that bring us together. The more we insist on them in our dealings with strangers, the better morale in the city will be," Auster explains.[97] To discuss weather conditions with a stranger is "to shake hands."[98] Smoking, sharing a cigarette together, like discussing weather, is elevated to philosophical prominence and becomes a sign of humanity, mortality, equality, and tolerance. That is how we (used to) relate to each other—by recognizing our shared human condition through these small but significant acts.

But an offered cigarette also plays other roles. It works to establish the atmosphere— of peace, of non-threat, of good intentions in an otherwise hostile environment (the war? the world? the streets of New York?). Sante explains it in the following way: although the cigarette itself can appear menacing (it is "a ceremonial dagger," "an ornamental emblem of power and a symbolic protection," "a colonial officer's swagger stick", "an exoskeletal limb with potential menace at its glowing tip"), to give it to someone means "to confer power."[99] Examples abound in the war literature (including in the novels of Ernest Hemingway, allegedly a non-smoker), where allied soldiers, and occasionally foes, greet each other by offering cigarettes in a friendly gesture. Shared on the battlefield, the cigarette can become a sort of calumet, smoked to seal a mutual covenant, treaty, or peace pact. It is a sign of reconciliation. Such is the power of tobacco to introduce peace that even amidst battles, "[t]he act of rolling and lighting and drawing at length on a cigarette establishes an intimacy that almost makes the enemy a guest …"[100] The cigarette does not kill. It saves lives.

Observe the way cigars are smoked in *Smoke* in silent reunion after a scene of argument—to confirm a peace treaty and turn the enemies back into friends. This happens first after Rashid's dispute with Paul, and later after the fisticuffs between Rashid, his father, and the others involved. After the storm—silence and calm. The hands and mouths of the characters are occupied with the smoking of cigars and cigarettes. As they inhale and exhale tobacco smoke, tranquility replaces the noise of the argument. Such moments are transcendental.

Cigarettes are "frequently represented as being democratic, international, cosmo-politan."[101] And, as such, they overcome the barriers erected by disagreement and even war. In his travel diaries, *Viajes por Europa, Africa y Norte América—1845/1847*, the Argentine activist, writer and one-time president Domingo Faustino Sarmiento called smoking "the sole habit that makes brothers of earth's people,"[102] comparing it to religions whose histories are often violent. Yet to be "democratic," "international" and "cosmopolitan" also requires one to be tolerant and accept diversity. How does smoking encourage that? Because the cigarette itself is "imperfect" (unhealthy, filthy, stinking), it tolerates imperfections also in those who smoke it. And, *vice versa*— tolerance on the smoker's part is a pre-requisite for smoking a cigarette.

Advocates of smoking would insist—or such is the implied argument—that one should tolerate smoking as a way of accepting that we human beings are imperfect in ourselves. Essentially, to be "smoker-friendly" means to tolerate one's impurities, faults, and bad habits. That correlation might be what once made the hard-drinking and hard-smoking Jeffrey Bernard conclude: "Nonsmokers tend to be more judgemental."[103] Smoking is not merely a sign of human imperfection but also a commendable tolerance of it.

It is a loving sign of the flawed. The imperfect characters of Auster's two films, all marked by a lack or absence of some kind (a missing arm, a missing eye, a missing father, a missing family, or a dysfunctional relationship), constantly signal their acceptance of these imperfections by smoking or not minding being surrounded by smoke. "Smoking and letting people smoke is a sign of … 'undogmatic behavior,'" writes González, referring to what Auster says in one interview.[104] For González, too, smoke as symbol seems to represent "human relationships, friendship as something intangible but present, constantly connecting and influencing the characters."[105]

This belief, that smoking, like human relationships, should be regarded from an unconventional and undogmatic viewpoint is emphasized not only by the sustained ideology of *Smoke* but also by other Auster texts, such as his 2009 novel *Invisible*, published after the adoption of public smoking bans in New York. In this text, the character James Freeman at one point wants to enjoy his Schimmelpenninck cigarillo, but hesitates since he is a guest at the house of an acquaintance he does not know well. Yet the host does not object to his smoking and finds an ashtray for him, which makes James describe her as "matter-of-fact, sympathetic," and "one of the last Americans who had not joined the ranks of the Tobacco Police."[106] Elsewhere, in his *Winter Journal*, Auster repeats the analogy between smoking and tolerance, and what he fears could be the consequent loss of both once tobacco is eradicated:

> The world is probably better off now with its militant anti-smoking laws, but something has also been lost, and whatever that thing is (a sense of ease? tolerance of human frailty? conviviality? an absence of puritanical anguish?), [I] miss it.[107]

The act of giving out cigarettes to people and in such a way encouraging smoking, which conceptual artist Sophie Calle implements under Paul Auster's direct instruction in their co-project "Gotham Handbook," becomes a gesture towards equality, freedom, and humanity, not unlike the historical march of smoking women during New York's Easter Parade of 1929. In that year, a group of young models, allegedly in an attempt to break the taboo against women smoking in public, walked down Fifth Avenue in New York, lighting their "Torches of Freedom"—Lucky Strike cigarettes—in their war for gender equality.[108] At this point, it does not even matter that what people witnessed back then was one of the first publicity stunts, ingeniously orchestrated by the "father of public relations" and Sigmund Freud's nephew Edward Bernays in order to increase the size of the female cigarette-consumer market. The association between smoking, liberation and equality stuck. The importance of this cigarette brand as a symbol for freedom and fairness is reiterated in *Blue in the Face* where the Lucky Strike-smoking Bob/Jim Jarmusch criticizes the ban on smoking in public places. Cigarettes, it seems, because of their subversive status in contemporary society, make a perfect weapon in the fight against restrictions on personal liberties, smoking being one of them.

Smoking itself has often been "oppressed." In the nineteenth century (when smoking was the exclusive prerogative of men), it was confined to specific places and restricted or banned elsewhere. It was banned in most public places, including outdoor spaces—a restriction originally justified by the danger of fire in cities that at that time consisted mainly of wooden houses.[109] When this justification no longer applied, writes Schivelbusch, the official prohibition of smoking in public places quickly became "a symbol of political oppression." He adds: "Once the streets, squares, and parks were 'liberated' for smoking, it assumed a symbolic character similar to that which it had had for the women's emancipation movement."[110] While for the oppressed the right to freely smoke in public is a symbol of liberation, the ruling authorities tend to regard it as "a sign of political recalcitrance," or rebellion.[111] For Corliss, the battle over smoking is always "part of a bigger fight"—it is "the crusade some people want to wage over regulating what other people are allowed to consume."[112]

Auster not only suggests one should be tolerant of smoking, but also seems to encourage making use of the cigarette's ability to offer support and help (as a small patch, a crutch ...). So the cigarette is also a sign of compassion. The busy and crowded streets of New York neighborhoods become Auster's testing site for humanity in several of his texts (*Smoke, Blue in the Face*, and also "Gotham Handbook") as cigarettes are handed out to beggars, distributed in telephone booths, and constantly consumed by everyone around, including minors. In the instructions that he gives to Calle in "Gotham Handbook," he urges her to hand out cigarettes to beggars (whole packs and not just one cigarette) because he understands the invaluable consolation that they provide to the smoker.[113] As Auster puts it, "Common wisdom says that cigarettes are bad for your health, but what common wisdom neglects to say is that they also give great comfort to the people who smoke them."[114]

Giving out cigarettes to people becomes an act of benevolence and sympathy rather than irresponsibility. And, conversely, anyone who condemns encouraging smoking fails to see or prefers to forget that cigarettes are, in Klein's words, "the traditional luxury of the poor—the ultimate consolation of those who are bereft, who sacrifice much of the little they have for the solace and comfort that cigarette smoking provides."[115] And so, as the "historian of humankind" V. G. Kiernan notes, cigarettes given to the miserable become signs of both "untold comfort to sufferers" and "innumerable small acts of kindness."[116]

Cigarettes and the poor go well together. In a way, one was meant for the other. Of all the tobacco products, it is the cigarette that was made largely for and by the deprived. Cigarettes are tobacco's leftovers, the breadcrumbs and table scraps that beggars get from the master's table as nourishment. Eric Burns reminds us in his social history of tobacco that the world's first "cigarettes" were made by Native Americans from leftover tobacco leaves wrapped in pieces of reed or straw and given to the poor (and the very old, and women). Later, in Medieval and preindustrial Europe, cigarettes were reinvented by beggars and outcasts from scraps of tobacco and paper found in garbage. In seventeenth-century Spain, snippets of discarded cigar butts wrapped in bits of paper were used to manufacture a "poor man's by-product of the lordly cigar."[117] It was designed for the poor man but also for the common man, the working man, as the new kind of smoke. Compact, easy to light and quick to burn, it demanded little effort and time for consumption amidst one's busy schedule. However briefly, it allowed escaping from the tyranny of time and pressures of everyday life.

The cigarette is indeed an escape—not only from the self, and not only for the writer-philosopher. It grants the same promise of getaway to every smoker: the illusion of being someone else, someplace else. This means forgetting, for the instant of smoking, one's current condition, which may be marked by physical or emotional misery. Smoking and escapism might be condemnable and cowardly activities to engage in. But there is also another association to be made, between smoking and bravery, which transforms the cigarette from a short-lived, mild anti-depressant into one of the most encouraging "things" in the world. The cigarette, on occasion, can make you feel brave.

Smoking means looking death in the face. Smoking kills, as tobacco packaging labels increasingly remind us. Every time a smoker takes a puff of smoke, the poison that is more deadly than heroin or cocaine takes him one step closer to terminal disease. There is, in a way, a small death with each cigarette. Jonathan Jones, who has explored the relationship between smoking, death and art, puts it this way: "for the truly cultured smoker, smoking is about knowing you will die."[118] Smoking constantly reminds one of one's own mortality, "the fragility of [one's] body."[119] And it is exactly the lurking presence of death that accompanies every smoked cigarette, and the courage to contemplate it—to accept it—that makes not only many soldiers but also writers, artists, and philosophers smoke. So, Corliss aptly calls nicotine the "Existentialist's drug of choice."[120] (And so would Auster, too, who describes his "art of hunger" as "an existential art"—"a way of looking death in the face ..."[121]) In a way, death is confronted, accepted, fought, and conquered in every instance of smoking. Smoking re-enacts dying. And if this deadly poison-drinking (for to smoke initially meant to "drink tobacco") can be stoically survived, then, perhaps, so can death itself.

This re-enactment of death culminates in the "last cigarette" customarily granted to the condemned before they face their own death by execution. As the cigarette is lit, its smoke starts to dissolve the boundaries between "here" and "there" of the earthly life, and "before" and "after" of the approaching death, making the transition easier. The comfort of the smoke's familiar embrace, the kick of nicotine rushing through the body ... "Courage! Pull yourself together!" the last cigarette seems to say to the ill-fated. And so they do, at least in their mind. Sir Walter Raleigh, a passionate smoker who introduced and widely advocated tobacco-smoking in seventeenth-century England, has been lauded for his courage in the face of execution for treason. Allegedly, Raleigh's last words as he was being led to be beheaded were directed to his executioner: "Let us dispatch. At this hour my ague comes upon me. I would not have my enemies think I quaked from fear."[122] Shortly after his execution at the Palace of Westminster on October 29, 1618, a small tobacco box was found in his prison cell bearing an engraved inscription in Latin: *Comes meus fuit illo miserrimo tempo*—"It was my companion at that most miserable time."[123] It is through stories like this that tobacco gained its connotations with bravery and encouragement, the final measure of which is to stand up to death itself.

Courage and comradeship, as well as a quiet resignation and the will to forget this world (yes, to "die"), are suggested by those who smoke in Auster's darkest texts, such as the early dystopian novel *In the Country of Last Things* and the more recent *Man in the Dark*. In the former, the simple satisfaction of smoking "real, old-fashioned cigarettes" attains a melancholic dimension as the devastated characters, Anna Blume and Sam, smoke themselves into forgetfulness. Smoking cigarettes brings one of the last consolations and small pleasures they can still indulge in:

> We would smoke them after it got dark, lying in bed and looking out through the big, fan-shaped window, watching the sky and its agitations, the clouds drifting

across the moon, the tiny stars, the blizzards that came pouring down from above. We would blow the smoke out of our mouths and watch it float across the room, casting shadows on the far wall that dispersed the moment they formed. There was a beautiful transience in all this, a sense of fate dragging us along with it into unknown corners of oblivion.[124]

In *Man in the Dark*, the smoke that leaves August Brill's and Katya's mouths becomes "the conspirational bond" that ties them together and takes them on the same kind of journey into oblivion, as they lie

> … side by side on the sofa, blowing smoke in tandem, two locomotives chugging away from the loathsome, intolerable world, but without regret … without a second thought or single pang or remorse. It's the companionship that counts … the fuck-you solidarity of the damned.[125]

Whenever smoking gets condemned, smokers indeed are damned. At the same time, the cigarette itself has become a bothersome thorn in the side of non-smokers. Yet the question that the cigarette's insistent presence in Auster's texts asks is not "Will you smoke me?" It is not even "Will you approve of me?" Rather, it seems to ask: "Will you let me be, and do my acting?" Not a health issue, but a moral one, it seems to be addressing the larger question of empathy for the flawed human condition. And in that sense, it seems to say, we are all damned.

González sees *Smoke* and other Auster films as "stories of moral responsibility where the characters need to consider the ethical implications of their acts."[126] And this pertains to smokers and non-smokers alike. However, Auster is not a conventional moralist, as González also recognizes. Traditional moral views (such as the perception of smoking as a harmful and degrading habit) get tested throughout the film and eventually turned on their head. The issue of selling the cigar shop becomes a moral dilemma whose outcome will determine the well-being of the whole neighborhood. As Auggie says to Vinnie, "go twenty blocks from here, and twelve-year-old kids are shooting each other for a pair of sneakers. You close this store, and it's one more nail in the coffin. You'll be helping to kill off this neighborhood."[127] In other words, Auster, who often toys with questioning the conventional moral "truths" of society (can stealing or lying be seen as acts of empathy and kindness?), fills the concept of smoking with a meaning and significance which urges one to look beyond established understandings and the obvious surface matter. An apparition of the legendary baseball player Jackie Robinson says to the dilemma-torn cigar shop owner: "[m]ind over matter," "that's what counts, Vinnie."[128]

Like other "dubious" things (double-stolen photo cameras, dirty money stolen from bank robbers, illegally sold Cuban cigars) in *Smoke*, cigarettes are needed to trigger moral responses from those who encounter them. All the thing-related incidents that take place in both films serve only as catalysts for the characters to change something in their actions and attitudes towards people around them, making them finally choose in favor of an altruistic gesture. This pushes their many narratives towards a positive solution. It is not all grim.

This optimistic thought—that "all the characters in the story are a little better off at the end than they were in the beginning"[129]—in fact is the prevailing motif in the Auster novel *The Brooklyn Follies* (which almost reads as the other side of the same coin in relation to *Smoke*), as well as *Man in the Dark*. Unlike the cigarette that accompanies the isolated writer, in these texts smoking equals shared experience and, as a positive affirmation, is present whenever the lives of the characters take a turn for better.

Smoke indeed marks turning away from the narrative and identity quests of self-obsessed writer-protagonists. It is a filmic production, a collaborative work, which suggests rhizomatic rather than arborescent relations, both within the project's authorship and within the text itself, where a variety of characters can claim their share of story in a more democratic and inclusive way. The cigarette, just like collaboration, in its essence means sharing—the sharing of a thing, of a ritual, of a habit, of a certain space and amount of time, of attention, of experience ... and of stories. Sharing not just the stories of redemption and reconciliation that the characters experience, but sharing the act of storytelling itself. And so, there is yet another way we can read both smoking and *Smoke*.

Smoke is the story itself

Tobacco has stories to tell. As Luc Sante puts it, every cigarette, from the American Marlboro to the French Gauloises and the hand-rolled Samson, has its own "biography" to tell.[130] This is what often makes smoking good subject matter for a story. And, even if "the lives of cigarettes" are "seldom interesting," they nevertheless, "like sundry zoological parasites, are the secret sharers of countless lives, of moments of impenetrable intimacy."[131] Cigarettes have "witnessed romance, rage, epiphany, confusion, elation, despair, serenity, chaos."[132] Significantly, as Sante also notes, cigarettes were "not just present in those moments, but according to their consumers they played an active role, either in enhancing the sensation or in attempting to assuage it."[133] Cigarettes and cigars have inspired, witnessed, and played a part in stories.

Apart from the invested symbolic meanings and associations of tobacco, the very act of smoking also "things." Smoking becomes part of storytelling by aiding the process. It is a visually compelling and dramatic action, in itself telling a little tale:

> So after inhaling you wait one beat and then release the smoke through your nostrils, do you? That's one way to do it, although it tends to communicate impatience. They make you look like a dragon, those twin jets rushing downward from your nose. It's the sort of exhale you might employ while negotiating with someone over whom you have an advantage, or when arguing with a lover. In a calmer or more tender moment, you are better off letting the smoke out though your mouth, in little puffs, like clouds for cherubim to ride upon. Yes, little puffs—a long stream of smoke is another matter altogether. It can often indicate

hostility, especially if you aim it at someone's eyes. By contrast, moments of poetic idleness are best conveyed with smoke rings.[134]

And how else? Both the smoke we blow and the words we utter come from the same place. Klein agrees when he says that "[s]moking cigarettes is not only a physical act but a discursive one—a wordless but eloquent expression."[135] He calls it is "a fully coded, rhetorically complex, narratively articulated discourse with a vast repertoire of well-understood conventions that are implicated, intertextually, in the whole literary, philosophical, and cultural history of smoking."[136] In other words, each cigarette that is being lit and the particular way it is being held, sucked on, smoked and stubbed out transmits associations with the many other cigarettes smoked in real and fictional lives. One cigarette may not look much different from hundreds of other cigarettes (it is, after all, machine-produced), yet the strength of each cigarette lies in this potential to evoke immediate powerful associations with imagery and stories derived from the entire history of smoking.

Cigarettes and stories. This combination sets up entire new connections, new ways of seeing Auster's two smoke-infused films. We might end up agreeing with Harvey Keitel, the actor who plays Auggie Wren in both films and who thinks that "*Smoke* is all about telling stories."[137] This idea, that smoking and storytelling form a natural pairing, takes us back to some of the conclusions derived earlier, and to some of the already established associations. Firstly, there is the point that the cigarette is a prosthetic element in the writer-character assemblage. And, secondly, that the cigarette is an actant with a capacity to bring and hold people together. Here, the two points are entwined as the cigarette works to assemble the idea of a storyteller—in essence a concept related to that of the writer—and of shared rather than solitary storytelling.

Forget about the lonesome writer confined within the empty space of his room. In *Smoke*, stories are not scribbled down in deceptive notebooks but are openly and generously shared, as a number of people engage in collective smoking and story-telling. The outcome is more positive than the solitary writer's struggle to write, and the characters' enjoyment in sharing a story is made obvious by the way they smoke. The shift that both *Smoke* and *Blue in the Face* make from the naked cigarette of Auster's writer-figure to the more enjoyable cigarillos (and implicitly Cuban cigars) is another way of signifying the transition from solitary agony to a shared pleasure. The smoke is the delectable words of the story—rich, fragrant and comforting. The smoke is the story itself.

For Auster, the writer-figure is unimaginable without a cigarette, which externalizes his inner being, and the typewriter, which assumes the function of materializing the story. Without the latter, the story could not be written down and would remain "locked" in the writer's mind. Or it would be uttered, only to evaporate like smoke. It is equally impossible for Auster, as both films show, to imagine the character of the storyteller and the process of storytelling without the cigarette or cigar. Heidegger suggests in *Being and Time* that the world (the physical reality consisting of objects) and the mind (our subjective mental world) cannot be separated. There is no split between subject and object—the two are one, he says.[138] Neither are tobacco and the act of smoking separable from the writer/storyteller and the act of writing/storytelling. That becomes obvious when you observe the many conversation-based episodes in the two Auster films.

In Auster's life-work, telling stories, like writing stories, is clouded with tobacco smoke. Tobacco plays a decisive and active role in making storytelling possible. It sets up the *mise en scène*, forms the atmosphere, and helps both the storyteller and his listeners fulfill their functions. Think about it this way: storytelling is not an abstraction, but an assembly of particular elements where every human and non-human element has a certain function and force. In order for the story to be told, there needs to be a combination of mutually complementing elements. If one of them is missing, then the network cannot function anymore and the storytelling becomes incomplete, if not impossible.

Tobacco serves as a tool of trade for the storyteller. It is what creates a story and also what provides a channel through which the story is communicated. To a storyteller, the cigarette, cigar or cigarillo becomes a substitute for the writer's pen. Gesticulating with it as he speaks, he is delivering his words into the air (he is "smoke-writing"). The process of smoking itself is a creative act, the "acting" out of a little stage performance that involves the smoker's gestures and facial expressions, bodily positions, the sounds made while smoking, and, of course, the exhaled ("theatrical") smoke. It is an emblem of creativity. Which makes me think: as such, the creative "act" of smoking is yet another way in which the smoker tries to substitute something for the "nothingness" of the cigarette as it burns down and vanishes. Smoking itself is not so different from writing, painting, acting, *storytelling*—which is why it is so often an indispensable attribute of creative types.

In the opening sequence of *Smoke*, even before the title appears on screen, Paul Benjamin enters a tobacco store and joins "a philosophical discussion about women and cigars" being held among the shop's owner Auggie and three loafers who regularly hang around the shop: Tommy, Jerry, and Dennis.[139] At this point, the agency of tobacco as a way of gathering disparate things together is condensed to maximum effect. This happens through the space of the shop that assembles a certain kind of people, through the shared act of smoking that presupposes a certain kind of interaction, and through "the matter of concern" itself, which is the focus of their attention—tobacco. Paul says: "I suppose it all goes back to Queen Elizabeth," and shares with everyone a story about Sir Walter Raleigh, who won a bet with the queen that he could measure the weight of smoke.[140] This Raleigh, historically credited for introducing and popularizing tobacco in Europe, himself makes good "story material." His name surrounded by myths and legends, he becomes a recurrent link between "tobacco" and "stories." *Smoke* does not speak of his courage, but praises his wit and sharp mind, implicitly associated with his passion for tobacco.

The story itself—a curious attempt to determine the weight of smoke—is a reminder of the mythical dimension and magical aura that has accompanied tobacco since its arrival in the Western world at the end of the fifteenth century. In their introduction to *Smoke: A Global History of Smoking*, Sander L. Gilman and Zhou Xun describe the smoke that a cigarette or cigar produces as "ineffable yet perceivable; real yet illusionary; present yet transient; breathable yet intoxicating."[141] The cigar(ette) itself changes from a tangible thing into something intangible; it visibly vanishes by transforming into smoke, which makes it "an object of pure essence."[142] Tobacco products have an aura of myth, magic, and mystery.

While the contents of Paul Benjamin's story reinvests smoking with the qualities of the mythical and sublime, the way the story is told emphasizes the importance of the act of storytelling that gets repeatedly performed by different "actors" throughout the film. A medium shot captures Paul in the frame and, for nearly two minutes, the camera motionlessly fixes on his body and face, as he slowly and expressively tells the others the story, gesticulating with a Schimmelpenninck cigar in one hand. Paul's story is occasionally disrupted by remarks from other characters outside the frame. But the camera is very still when the dialogue takes place, and refuses to show the impact of the story on Paul's audience. The typical inter-cut close-ups are absent. This undivided attention given to the storyteller clearly foregrounds the act of storytelling.

A number of agents work to make this episode possible, to construct the "story-telling situation": a space that accommodates a sustained conversation like this, a storyteller and his listeners, and the smoking of tobacco that is shared between them. An analogous set-up appears in Paul's apartment between Paul and Rashid; in Auggie's apartment between Auggie and Paul; in Auggie's tobacco shop between numerous characters; at the roadside opposite Cyrus' gas station between Cyrus and Rashid; and at the end in the diner between Auggie and Paul, where the former tells his climactic Christmas story.

Similarly, in *Blue in the Face*, story-based conversations mainly take place between the smoking characters (Man With Strange Glasses, Auggie, Bob) within the tobacco store, while rows and arguments are set in the chaos-filled space of Brooklyn street corners. These socio-spatial and associative arrangements gain significance through repetition, so that smoke defines the world of Auster and designates the space where stories are told. "WHERE THERE'S SMOKE, THERE'S AUSTER," announces the headline of a critical review of the two films. And, we could add, where there is SMOKE/AUSTER, there are stories, too. Smoking = "Austering" = storytelling.

In one episode in *Blue in the Face*, Bob (played by Jarmusch) in conversation with Auggie mentions other iconic combinations associated with the cigarette. Bob, who is planning to quit, comes to the tobacco shop in order to share the experience of smoking his "last" cigarette with Auggie, and laments the bliss he is about to lose by eliminating smoking from his life: "sex and cigarettes, you've got to admit ... that's one thing I'm really going to miss ... [h]aving a cigarette after sex ... that's like ... a cigarette never tasted like that. You know, share a cigarette with your lover..." To which Auggie responds in agreement: "That's bliss." And Bob continues: "That's what I'm going to miss ... and also with coffee. Coffee and cigarettes, you know? That's like 'breakfast of champions.'"[143]

The same Jarmusch is known as the director of a number of short films devoted to a similar assemblage where cigarettes play the key role. *Coffee and Cigarettes* (2003) is a compilation of these, and bears close resemblances to *Blue in the Face*. The comic vignettes that feature the coffee-drinking and smoking characters are but a series of short, absurd conversations, which, like Auster's film, have been partly improvised by actors that include iconic rock musicians and other celebrities.[144] All the encounters and situations we witness are born out of this particular combination: coffee plus cigarettes plus a table plus people.

Here, the table, like the cigarette, is another Heideggerian thing that "gathers" others around it and marks the stage for conversational performance. In the essay I mentioned earlier, "Reflections on a Table," the authors rhetorically ask: "Imagine there were no table between us; how could we begin to talk to each other?"[145] The table is "a born negotiator: It draws us together; it holds us apart."[146] In other words, the table is a prerequisite for conversation, like coffee and cigarettes for Jarmusch, or tobacco for Auster. Recall the philosophical debate about Don Quixote between Quinn and the character Paul Auster in the early novel *City of Glass*: this situation would not have been possible if "Auster" had not been sitting on his sofa, puffing away on his cigarette. But what distinguishes Auster's films from his novels is the new physicality and the power of visual manifestation that has been granted to objects. The role of object as actants becomes obvious. It is literally shown to us.

The omnipresent element of smoke in both of these Auster films dominates the screen by filling the spaces and surrounding its characters. In this way, what cannot be conveyed in written form is manifested in visual terms. In a book, the fact that all the characters constantly smoke would not be recognized in terms of plot ("what is happening?"). In the film, smoking is not only seen as part of the *mise en scène*, but also appears as "action," something that characters do all the time, while also doing something else, which is mainly talking and/or listening. This signals that *Smoke* is all about smoking and talking. It stands out with its peculiar reliance upon a certain type of conversation, clearly marking Auster's authorship of the film as its scriptwriter. To a great extent, the film pushes the narrative forward through dialogues rather than action. All background information about the characters is revealed not by the camera or a voice-over narration but simply through what can be heard in conversation. This is a shift from Auster's usual style of writing, which is almost free of dialogue (and whatever dialogue there is tends to be criticized by reviewers as unconvincing).

Instead of foregrounding story-creating and storytelling by deliberately making the narrative techniques conspicuous and self-reflexive (as we see in texts such as *City of Glass*), *Smoke* thematizes storytelling by substituting a lot of action with stories that the characters literally tell each other. Except for a few climactic scenes (like Auggie and Ruby's verbally abusive encounter with Ruby's pregnant crack-addict daughter Felicity, or Rashid's confrontation with his dad Cyrus, which ends in fisticuffs between the two), all the other episodes in *Smoke* are played out through conversations. Those themselves either contain "stories" that explain the life of the film's characters or are half-mythical stories about unusual incidents from other people's lives narrated mainly by Paul.[147]

So when Ruby storms into Auggie's cigar store we listen to the two of them conversing and through that dialogue are exposed to the history of their relationship, as well as an unexpected twist, which is that, years ago, Ruby gave birth to a girl whose biological father might or might not be Auggie. Likewise, unaware that he is speaking to his long-lost son Rashid, Cyrus tells him, and us, the story of how 12 years ago he lost his family and his arm in a drink-driving accident. He now has an artificial limb with a hook in its place.

Note that both Ruby and Cyrus look like odd types (but so does pretty much everyone else in these two films). They are visually marked as characters with an embedded story to tell, their looks signaling extraordinary experience. Their missing arm and missing eye are but visible stories waiting to be told. Seeing Ruby's eye-patch that has replaced a glass eye she has apparently lost, Auggie cannot resist a bitter remark: "What's with the patch, anyway? What'd you do with that old blue marble—hock it for a bottle of gin?"[148] We never learn how Ruby lost the glass eye, or her natural eye in the first place. But this object—the pirate-like eye-patch—defines and immediately positions her as someone with a story to tell (and, as it later turns out, confirms Auggie's assumption that she is broke). Cyrus' hook is no less intriguing and serves as a catalyst for his story of the past. So, when Rashid asks him about the arm, Cyrus unfolds his tale in the traditional manner of oral storytelling:

> Twelve years ago, God looked down on me and said, 'Cyrus, you're a bad, stupid, selfish man. First, I'm going to fill your body with spirits, and then I'm going to put you behind the wheel of a car, and then I'm going to make you crash that car and kill the woman who loves you. But you, Cyrus, I'm going to let you live, because living is a lot worse than dying. And just so you don't forget what you did to that poor girl, I'm going to rip off your arm and replace it with a hook … Every time I look at this hook, I remember what a bad, stupid, selfish man I am. Let that be a lesson to you, Cyrus, a lesson so you can mend your ways, a warning.'[149]

But Ruby and Cyrus represent common people. They wear an eye-patch and a false arm not because they are "eccentric odd balls," like the eye-patch-wearing housewives and one-armed men from Quentin Tarantino's *Kill Bill* series or David Lynch's *Twin Peaks*. They do so because their ordinary lives were marked by extraordinary experiences, investing them with material for interesting stories.[150]

Stories/storytelling become the film's central axis around which all episodes revolve, and they are always accompanied by smoking. What matters is a good story; what does not matter is whether it is true or false. The last we see of Auggie before the final poetic scenes with Tom Waits' "Innocent We Dream" is a medium-range shot of Auggie's mischievous smile amidst curls of rising cigarette smoke. Auggie has just finished telling his Christmas story to Paul, who looks incredulous but affected. Here, Auggie reminds me of Messer's portrait of the smoking, storytelling Auster whose improbable stories often leave the same kind of doubt in the audience's mind. The little dialogue that takes place between Auggie and Paul at the end is more than a self-reflexive commentary on Auggie's story. It sums up Auster's aspirations as a smoker-storyteller.

PAUL [cont'd]: Bullshit is a real talent, Auggie. To make up a good story, a
    person has to know how to push all the right buttons. *(Pause)* I'd say you're
    up there among the masters.
AUGGIE: What do you mean?
PAUL: I mean, it's a good story.[151]

Auster's fascination with extraordinary stories (that are either true or "true") is
apparent through his entire life-work. It makes me think of the famous four-part
collection of "true" tales entitled *The Red Notebook* (2000). In these, Auster relies on
his own life as well as the lives of his friends and acquaintances to recount anecdotes
molded in the form of pure storytelling. These are stories about objects and things that
"act," inviting the reader to ponder the relationship between human and non-human
actors. There is a story about a book, about a lost-and-found dime, about a burnt
onion pie, about a scrap of paper discovered in a Paris hotel room … These little
encounters all testify to the mystery of coincidence and document the bizarre if not
catastrophic turns of everyday reality. They claim to be true, while also reappearing in
identical or slightly modified versions in Auster's fictional texts (like, the story of the
"wrong phone number," which also "starts" the story of *City of Glass*).

It also reminds me of NRP's *National Story Project* (a.k.a. *True Tales of American
Life*), a collection of real-life stories about the coincidences and absurdities of life.
Written this time by ordinary American people, the stories were selected for publication and edited by Auster. The project's authorship exceeds more than 3,000 people,
who sent in their tales from all over the country, and Auster sees these stories as
"vindication" against accusations of his own work being too "unbelievable." Auster,
who believes that reality is stranger than fiction ("[the] unexpected occurs with almost
numbing regularity in our lives"), uses ordinary characters to prove this claim.[152]

Auggie Wren, from *Smoke* and *Blue in the Face*, likewise a seemingly unremarkable
man in charge of a small cigar shop in Brooklyn, is made "special" by his unusual
photography project, to which he refers as his "life's work."[153] Apart from a story of
his tobacco store, told through 30 years and thousands of photographs, there is also
the afore-mentioned "Christmas story" about bonding with a strange woman, which
he tells to Paul at the end of the film. Here, Auster comments on the commonality of
story material: "Working behind a cigar store seems like such a nothing job … But is
it really? Everyone has a story. Everybody is interesting, no matter what they do. If you
just keep your eyes and ears open, someone very ordinary becomes quite amazing."[154]
Paul's otherwise habitual life as writer is shaken by a tragedy when his wife gets
gunned down during a bank robbery. It is a death "unusual" for "ordinary people," but
the Hollywoodesque death of his wife does not make Paul special—it makes his story
special. And so, each of the characters has "a story of their own" to tell, including, of
course, Paul Benjamin himself, who like Paul Auster, is an occasionally blocked writer
with a fascination for extraordinary stories.

Apart from the anecdote about Raleigh and the weight of smoke, there are two
other vivid stories that Paul tells the others in *Smoke*. In their presentation, these tales
do not differ much from the story about smoke that I referred to earlier. These same

two stories also reappear in two other Auster texts—the early novellas *The Locked Room* and *Ghosts*. That should no longer come as any surprise to us. Different texts and agents may be used to transmit these stories, but there really is no difference between these texts or the characters who recount them. The voice of the smoking storyteller clearly belongs to Paul Auster/"Paul Auster."

I mentioned the first story earlier, in passing. It concerns the Russian linguist Mikhail Bakhtin and his cigarettes, and the correlation between the two that this time spins off in a reversed direction. Trapped in his apartment in Leningrad during the 1942 German siege, Bakhtin smokes heavily and writes a study of the German novel in the eighteenth century (the *Bildungsroman*). He calls it *The Novel of Education and Its Significance in the History of Realism*. He has been working on it for 10 years. Yet, due to the paper shortage, he eventually chooses to tear his manuscript up, page by page, to make wrappers for his "endless chain of cigarettes."[155]

> RASHID: *(Incredulous)* His only copy?
> PAUL: His only copy. *(Pause)* I mean, if you think you're going to die, what's more important, a good book or a good smoke? And so he huffed and he puffed, and little by little he smoked his book.[156]

In a Sartrean rather than Raleighian way, Bakhtin weighed "a good book" against "a good smoke," and understandably chose the latter. He literally consumed his own creative work, and it "went up in smoke when he used it for cigarette paper."[157] In some sense, you could say that it went back to where it came from—i.e., tobacco smoke.

The other story that Paul recounts is about a man who went skiing in the mountains but was buried in snow, only to be discovered frozen in Alpine ice years later by his son, who by that time already looked older than him. What are we to make of these stories? We could try and read them in relation to the film's main narratives, as a sort of *mise-en-abymic* meta-commentary. We could note the relation between the frozen man and Paul's apathetic state after the death of his wife and child, or make similar speculations. But the way these stories have been presented rather shows us the author's fascination with good story material and the skill of storytelling.

Smoke ignores the Hollywood tradition of visualizing the re-telling of a story by using flashbacks, which brings it closer to a literary narrative. Auster, who has complained about the medium's two-dimensionality, where the spectator, unlike the reader, has been left without any room for imagination, has minimized this intervention on the spectator's perception. The spectator sees the speaker's face and hears his voice, but the story itself is not "shown" through visual means. The climax of *Smoke* is the ending sequence of the film, where Auggie's ten-minute long Christmas story is delivered to the spectator in a single long take. The camera fixes on Auggie's body, drawing closer to his face as the narration progresses, until at one point we only see his lips move as he talks. The story is transformed back into its original ancient form of oral storytelling. Without any montage tricks or special effects to rely on, everything depends on how well it is conveyed by the speaker.

This is Auster's critique of film's reliance on the image and its overuse of all kinds of cinematographic techniques (montage, sound and soundtrack, lighting, camera angles, etc.) that manipulate the reader's perception of the story and turn him into a "passive" recipient of it.[158] In *Smoke*, the story is preserved in its purest form so that the spectator, while listening to it, has to use imagination, just as when reading a book. The film wants me as spectator to be "actively involved in what the words are saying."[159]

In the interview with Annette Insdorf that complements the book of the two screenplays, Auster talks about his problems with the cinematic medium, which he mainly attributes to its two-dimensionality.[160] For Auster, the movies are "flat pictures projected against a wall," "a simulacrum of reality," and "not the real thing."[161] For Auster, the "real thing" is the book where, through the use of imagination, one can "smell things," "touch things," "have complex thoughts and insights," and in general "find [oneself] in a three-dimensional world."[162] Hence also the frequent use of smoke on screen in *Smoke* and *Blue in the Face*—it not only symbolizes the five human senses (as Tempel suggests) but also obscures the view and adds depth and another dimension, mystifying the objects and persons seen in its midst.[163]

Imagination is reality: that explains Auster's self-perception as a "realist writer." Auster tries to add more "real" substance to the medium of film not by packing it with cinematic effects but by stripping the stories bare in order to bring the film closer to an oral or written narrative. In the interview with Larry McCaffery and Sinda Gregory, he once admitted that the greatest influence on his work has been fairytales and the oral tradition of storytelling.[164] Possibly, what Auster admires in these stories is "their economy of bare-boned narrative and lack of detail which leaves enough space in the text for the reader to inhabit it," as Dragana Nikolic suggests.[165] "The text acts as a 'springboard of imagination' and it is up to the reader to complete it."[166]

González, in his article "Words versus Images: Paul Auster's Films from 'Smoke' to 'The Book of Illusions'," observes that *Smoke* is basically Auster's attempt to re-create and add the missing third dimension to film. That is mainly achieved through a peaceful, slow and "natural" pace, the emphasis on conversations and long takes rather than action and editing. González notes that *Smoke* follows the "realistic" approach in cinema as manifested in works by such directors as Jean Renoir, Yasujiro Ozu and Robert Bresson—directors who all favor, in Auster's words, "telling stories over technique" by letting their characters speak for themselves and giving them time to show their emotions so that they can "unfold before our eyes" on screen and "exist as full-fledged human beings."[167]

Elsewhere, Auster admits: "We wanted to make an Ozu film, but with Americans ... Hence the little bracketing shots of the Brooklyn subway train, which echo Ozu."[168] The film is dominated by space that, whether private or public, indoors or outdoors, "encourages" conversations (and often also smoking)—a cigar store, a Brooklyn street corner, a bar, the living room of a writer's apartment, a bookstore ... The locations are set "mostly indoors with just faces and bodies, and their story to tell."[169]

Stories, of course, take time to be told, and there is plenty of it if everyone smokes. Smoking slows things down, and so, in a way, it too becomes a cinematic technique. The narration belongs to the smoking characters, not the camera. In an Ozu-like manner, a nearly static camera captures characters in mid-shot, letting them speak uninterruptedly for five or ten minutes. In fact, time in this film should not be counted in minutes, but in the amounts of consumed tobacco, puffs taken and smoke exhaled. For it is not the clock time but the transcendental time of smoke that sets the pace for the film. Remember Auggie's advice to Paul, who initially fails to understand the meaning of his photo project that involves more than 4,000 pictures of the same place (the tobacco shop photographed from across the street), "You'll never get it if you don't slow down, my friend."[170] This advice is given to the spectator as the key to understanding the entire film. Like the Christmas story, this episode becomes a self-reflexive comment, and for director Wayne Wang is "the heart of" the film.[171] It is slow-beating and pensive.

Tobacco, especially a cigar, is meant to be enjoyed slowly, and savored for its feel, taste, and aroma. When one smokes for pleasure, the activity presupposes a myriad of other co-existent processes and conditions. It is a certain mental and physical condition, which creates a relaxed and tranquil atmosphere, while stimulating mind and spirit. For centuries, artists have been using smoking as a symbol of pleasure and "timeless contemplation."[172] Describing Manet's painting of Mallarmé, discussed earlier, Tempel notes how the cigar, in combination with the poet's posture, neatly illustrates "bodily calm and spiritual stimulation" through the supposed effect of nicotine.[173] The transcendental atmosphere of smoke/*Smoke* is captured by Jackie Robinson's words to Vinnie: "mind" over "matter."

Several moments in *Smoke* vividly portray such calm—like the peacemaking episodes we looked at earlier. The scene following Rashid's culminating fight with his long-lost father Cyrus is a contrasting moment of tranquility and peace as the group of characters sit around an outdoor table smoking cigarettes and cigars, evoking in the spectator recognition of the symbolic and ritual meaning of smoking as inducement to peace-making. An analogous moment takes place in Paul's apartment after his quarrel with Rashid, when the two of them are portrayed sitting in the room, watching a baseball game on TV and silently puffing away on cigars. Same as the previous episode, it is devoid of any speech, a moment of silence and reunion with an almost transcendental quality.

In setting up the scene, smoking in Auster's texts is associated with certain quietness, contemplation, or non-aggressive conversation. In other words, what Auster throughout the film seems to be emphasizing is the emotional reality over superficial realism, human time over mechanical or natural time, the "mind" over the "matter," which smoking-related objects and activities capture better than any other element in Auster's life-work assemblage.

But, in the end, it is impossible to sum up the work of the cigarette. A small "thing," it nevertheless has the potential to contain "the entire world" within it, or open up another temporal dimension. The cigarette is an over-determined signifier that cannot be contained in a singular reading. It is always fluid, ambiguous, contra-dictory, multiple, and irreducible to a single type of association. It is, as Sante puts it, "like the language of flowers, or of postage stamps, in which every nuance is pregnant with significance, and there is no possible communication that does not entrain a string of secondary and tertiary meanings."[174] That is what makes it such a perfect tool for exposing the multilayered texture and interpretive dynamics of Auster's own rhizomatic texts.

What would happen if Auster quit smoking—in fact, if all the smoking writers stopped puffing away at their desks? Perhaps, not only their bodies but also their bodies of work would fall apart. Smoke is a binding substance, as we saw. Indeed,

what will happen once cigarettes (soon) become extinct? How would we express and recognize that mind embodied by tobacco, if we stopped believing in its associations—ones that we already deem inappropriate for the safe world we want to live in? There would still be a mind and a matter to write about, but it would be a different mind (a non-smoking writer's mind). How would it be able to look death in the face without the help of the burning cigarette, that phantom of death's image? There would still be a mind and matter to write with, but what kind of device it would be, and how, and what kind of writing it would do, remain to be seen.

Such nostalgic thoughts surround another vanishing tool that Auster works with. What if the writer also lost his typewriter? Seemingly a thing of the past, its presence is already more ghostly than dreamlike. Yet Auster is attached to it no less than to his Schimmelpenninck cigarillos. "I write by hand then I type it up on an old manual typewriter,"[175] says Paul Auster on his process of writing. It is a widely advertised fact that he rejects computers in favor of fountain pens, spiral notebooks, and vintage typewriters.[176] Auster claims that since the day in 1974 when he bought for $40 a used, manual Olympia SM-9 typewriter from his acquaintance, "every word that [he] ha[s] written has been typed out on that machine."[177]

This little technical aspect of his writing process has come to define Paul Auster as a writer, and, unsurprisingly, also his writer-characters (Quinn from *City of Glass*, Blue from *Ghosts*, Sam from *In the Country of Last Things*, Sachs from *Leviathan*, Fogg from *Moon Palace*, Zimmer from *The Book of Illusions*, Martin Frost from *The Inner Life of Martin Frost*, Paul Benjamin from *Smoke*, and …). This fact, that both Auster and his textual stand-ins choose old Underwood, Olympia or Smith-Corona typewriters as their writing tools, raises questions about the significance and function of this object in Auster's writer-figure assemblage. How much of Auster's intratext that we see is the result of the work of a typewriting machine? The typewriter is clearly another suspect on my list.

2

The Story of the Typewriter

The chain-smoking, typewriting writer. I encounter this assemblage, which can be reduced to three core elements—a male figure, a cigarette, and a typewriter—in nearly all of Auster's literary and filmic works. It is what Deleuze and Guattari would call "an extensive multiplicity."[1] The *mise en scène* the figure is placed in is equally consistent in Auster's oeuvre—a bare room in a New York apartment, ascetic in its simplicity, and consisting of a desk, a few books, some paper, a fountain pen, a spiral notebook (Portuguese, preferably), as well as perhaps a bed and a telephone. Images that supplement Auster's written texts depicting this assemblage of objects and spaces, like those of *City of Glass: The Graphic Novel*, could be replaced with analogous shots taken from his films (e.g., *Smoke* or *The Inner Life of Martin Frost*), or with textual descriptions from his books. The contents they all signify are alike.

When Paul Benjamin from *Smoke* is working, he is

> writing in longhand, using a pad of yellow legal paper. An old Smith-Corona typewriter is also on the desk, poised for work with a half-written page in the roller. Off in the corner … a neglected word processor. The workroom is a bare and simple place. Desk, chair, and a small wooden bookcase with manuscripts and papers shoved onto its shelves. The window faces a brick wall.[2]

Blue, in the early novel *Ghosts*, "sets his typewriter on the table and casts about for ideas, trying to apply himself to the task at hand."[3] His study space appears identical: "Pencils, pens, a typewriter. A bureau, a night table, a lamp. A bookcase on the north wall, but no more than several books in it …"[4] Auster himself prefers to work in "a little apartment" in his Brooklyn neighborhood, which he has created as "a very Spartan environment," "a rougher, meaner environment" (presumably it involves the same minimum necessities for writing—a desk, some pens and pencils, a notebook and a typewriter …), because he feels "happier in a bare space."[5] He explains in *Winter Journal*:

> Spartan surroundings, yes, but surroundings have never been of any importance as far as your work is concerned, since the only space you occupy when you write your books is the page in front of your nose, and the room in which you are sitting, the various rooms in which you have sat these forty-plus years, are all but invisible to you as you push your pen across the page of your notebook or transcribe what you have written onto a clean page with your typewriter …[6]

Figure 2.1 The Auster-assemblage. "Mr Coincidence," by Sam Messer, oil on canvas, from *The Story of My Typewriter*.

We will return later to this idea of the writer's solipsistic room, and the interaction between the mind and the "matter" that takes place there. But for now, we should merely notice: the typewriter is ambiguously placed as "an 'intermediate' thing" (to use Heidegger's terminology).[7] It is always in-between, between the thoughts inhabiting the writer's mind and those expressed on paper, "between a tool and a machine."[8] It is, as Martin A. Rice notes, between "a tool" and "the finished product."[9] And it is also between a machine and its operator—the word "typewriter," after all, can mean both.

It is literally a mediator, an agent of textual transmission, installed between the one who types and the typed text.

How does this agent mediate the thought? Does it mediate, or does it, perhaps, create? And, as I am typing up these words on a silent Royal I acquired in Riga years ago, I find myself indeed in a state in-between: between what I want to say, and what the machine says to me. It is a thing symbolically so laden, so ambitiously complex and versatile, that its heavy steel presence threatens to overwhelm my own thoughts. And still it urges me to write. I have not yet written much, but, somehow, the machine makes me feel I will. Its square body seems impregnated with writing-to-come. The typewriter begs me to be a writer and do some writing. "Just press me," the keys plead in unison, "pick any one of us." Too steely, too confident to tolerate any mistakes, it scares and thrills me in equal parts.

It makes me feel like a writer more than a computer does, whose associations are too boundless and scattered to have the same effect. Like the pen, which for centuries dominated the cultural history of writing as a symbol of power associated with authority and authorship, the typewriter has become a visual cliché signifying writing and those who write. Sitting at the typewriter, any humble "writer" gets the reassuring company of Ernest Hemingway, Raymond Chandler, Charles Bukowski, Don DeLillo, Daphne du Maurier, George Orwell, John Updike, Arthur Conan Doyle, Marguerite Duras, T. S. Eliot, William Faulkner, Hermann Hesse, Alfred Hitchcock, Aldous Huxley, Jack Kerouac, Agatha Christie, Sylvia Plath … and Paul Auster, of course. Such connections alone encourage writing.

Typewriter associations

The associations evoked by the typewriter not only embody and express the idea of "true," laborious writing (which originated around the nineteenth century), but also work to fill the outlines of otherwise flat Auster characters with a certain semiotic content. The classical writing tools of pen and paper, of course, have long lost their significance as symbolic and practical evidence for supporting one's position as a writer. Industrialization at the beginning of the nineteenth century simultaneously nullified writing by hand and handiwork.[10] The handwritten word has come to be seen as neither credible nor lasting. Recall the misleading nature of Auster's notebooks that we dealt with earlier. What was required instead was a tool that was sufficiently objective, trustworthy, distanced and stable that in the process of being copied the written word could materialize. This function has historically been fulfilled by the typewriter, as I discovered. Also in Auster's case it works to validate the statement: "I am a writer."

The many histories of the typewriter (by Michael H. Adler, Friedrich A. Kittler and Darren Wershler-Henry, among other scholars) reveal how the typewriter acquired its many functions that shape its "thingness." That is the question of the "whatness" of the thing, the question of its "eidos," which translates from Greek as "form" and is related to the Greek word for "idea."[11] It means that the thing's essence is shaped by its form or "type"—what type of thing is it and what does it allow me to do? So we have to consider what philosopher and collector of old writing machines Richard Polt calls the "eidetic limits [and possibilities] of typewriterness."[12] Those are revealed through strands of the typewriter's cultural history.

And this is what we can trace there. Akin to the first typewriters were pantographs—devices invented in the mid-seventeenth century that could accurately copy a handwritten text for use by lawyers, scriveners, merchants, scholars, registrars, clerks, and the like. It guaranteed precision in the act of copying as well as prevention of falsification. These qualities attributed to early pantographs later worked to form the typewriter's associations with production and transmission of the truth—an idea which continued to dominate in the typewriting discourse for the next few centuries. Typewriters were assumed to be neutral and objective, unmarked by the biases and idiosyncrasies of a dictator or of an amanuensis (who is employed to take dictation or copy manuscripts). The typewriter was capable of delivering the "truth." It is not a coincidence that the word "polygraph" (the correct term for a fixed-width pantograph) is also the official name of what is generally known as a "lie detector," the machine used by law enforcement bodies to test whether a subject's claims are truthful.[13] Because of these claims to accuracy and authority, the typewriter became an apotheosis of rational thinking and writing, and came to be seen as a machine that produces and/or verifies the truth.[14]

It seems to me that for Auster, who is known to write his first drafts by hand, typewritten text is required to finalize and verify his story. The typewriter becomes both "a tool and the finished product, tangible."[15] Because Auster's texts so often expose the process of writing as a struggle to produce a text, the typewriter and typewriting, which are used by these characters, become marks of the progress of their (embedded) narratives. The typewriter makes possible the solution to the protagonist's creative crisis by materializing his *mise en abyme* story, which until then existed only in his mind—unverified, unreliable, and intangible.

Besides, a book is never finished when it is written by hand. That is an illusion—"a book of illusions." Typing up the manuscript allows Auster "to experience the book in a new way, to plunge into the flow of the narrative and feel how it functions as a whole."[16] At this stage, writing becomes the writer's conversation with the typewriter where the machine's responses to the writer's thoughts, extracted from his sketchy notebook and channeled through his typewriting fingers, appear in typescript in front of him. That response changes the writer's thoughts. "Amazing how many errors your fingers will find that your eyes never noticed," Auster says. "Repetitions, awkward constructions, choppy rhythms."[17] He calls his typewriting "reading with [his] fingers"[18]—braille-like, it requires finger dexterity and allows the writer to sense the physicality of the word. "It never fails."[19] The process of typing is simultaneously writing, reading and editing, and, as such, is slow-moving. The pen does not have the machine's patience—it always urges one to move forward; its ink wants to flow and spill.

The text's wholeness that the typewriter suggests has something to do with the fact that the process of typing turns conceptualized or hand-written text into "an official and standardized communiqué: the typed document conforms to 'type.'"[20] Hence, for Polt, typing is "the act of recognizing types, or forms."[21] A type-written text appears

Figure 2.2 I am a writer, and I use a typewriter. Two frames from *City of Glass: The Graphic Novel*, by Auster, Paul Karasik and David Mazzucchelli.

more book-like than a hand-written text in a notebook (which is a book of notes, after all). Typewriting creates a book type, the rules of which dictate that it needs a clear beginning, a designated end, and a consistent body. Typing gathers notes into a book by, first of all, pulling them together into a coherent whole. The text becomes ready to be bound and squashed in between its two hard covers. The type-written text now "feels" like a book whose form it starts to take.

You can see this "action" of the typewriter of finalizing and verifying a story in two of Auster's collaborative works—a film and a comic book. A frame in *City of Glass: The Graphic Novel* equates the telling of a particular story with the process of typing it up. A similar shot at the end of the film *Smoke* informs us that Paul Benjamin has produced the desired piece of text, marking the moment of resolution of his writer's block (the major conflict of the film's subplot). This is signaled to the spectator by a single shot in which the writer types up—on what is presumably his manuscript's title page—his new story's title and his own name. We are to read this as an affirmation of the final stage of writing.

The ability to materialize and verify a story not only distinguishes the typewriter from pen- and hand-writing, but also from the computer, towards which Auster displays a certain scepticism. A computer-typed word that appears on screen never seems "finished." Although Auster admits in interviews that, at times, he has felt tempted to follow technological progress and purchase "one of those marvels," the writer worries about the instability, fragility, disruption, and unreliability that he associates with computers as tools of text-production and storage. Auster has no doubt mythologized the computer no less than he has the typewriter, but his attitude towards the former has been mainly shaped through secondary experiences. From his friends, Auster has heard "too many" computer-related horror stories about "pushing the wrong button and wiping out a day's work—or a month's work" and about "sudden power failures that could erase an entire manuscript in less than half a second."[22]

The sensitivity and intangibility of digital text and the frailty of the machine itself turn computers into "un-reality," "the stark opposite" of the typewriter.[23] In his tribute to the typewriter, "Amor me Jubit Mechanoscribere (Love Bids Me Type)," Martin A. Rice mocks the fragility of the modern-day computer: "[d]rop an Underwood 5 on a laptop and see which survives … You can beat a computer to death with a typewriter, but, as with implication, the converse does not hold!"[24] Unlike any computer, Auster's Olympia, in his own words, remains "dependable" and "indestructible."[25] Whenever asked about his outdated writing machine, Auster makes sure to remind the asker that this "relic" that he bought secondhand forty years ago, and that was built in a West German factory more than half a century ago, "will no doubt go on functioning long after [he is] dead."[26] We can interpret this affection of the writer towards his old typewriter as his desire to leave a lasting imprint behind—one that a computer cannot secure.

Auster, therefore, uses a fountain or ballpoint pen for writing and—as the next step—an old and rattling typewriter, which allows him to literally and physically leave his author's imprint on the white page, either through the tactile experience of "dig[ging] the words into the page" with his pen or by striking them onto the paper through an inked ribbon.[27] The handwritten word must be later consolidated into typescript, because the typewritten word "forces itself onto the paper" so that "[t]he paper has no choice."[28] One of the first typewriters, which has been identified as an inaugural object in typewriting history, was patented by the British engineer Henry Mill in 1714 and described at that time as "an artificial machine for the impressing … of letters …, as in writing," with "the impression being deeper and more lasting than any other writing, and not to be erased or counterfeited without manifest discovery."[29] A machine of a solid and durable type, it produces "solid" and "durable writing."[30] Or, in other words—a textual signature that will last. This desire to "sign" his text manifests itself in an interesting, unexpected and possibly unintentional way in Auster's films as well. First of all, Auster emphasizes his partial authorship of *Smoke* by inserting a shot in the film that shows his hallmark signature (a typing writer) placed under the film's main *mise en abyme* story about a writer's productivity ("Auggie Wren's Christmas Story"). We know that the writer has regained his ability to write because a close-up shot shows the title of the story typed by a typewriter on a white sheet of paper:

AUGGIE WREN'S CHRISTMAS STORY
BY
PAUL BENJAMIN

The spectator cannot see the writer's face but sees only two hands, loudly striking the keys and, letter by letter, almost melodically arranging the words until they form the title. Not many know that the hands in these frames belong to the "real" writer Paul Auster. This quick shot not only allows Auster to place his signature in the film, but also brings him closer to the character of Paul Benjamin, with whom he shares a not entirely comprehensible relationship, because Benjamin seems to be Auster's prototype, while at the same time he has "nothing to do with [Auster]" and is "an invented character," as Auster himself insists.[31]

Apropos of filmic signatures, this small and concealed cameo appearance becomes more significant if we notice that each of the four Auster films contain similar "signs," in the form of episodic roles played either by Auster or by one of his family members (other "Austers"). Apart from Auster's hands, *Smoke*'s cast includes his son Daniel in the role of book thief. Auster's daughter Sophie appears in *Lulu on the Bridge* as Sonia Kleinman and also in his filmic production *The Inner Life of Martin Frost* as one writer's clumsy muse, Anna James. And in the ending sequence of *The Music of Chance* we see Paul Auster himself again. It does not even matter if some of these cameos, which serve as the author's signature, were unintentional—they have already become a kind of hallmark, similar to the fleeting appearance of Alfred Hitchcock in all of his films.[32]

But, as concerns signs expressed through "word processors," the differences between computers and typewriters stretch far beyond their physical nature or the materiality of the finished text. The fundamental difference is this: they are different thinking tools. A computer (especially a laptop), which may be physically reminiscent of the typewriter, is not the latter's more advanced sibling but an object of a different kind, because it operates according to a different logic or mode of "thinking." The differences between these thinking modes—what Michael Foucault calls a "discontinuity" and what Wershler-Henry describes as the "space that appears between modes of thinking (and the technologies that help to create and propagate them)"[33]—is what distinguishes different writing styles. Auster puts it simply: "talking about writing in the book is talking about thinking, finally. Talking about how you tell the story because that really is what it's all about."[34] And Auster, I think, thinks through the typewriter.

Nicholas Carr and Sven Birkerts are among the many who have written on the computer's impact on the way a subject thinks, reads, and writes.[35] An electronic medium like the computer seems to disrupt the logic of linear thinking that has come to be associated with print, partly because it is so forgiving of the writer's mistakes—"[i]t might even correct them for you."[36] Because it does not demand the discipline of thought and ability to think ahead, like in chess, the computer is "tailor made for soft and fuzzy thinking."[37] The lack (or "pure avoidance," in Rice's words) of required effort in thinking, and, by implication, in writing, and the absence of "physical character" makes computer-assisted writing appear ethereal, false, misleading. Un-real. A computer-typed text is "un-reality" in contrast to a typewritten text.[38]

If the computer is "un-reality" then the typewriter is "reality" because neither reality nor typewriters "tolerate fluff, or slop, or laziness."[39] Auster knows that: "With a computer, you make your changes on the screen and then you print out a clean copy. With a typewriter, you can't get a clean manuscript unless you start again from scratch."[40] Typewriting is "like logic—hard, cold, brutal, unyielding,"[41] and it is exactly in the act of typewriting that the typewriter machine starts to exert its influence over the thoughts of the one operating it. When Friedrich Nietzsche sat down at his "Schreibkugel" (a Malling Hansen "writing ball," patented in 1870), he soon observed that the machine had a curious effect on his thinking and writing style. "Our writing tools are also working on our thoughts," Nietzsche famously typed.[42] He had received the typewriter as a Christmas gift from his mother and sister in 1881 and initially was not impressed. "Maybe the Nietzsche women wanted to change Friedrich's writing [thinking!]," Polt playfully remarks.[43] Apparently, the women, *the machine*, succeeded in changing it. The philosopher, writes the media technologist Friedrich A. Kittler,

> changed from arguments to aphorisms, from thoughts to puns, from rhetoric to telegram style. That is precisely what is meant by the sentence that our writing tools are also working on our thoughts. Malling Hansen's writing ball, with its operating difficulties, made Nietzsche into a laconic.[44]

A similar observation about the effect of typewriting was made by T. S. Eliot, whose writing under the influence of a typewriter became more "lucid." Wershler-Henry notes how Henry James gradually "adapted" his "speech patterns" to the "necessity of typewriting" (as his typing secretary Theodora Bosanquet observed).[45] It is nothing but "the effect of its technology on style," concludes Kittler.[46] After all, August Dvorak himself (the inventor of the Dvorak keyboard) perceived typewriting as "designed to develop you into a thinking machine," as he put it in his *Typewriting Behavior: Psychology Applied to Teaching and Learning Typewriting.*[47]

Barry Lewis describes Auster's style of writing as combining "both the dryness of a clinical report and the inventiveness of fiction."[48] It is often characterized as austere and laconic—a peculiarity for which you can blame the writer's collaboration with his Olympia typewriter. Because of the typewriter's involvement in the writing process, Auster's texts have managed to retain their desired lean type and certain "flatness," while leaving enough room for the reader's imagination, so that in the reader's mind the text could acquire the desired "third dimension." The typewriter in its interaction with the writer also seems to command the tempo of story-writing by keeping a steady beat (not unlike the cigarette does it for story-telling). This metronome dictates that writing is a painstakingly slow and "incredibly tedious process," says Auster.[49] Typewriting is also laborious: "It's bad for your neck, bad for your back, and even if you can type twenty or thirty pages a day, the finished pages pile up with excruciating slowness."[50] Yet the patience and labor on the writer's part awards his text an aesthetic quality that computer-written texts seem to lack. Because of the effort invested in producing a typewritten text, every word in typescript appears to carry greater significance, and this quality applies to the whole text (for what is a text but an assemblage of words?). This leads to the typewriter's associations with arduous, "real" writing, and explains how the machine itself became a symbol of "unalienated labour."[51]

If the typewriter ascribes to the typing subject logical thinking and hard work that results in "real" writing, and if it has the ability to produce legible, meaningful truth, then it is little wonder that the typewriter itself becomes viewed as a possible source of some confidence and stability in a world which is otherwise dominated by confusion, disorder, and instability—i.e., in a computer-dominated world. Wershler-Henry thinks that is one of the reasons why some writers are reluctant to move from typewriting to computer-writing: "[t]he consequences of hewing to the old order from within the new one are not simply aesthetic; they're also ontological."[52] Naturally so, because things evoke their worlds—especially archaic things, whose worlds are otherwise out of reach to us, and, as such, not taken for granted. Polt even attributes "magical power" to a thing of the past because it is "a window—a hole in the wholeness of our world (which is never a seamless wholeness), through which we can imagine another world."[53] Auster evidently uses this typewriter-window to connect to a bygone era that is ontologically safer, and to the writers, books and ideas that belong to it.

The typewriter evokes associations with "the mythical time when words had unequivocal meaning, and the machines used to produce them were free from error or duplicity."[54] A time which vividly contrasts with the diegetic setting of Auster's *City of Glass* or *In the Country of Last Things*, in which things have lost their meaning because the link between the signifier and the signified has been broken. These texts portray a world that is disintegrating and falling apart.

In the dystopian novel *In the Country of Last Things*, the protagonist Anna Blume makes her living by "scavenging" for broken and half-forgotten things on the city streets because objects that have a capacity for being reused or recycled are collected and "salvaged." At some point, she stumbles upon a crippled old typewriter, which has become just another piece of discarded junk. Blume's universe is a place marked by instability and uncertainty, where "things fall apart and vanish" before one's very eyes, and "[e]ntire categories of objects disappear—flower-pots, for example, or cigarette filters, or rubber bands—and for a time you will be able to recognize those words, even if you cannot recall what they mean."[55] The rediscovered typewriter's strength lies in its promise that not will only the typewritten text not perish, but it will remain readable and meaningful (unlike the notebook from *City of Glass*, whose contents narrators, characters and readers are unable to "decipher").

It seems to me that Auster needs the typewriter to anchor this fragile sense of stability and order as much as he needs the figure of a detective (embodiment of truth and order), which also keeps reappearing in his works. "Everything breaks, everything wears out, everything loses its purpose in the end," writes Auster in *The Story of My Typewriter*, "but the typewriter is still with me."[56] Elsewhere in the same book, he describes his typewriter as "battered and obsolete, a relic from an age that is quickly passing from memory."[57] Nevertheless, "the damn thing has never given out on [him]."[58]

Curiously, for Auster his typewriter mutates from a mere working tool into something more personally meaningful after the writer starts to realize that the machine is a relic from an era of writing that is about to disappear. "It was simply a tool that allowed me to do my work, but now that it had become an endangered species, one of the last surviving artifacts of twentieth-century *homo scriptorus*, I began to develop a certain affection for it," admits Auster.[59] And that is the moment when the typewriter moves beyond its primary function of reproducing a typescript copy of a text and starts to operate on a more metaphorical level.

In his essay "The Things We Carry," Joshua Wolf Shenk questions the value of things, of antique objects (their "intrinsic versus market worth"), and the ways they become commodities.[60] Although the machine's material worth is undermined by its "modernity," in Shenk's house (as well as in his imagination) his grandfather's Hebrew typewriter takes an honorary place. The vintage machine has lost its mechanical functionality; it is even out of order—"the ribbon is dry, the platen so hard that it could crack the type."[61] This thing, "built to make meaning through language," is not used for writing anymore—it just "sits [there] idle and stares."[62] And yet, as Shenk suggests, a thing like this old typewriter, is "made to breathe and speak."[63]

When a piece of equipment loses its functionality, it does not immediately become "a mere object." Instead, as Richard Polt explains, it "draws attention to its world," "evokes its world, speaks of it, by appealing to our imagination."[64] It announces "what is missing," says Shenk, "the world that created them, the person who used them;" it is a "portal."[65] Because Shenk's grandfather is also part of the same typewriting world, the typewriter becomes a sort of a "monument"[66] with symbolic value closely tied to him. Its value, Shenk suggests, is "in *feelings* that can be evoked by [this] thing[] but not counted, transferred, or … represented," that "can be imagined but never confirmed," because it links to a past never known (his emphasis).

"If I strain, I can picture my grandfather hunched over it, striking its keys. But I am touching an absence," writes Shenk. "The typewriter speaks of my grandfather but is, for me, forever silent."[67] It resembles Auster's barren efforts to grasp the essence of his deceased father's identity from the things and objects Samuel Auster left behind. The apparent promise of objects to reveal something more about the identity of their users (as if in those objects one could read traces left there by their user) is illusory. Things are "inert" for Auster; they have meaning "only in function of the life that makes use of them. When that life ends, the things change, even though they remain the same. They are there and yet not there: tangible ghosts, condemned to survive in a world they no longer belong to."[68]

But, paradoxically, that is also the strength of such "things in-between," and Auster must know this. If a ghostly object fails to recall its owner from death, it can nevertheless work to help summon it through imagination. The grieving Zimmer from *The Book of Illusions* tries to evoke the sense of presence of his dead wife through sensations and memories associated with certain objects once used by her. He tries on her clothes and puts on her perfume. "It was a deeply satisfying experience…"—even if only for a while.[69] And so we learn from these accounts that the true value of the thing is not tied to itself, or its "memory," but "'what it can conjure,' its invisible connections, what it ushers forth …"[70] Those are the same windows—shortcuts to other worlds—that I spoke of earlier.

These "portals" not only open the way to an imaginative or recollective experience of a world gone past. They also allow connection with other actants, things or notions from the same milieu. An object like Auster's own typewriter becomes a sort of gateway connecting two realms—the real and the imaginary, the present and the past, the external and the internal. It makes it possible to explore both sides of the Möbius strip. Therefore, it is also one of the central elements in Auster's *The Inner Life of Martin Frost*, a film which investigates the process of writing and the relationship between reality and imagination, constantly crossing the threshold between the two.

What is this world that the typewriter "speaks of" to its present-day user? It is an imaginary past "when things—in this case, writing—'meant something' and it was possible to ask the big questions without wondering about the presumptions involved."[71] From a cold, 40-pound iron-cast industrialized machine, the typewriter has become a poetic symbol of "true" modernist writing. It allows the one who sits at it and types to access an imagined cultural experience of the past, the space that Wershler-Henry describes as

> a non-existent sepia-toned era when people typed passionately late into the night under the flickering light of a single naked bulb, sleeves rolled up, suspenders hanging down, lighting each new cigarette off the smouldering butt of the last, occasionally taking a pull from the bottle of bourbon in the bottom drawer of the filing cabinet.[72]

The typewriter, like the cigarette, is a "thing that things," or "gathers," but the typewriter's gathering works predominantly on the level of the imaginary. The cigarette—a social object—gathers smoking people around it. The work of the typewriter, like that of the writer, presupposes a solitary experience. Its "thinging" takes place in the writer's mind, where it acts to create "invisible connections" with other typing writers of the past. Martin A. Rice, another typewriter devotee, explains: "When I type, I'm linked to all the hard thinking men of the past, the Raymond Chandlers, the Erle Stanley Gardners, the Dashiell Hammetts, the Russells, the Moores and the Searles."[73]

For Auster, however, it is not so much the typewriter itself as the kind of shared solitary experience that (type)writing requires and suggests that allows him to connect with other writers with whom he feels a strong affiliation. As he notes in the interview with McCaffery and Gregory, "the more intensely you are alone, the more deeply you plunge into a state of solitude, the more deeply you feel that connection."[74] The typewriter as a writing tool first provokes, then externalizes, these connections which serve as a source of inspiration for Auster and so generate intertextuality:

> No matter how apart you might find yourself in a physical sense—whether you've been marooned on a desert island or locked up in a solitary confinement—you discover that you are inhabited by others. Your language, your memories, even your sense of isolation—every thought in your head has been born from your connection with others ... That's why the book is filled with so many references and quotations, in order to pay homage to all the others inside me.[75]

As a young writer, Auster would wonder about the "eerie, disembodied quality" that characterizes his narrative voice, and in particular the third-person voice: "Where are the words coming from? Who's saying this? … It seems to come from nowhere and I found that disturbing."[76] The typewriter emphasizes what the narrative voice already has done: it further disembodies and de-personalizes the author, separating him from his words. The space created through this split does not remain empty. Throughout the discourse of the history of typewriting it can be observed that the typewriter, since its genesis, has always been connected with a "sense of uncanniness that … some force inside or beyond the machine is actually doing the composing"[77]—whether, as in Auster's case, it is one of "the others" inhabiting his mind, or someone or something else.

As Wershler-Henry points out, the idea of the typewriter as potentially channeling someone Other from elsewhere probably stems from the invention and construction of semi-automatic machines (writing machines, clocks, and similar objects), which temporally coincided and partially overlapped with the advent of the typewriter, and which, like the latter, seemed to manifest autonomy and independence from human intervention in carrying out certain tasks. As more and more people rejected the pen as a symbol of authorship and authority, and turned to the typewriter as a means of text-production, the question of "exactly who—or what—was doing the thinking that produced typewriting" became increasingly prominent.[78] And so we have learned: nobody is ever alone at the typewriter, and to engage in typewriting is never an innocent act.

The typewriter-assemblage

The typewriter is ambiguous. Since its coinage, the word "typewriter" itself has denoted two entities—that of the writing machine and of the person operating it. Or, from a slightly different way of looking, there is always someone or something typing ("type-") and someone or something writing ("-writing"). Is "writing" the same as "typewriting"? If yes, who or what is doing the job of (type)writing? Confusion arises because the typewriter always demands an assemblage; it cannot function on its own, as computers do (and even then, a computer always presupposes a human being who has assembled it to function). For a (manual) typewriter to do its typewriting, it first needs a human touch—the spark of life passed on from an outstretched fingertip. (It is different with electric typewriters, "other machines, computers and so on," whose soul is "hooked into the wall," as the "Typewriter Man" Martin Tytell explains.[79])

Either way, the name suggests that what one gets with "typewriting" is "a package deal," an assemblage of a human and a machine. This means that typewriting is a kind of collaboration. A week of typewriting was enough to plant the half-blind Nietzsche "into an assemblage with the machine that, as Henry Ford fantasized, would do away with the shortcomings of the flesh … [Nietzsche wrote:] 'the eyes no longer have to do their work.'"[80] In other words, the two become one, and the border between the non-human and the human is erased. In the same year that Nietzsche recognized the impact of his writing machine on his thoughts, he typed a poem about his "writing ball":

THE WRITING BALL IS A THING LIKE ME: MADE OF IRON
YET EASILY TWISTED ON JOURNEYS.
PATIENCE AND TACT ARE REQUIRED IN ABUNDANCE
AS WELL AS FINE FINGERS, TO USE US.[81]

Wershler-Henry derives a syllogistic conclusion from the poem: "If the writing ball is a thing—an object—so too is the philosopher: 'A THING LIKE ME'. If the philosopher is alive, so too is the writing ball."[82] Typewriting results in mutual impacts—a part of the typing human becomes de-humanized, machine-like, and a part of the machine gains human characteristics. Auster, for example, has trouble "thinking of [his]

Figure 2.3 A set of fine fingers at work. Stills from *The Inner Life of Martin Frost*.

typewriter as *it*. Slowly but surely, the *it* has turned into a *him*"[83] (his emphasis). His Olympia "has moods and desires now, it expresses dark angers and exuberant joys, and trapped within its gray, metallic body, you would almost swear that you could hear the beating of a heart."[84]

The reverse process also takes place as soon as Auster or his characters start typing. Recall one of the final shots in *Smoke* which shows Paul Benjamin/Paul Auster typing, or the almost-identical shots of typewriting from *The Inner Life of Martin Frost*: a close-up of two hands whose fingers are dancing on the machine's keyboard. Those are hands that have been severed from the writer's body. And this image of the dehumanized, typing hands which have merged with an old Smith-Corona typewriter reminds me of prosthetic hands at work. The organic and the inorganic fuse into "US," with the machine becoming human-like, and the human more like a machine—an assemblage of iron and meat, becoming, in Wershler-Henry's words, "one continuous instrument at the disposal of an entirely other set of 'FINE FINGERS.'"[85]

The comparison of a typewriter to a prosthetic limb is an apt one. After all, the first writing machines were invented to give blind people access to the written truth and let them proclaim the truth through their own (type)writing. (This thought takes us back to the typewriter's alleged ability to produce and channel the truth.) The inventor of Nietzsche's writing ball, Hans Rasmus Johann Malling Hansen (a.k.a. Malling Hansen) apparently conceived of his machine as a prosthetic device to aid the visually impaired. In fact, as Kittler bluntly puts it, most technical media (the typewriter, the telephone, the gramophone) were invented as prosthetic tools designed for and by "cripples and handicaps."[86]

A prosthesis seeks to compensate for a lack of something. In Brian McHale's words, it simultaneously "extends a human organ or capability and replaces it."[87] McHale refers to David Wills, whose "provocative" account of it, as he puts it, "disturbingly combines natural and artificial, human and mechanical, the spontaneous and the contrived, overriding the distinction between these categories."[88] Typewriting is prosthetic because the production of the text involves an assemblage, in which, in Wills' words, "a human [is] attached to a writing machine."[89]

But typewriting is also prosthetic because the typewriter's imposed rules, limitations, and possibilities, its "algorithms," likewise simultaneously extend and replace handwriting. During the typewriting process, Auster and his fictional stand-ins become part humans, part machines, cyborgs, Auster-machines. This process is never innocent. Typewriting, like any other machine-writing, always creates ambiguity, representing, to use McHale's words, "a case in which machine mediation becomes indistinguishable from machine generation."[90]

Typewriting, then, makes the question of authorship even more difficult to determine because it removes the illusory certainty that a handwritten manuscript offers. With typewriting, as Heidegger lamented, the script is torn from "the essential realm of hand—and this means the hand is removed from the essential realm of the word. The word itself turns into something 'typed.'"[91] It becomes no less than "a type"—a template, in other words. Typewriting de-humanizes. For Heidegger,

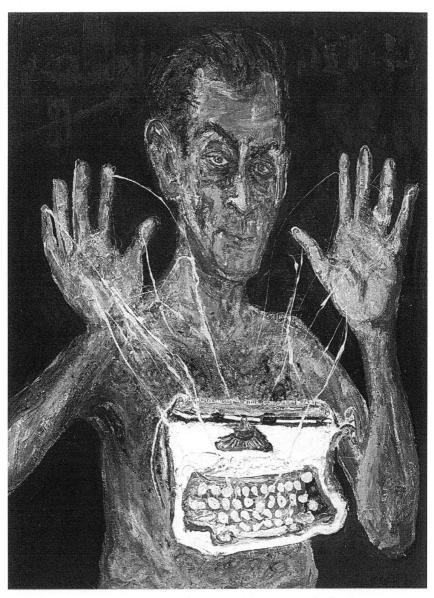

Figure 2.4 "Which is the puppet and which is the puppeteer?" asks Darren Wershler-Henry. Paul Auster and his typewriter in "As One," oil painting by Sam Messer, from *The Story of My Typewriter*.

for whom the hand, together with the word, formed "the essential distinction of man"—"Man himself acts [*handelt*] through the hand [*Hand*]"[92]—the two were inseparable. Auster could sense that. With a pen in his hand, he felt "the words ... coming out of [his] body," and not from "nowhere" anymore.[93] The typewriter does not subscribe to this idea that a medium could somehow be natural to a human body. The typing machine cannot be grasped or held in one's hand like a pen: it does not confer its power to the hand that operates it.

Two hands are used in typewriting instead of one, and nine fingers. They move in at least two directions each—upwards, downwards, sideways, sometimes (if the user lacks skill) crossing their paths. This, by the way, explains the association between the writer's many fingers engaged in typewriting, and the multitude of hands that are "writing" in Messer's two portraits of Auster. The arachnid hands dancing on the keyboard weave a rhizomatic text, just as the increase in the number of fingers engaged with the writing tool enacts the tool's tendency to multiply the written text.

From a pen-writing hand, the text flows onto a paper as a never-ending stream of consciousness, and it is the writer's mind, and the hand, that decide when and how to control it. In typewriting, the words (and the thoughts) are broken even before they are written. They must be assembled from a set of types, letters, characters laid out before the writer in four or more rows of the (typical) QWERTY keyboard layout. There is no flow, only quick assemblages, followed by more assemblages that must be mobilized in an army of straight, machine-defined lines. It is a different "type of writing." The machine interrupts the flow of thought and imposes itself on the writer. It clearly wants to claim its part in writing. So the question remains: when an Auster film shows Martin Frost or Paul Benjamin working at the typewriter, are they "typing" or are they "writing"? And if we accept that the typewriter-assemblage not only presupposes the human becoming machine-like, but also the machine becoming more human-like—who or what is the author then, and where does the dictating voice come from?

Wershler-Henry remarks that the bipartite division of the typewriter-assemblage into a machine and its operator is in itself a categorical mistake.[94] Typewriting, after all, includes not only the process of copying or recording a dictated text, which is done in collaboration between a human and machine, but also the dictator itself. Apart from the machine, there is a writer and a human typewriter, an author and a scrivener. The first element in the typewriter-assemblage therefore is the typewriter, the actual machine that makes writing possible. The second one is the amanuensis or the other "typewriter," the one who copies, who types, through which the words that come from the dictator are channeled into the writing machine. The hands that we see typing then (even when in *Smoke* they are Auster's actual hands) are no longer the same hands as those of Paul Auster the dictator, the author. They belong to the obedient amanuensis, the scribe, the typewriter.

The third element is the dictator, the dictating voice and the "source" of the words dictated.[95] This triangle, Wershler-Henry explains, was most evident in the middle of the nineteenth century, when typewriting became prominent in office work and the dictating person entrusted recording of the dictated text to a secretary (a.k.a.

typewriter). Although this division appears simple in itself, the problem is that the typewriter creates a schizophrenic situation where the identity of the dictator (the dictated "I") fluctuates back and forth, interacting with the identity of the amanuensis (who is forced to write this "I"). "[D]ictation weaves them [both] together in a manner that makes their writing styles indistinguishable,"[96] writes Wershler-Henry. The text begins to resonate with a multiplicity of voices, some of them unforeseen. It starts to appear "haunted."

Do Paul Auster and his writer-characters dictate to anyone, or do they themselves take dictation? For our solipsistic subject of investigation, the process of writing takes place in a solitary environment. Yet that does not mean that he is "alone," as we saw earlier. Present always, as Wershler-Henry notes, is "someone or something, even if it's just another part of ourselves," who "dictates to us, tells us what to write until we internalize it and forget about it ... No one is ever alone at a typewriter."[97] He suggests that within the categorization that includes three elements one can distinguish at least four forces that all participate in the typewriting situation: the machine, its operator or the amanuensis, the dictator, and this dictating, inspiring voice, which could claim to have the authorship and which could originate in any of the three above-mentioned sources. The typewriter renders authorship ambiguous. And that, in turn, could be yet another reason why Auster stays loyal to the typewriter. The typewriter defies origins. It makes possible rhizomatic text-generation, where authorship is always obscure and shared.

On the desk in front of me, I have placed Auster's *The Story of My Typewriter* (2002), which, as the name suggests, is a book dedicated to his old Olympia typewriter. It is a compelling text. Visually reminiscent of a children's book, it is part textual book, part art book. Set in large type and accompanied by Sam Messer's colorful oil paintings of Auster's manual Olympia, it tells a story of how Auster acquired, and grew affectionate towards, his typewriter. Together, the text and the images are also telling of the kind of ambiguous relationship that has come to exist among the three of them: "[b]etween a writer and an artist. Between a writer and his typewriter. Between an artist and his obsession with the writer's typewriter."[98]

The book is therefore a collaboration between Auster and his acquaintance Sam Messer. Yet Auster claims that his typewriter "talks" to him, has a mind of its own, and that, in fact, the book was written not by him but by the machine—"Letter by letter I have watched it write these words," he writes.[99] Auster attributes a soul to his Olympia—a soul which he believes the typewriter laid bare when posing for Messer for the paintings and which has now "possessed" the machine.[100] Hence, the possibility for the ambiguous fourfold authorship—Auster, Messer, the Olympia and "whatever 'spirits' might be possessing" it.[101]

The idea that a writer's tool (be it pen or typewriter) is possessed and capable of transmitting to the writer an inspiring or dictating voice from somewhere else, an intervening outside source, is not new to the discourse of typing writers. Kittler and Wershler-Henry both point to exemplary documented cases of what can be called "ghostwriting." Henry James, for example, allegedly felt he had channeled the ghost of Napoleon Bonaparte during a typewriting session with his typist Theodora

Bosanquet, when he dictated to her in a clear and coherent manner two letters that Bonaparte wrote to one of his married sisters.[102] After James' death, it was Bosanquet who, while (type)writing (presumably on James' old Remington Priestess) her biography of James, *Henry James at Work*, claimed to have encountered his ghost, who dictated to her the contents of the book. Inspired by the idea that a typewriter could channel authorial voices, American author John Kendrick Bangs in 1899 wrote a collection of short stories, *The Enchanted Typewriter,* whose authorship he largely attributes to the late James Boswell. The dead writer "spoke" to him via the typewriter. Who wrote the stories? This collaboration between the living, the dead, and the typewriter results in a situation where the typewritten text's authorship can no longer be distinguished.

Rhizomatic typewriting

Yet the typewriter situation does more than confuse the authorship of a single typewritten text. It seems to affect the whole network of texts it has (co-)produced. In the case of my suspect, Paul Auster, this entanglement surrounding authorship and textual origins is passed on from one text to another, problematizing the structure of his whole body of work. From the typewriter-actant perspective, it is the typewriter's tendency to first depersonalize and then reproduce copies of texts that seems to fuel the rhizome-generating machinery. After the typed text with its austere laconism and uniformity of typescript has eliminated any remains of individual authorship, the detached text, stripped to its bare essentials, gets reproduced, duplicated or recycled to reappear in a variety of forms. Auster's use of a limited set of elements to create the same story with slight variations resembles the prosthetic writing that McHale describes.[103]

McHale's observation that the aesthetics of prosthesis does not differentiate between genres explains the multidisciplinarity and multimediality of Auster's texts.[104] Prosthetic writing "systematically blurs that genre distinction" so that "the output of algorithms is just as likely to be one as the other."[105] All the distinctions of genre and discipline erode, and "what remains is an extra- or supra- or infra-generic practice of *writing,* which may include discourses of nonverbal media. Prosthesis seems to promise (or threaten) a realignment of genre categories," writes McHale (his emphasis).[106] And so, in Auster's work, as Markus Rheindorf also notes, there is a "change of shape, an outward metamorphosis that [nevertheless] leaves the core intact."[107]

This is a purely prosthetic quality: Auster's texts, through duplication, form a rhizome that spans genres, disciplines, and media, erasing all borderlines between them. The writer, for example, insists that his memoir-like *Winter Journal,* which is "really not a memoir," has "no genre whatsoever."[108] Prosthetic writing results not only in such genreless texts but also in textual hybrids such as "graphic novels" (the graphic adaptation of *City of Glass*) and "written films"[109] (such as the ones included in *The Book of Illusions*). Moreover, this remolding of a story from one genre or discipline to another is a process that is often reversible.

So, in Auster's film *Smoke,* the duplication of "Auggie Wren's Christmas Story" from oral narration to a typed-up story, and then from typescript to a film is, in the words of Jesús Ángel González, "a metafictional paradox: images become words (because the pictures taken by Auggie create stories and emotions in Paul's mind and are then transformed into words) and words become images (because Paul Benjamin's story for the newspaper is shown in images)."[110] At the same time, the black-and-white sequence at the end of *Smoke*, which shows words becoming images (or the novelist becoming filmmaker), appears like "the other side of the coin" of *The Book of Illusions*, where a reverse process is happening. David Zimmer, the novel's main character, presents to the reader a silent movie … through the written word, thus turning from a film maker into novelist.[111]

The "written films" of *The Book of Illusions* that as *mises en abyme* take up to one-third of the book's length appear unlocatable within any of the distinguished genres and text types. One of them, *The Inner Life of Martin Frost*, is presented in the book neither as a film script for silent movies nor a filmic review or description of scenes. It is an ambiguous amalgamation of both. As González points out, "Auster does not just describe images, he also summarizes, describes, and provides shot description using the specialized language of the most common way of translation between film discourse and literary discourse: the language of scripts."[112] Yet he also offers "the interpretation of the images," "the critical commentary and, very significantly, the audience reaction."[113] This brings us back to the idea that the the the rhizome is not characterized by filiation but by alliance, not by the pretension "either … or" but by the conjuncture "and … and … and …"

A hybrid text itself, the "written film" of *The Inner Life of Martin Frost* that is included in *The Book of Illusions* predictably exists in multiple other copies within Auster's oeuvre. One could say that this text has multiple entry points for the reader or the spectator. Let me point out a few. Entrance number one (an "unreachable" entrance that, nevertheless, "exists"): in *The Book of Illusions* (2002), the character of Hector Mann, a film director from the bygone era of silent movies, allegedly makes a film of the same title, and the narrator-protagonist Zimmer is one of the few to be able to view the film before its destruction. Through Zimmer's narration, Mann's film becomes a "written film" (number two) which is neither a review nor a detailed description, neither a film script nor the director's commentary, but simultaneously all of these combined. The film's authorship is unclear. Moreover, one of the book's interpretations suggests that both Zimmer's meeting with the film director and the viewings of his films are in fact invented by Zimmer and happen in his imagination. I will get back to this shortly. Number three: back in 1999, Auster wrote *The Inner Life of Martin Frost* as a screenplay for a 12-film project called *Erotic Tales*, which he eventually pulled out of.[114] Number four: this unused script later grew into a full screenplay (published in 2007; number five), and a film of the same title (number six), directed by Auster himself (2007). And seven: this title also belongs to a collaboration project between Auster and graphic artist Glenn Thomas—half art book, half large-scale textual book (2008), whose subtitle informs us: "From *The Book of Illusions*." We can count at least seven different "copies" of *The Inner Life of Martin Frost*, each of which have a slightly different appearance.

But never mind the nuances—when I take a closer look at the story, I see the same algorithm at work. I am given yet another slightly altered version of Auster's meta-story about the crisis-stricken writer. A story that is set and unfolds within the same familiar assemblage and according to the same principles. Besides, the constant self- and cross-referentiality that exists between the story of Martin Frost and all of Auster's other texts arranges them in a complex rhizomatic network where each text not only becomes a copy of another, but also "a multiplicity" and "a part of" one another. For example, the protagonist Zimmer in *The Book of Illusion* learns that Hector Mann has written a book called *Travels in the Scriptorium*. But in the embedded narrative of the same book (the "written film" of *The Inner Life of Martin Frost*) the character of Claire tells Martin that *Travels in the Scriptorium* is the best novel he has ever written. In the "real" novel *Travels in the Scriptorium*, written by Auster and published in 2006, the reader is told that Zimmer from *The Book of Illusions* has married the protagonist of *In the Country of Last Things*, Anna Blume. And so on, and on.

Within Auster's rhizomatic network, the hypodiegetic text of each novel or film serves to comment on or augment the master-narrative, and the resulting Chinese-box effect makes them all indistinguishable from each other. This method for constructing stories matches Auster's own observation about the nature of reality given in his pseudo-autobiographical work *The Invention of Solitude*: "Everything seemed to be repeating itself. Reality was a Chinese box, an infinite series of containers within containers."[115] And so we are back to the metaphor of texts as "containers."

The Book of Illusions, as I just noted, is based on the same emblematic Auster story of recovery from existential and creative loss. A woman is needed for this story to work. And there is one—Alma—who unexpectedly turns up in Zimmer's life and takes him with her to a ranch at the other end of the world, in order to meet the legendary film maker Hector Mann. Alma, who becomes Zimmer's lover, brings him back to life and writing, but dies at the end. One of Mann's silent movies, *The Inner Life of Martin Frost*, focuses on the protagonist Martin's struggles to regain his ability to write, and so exposes the process of literary creation. A strange woman also appears in Martin's life, and she too plays a crucial role in his recovery. As we learn at the end, this woman is Martin's invention, his self-made muse, who, unsurprisingly, dies once Martin finishes writing his story.

Most of the story, then, appears to have taken place in Martin's mind. This *mise en abyme* adds an extra layer of signification to the extradiegetic story of the book (i.e., Zimmer's narration). The story of Martin Frost becomes "much richer" than in its previous isolated form, because it "interacts with the main story of the novel" and "acts as *mise-en-abyme* of the diegetic story by means of a semantic network of analogies and contrasts."[116] It opens up the possibility for a new reading of *The Book of Illusions* by suggesting that what the reader perceives as happening to the protagonist Zimmer throughout may well have taken place in the writer's mind. There are other clues in his story that are equally suggestive of its imaginary nature—like the name of the ranch that he supposedly visited, Tierra del Sueño, which is Spanish for "land of dreams." González:

... if Claire in the film [*The Inner Life of Martin Frost*] is 'a spirit,' ... Alma's name also suggests her spiritual, dream-like nature ('Alma had walked in and out of my life so quickly, I sometimes felt that I had only imagined her' ...) ... As a matter of fact, all the clues about the nature of perception that suggest the unreal quality of the Martin Frost story may be applied to *The Book of Illusions*, explaining one possible meaning of its title. The entire Alma-David story, including their trip to Tierra del Sueño ..., might have been an illusion, a fantasy created by David Zimmer himself.[117]

Perhaps this story of a writer's "inner life" is a commentary on the nature of any Auster text. What you witness here is but the writer's wizardry at work, "the invention of illusions" (as González and Stefania Ciocia would say). Like most of Auster's texts that aim to "open up the process" and "expose the plumbing"[118] of writing, *The Book of Illusions*, too, appears as a self-conscious writing exercise. Its title, as González also remarks, is no less suggestive than that of Tierra del Sueño. And the protagonist's name, Zimmer, itself bears strong connotations of the kind of imaginary spaces in which Auster's characters locate themselves to come up with their solipsistic stories.

Zimmer means "room" in German and a room in Auster's oeuvre often functions as a metaphor for the writer's mind, denoting a kind of domain where the internal and external worlds meet.[119] Rheindorf has described the room of Auster's works as "the image and *locus* of his characters' descents into solipsism,"[120] a place where "the spirit can project itself against the walls,"[121] a site, a landscape, a "sanctuary of inwardness."[122] It is not only the bare physical room in which the writer-assemblage does its work, but it is also "the room of the book," as in Auster's "The Book of Memory" (the second part of *The Invention of Solitude*). It is a space where, in Stephen Fredman's words, "life and writing meet in an unstable, creative, and sometimes dangerous encounter."[123]

When recounting his time spent in Paris, where he met a composer by the name of S., the protagonist of "The Book of Memory," A., gives a description of the composer's room that, although physically a claustrophobic space, is infinitely generative for the mind and can possibly contain the whole universe (just like Sartre's pipe):

> For there was *an entire universe in that room*, a miniature cosmology that contained all that is most vast, most distant, most unknowable ... *the representation of one man's inner world*, even to the slightest detail ... The room he lived in was *a dream space*, and its walls were like the skin of some second body around him, as if his own body had been transformed into a mind, *a breathing instrument of pure thought*.[124] (my emphasis)

When Zimmer from *The Book of Illusions* is working on his book about Hector Mann, he "hole[s] up in that small apartment" he has rented in Brooklyn, and, entrapped in that solitary space without a telephone, TV, or any social life, works "seven days a week, sitting at the desk from ten to twelve hours a day."[125] Except for small excursions to Montague Street "to stock up on food and paper, ink and typewriter ribbons," he rarely leaves his studio.[126] Yet, as Zimmer confesses, he "wasn't really in Brooklyn either."[127] Instead, he types, "I was in the book, and the book was in my head, and as long as I stayed inside my head, I could go on writing the book."[128] As Zimmer says later on about another house that he has bought in the outskirts of the city, "to inhabit those blank, depersonalized interiors was to understand that the world was an illusion that had to be reinvented every day."[129] That space is not unlike "the retreat" that Martin Frost visits: "The house was empty…"

Everything that is inessential must be removed from the given space/room until it resembles a white sheet of paper, or the writer's mind before writing. That is why Auster's room, in which the typewriter functions, always must be set up in laconic and bare style. The room, which, like the typewriter, is a "thing in-between" (between the graspable, physical reality and the elusive nature of imagination), allows Auster's work to retain a kind of ever-present epistemological ambiguity. Rheindorf describes this duality in the following way:

> Intricately bound up with the principle of a connected whole, the process of a partial or complete transformation between interior and exterior (and vice versa) can be taken as [another] organizing principle of Auster's work. Like the former, it often finds expression in characters' thoughts, as it does in Marco Fogg's realization that 'the inner and the outer could not be separated except by doing great damage to the truth'.[130]

In a sense, in Auster's rhizomatic oeuvre, where authorship is always dispersed and decentered, there is no identifiable site of textual origin other than the bare room, which may or may not reflect the physical reality, and the writer-assemblage within it. Somewhere, in the space of that room, the writer hears the dictating voice. It comes from his typewriter. It comes from his muse.

The machinic muse

Paul Auster has sole-authored and directed two films, *The Inner Life of Martin Frost*[131] and *Lulu on the Bridge* (which can be seen as slightly different versions of the same story),[132] and both are, more than any other Auster text, interested in exploring the fragile boundaries between reality and imagination, and the "plumbing" of the creative process of writing/filmmaking.[133] Both films also introduce a new element to the Auster assemblage—the female figure that functions as a muse. It quickly becomes apparent that this female, like the typewriter, is required for the protagonist's recovery from his (creative) crisis. But there is a tension, a curious relationship between the functioning of the muse and the text-generating typewriter. This tension goes deep. The simultaneous co-existence of the two appears to be impossible. But why?

Female characters are usually either absent or marginalized in Auster's life-work.[134] It always focuses on a male protagonist, with the (problematic) exception of *In the Country of Last Things*, where the narrator-protagonist has a female voice. Yet for some scholars, such as Markus Rheindorf, even this voice appears unconvincing from a gender perspective.[135] Whenever a female character is introduced in an Auster text, she is "inevitably defined as the 'female other', and only in relation to [Auster's] (and his male narrators') concept of maleness."[136] Her usual attribute is this: the woman is something that the male protagonist has lost, or she is the missing element. Once she appears, she usually takes the role of a rescuer, "truly deified as a saving presence,"[137] or, as Marco Fogg says about Kitty in *Moon Palace*, "an angel from another world."[138]

The prototype for this character might be Auster's own wife, the Norwegian-American writer Siri Hustvedt, whose fictional doublings play episodic roles in the novels *City of Glass* (where the fictional Siri appears together with Paul Auster and his son Daniel) and *Leviathan* (as a character named Iris who marries the protagonist Peter Aaron—note the anagram of her name and the initials PA). As Auster confesses in *The Red Notebook*, his novel *City of Glass* with its self-negating, self-destructing character Quinn is in fact his attempt to imagine what would have become of himself, and his life, if he had not met his wife.[139] The irresistible, overpowering female character, which always shows up at the moment when the protagonist experiences a crisis or creative blockage, seduces the passive male figure and brings him back to both writing and life, only to die herself at the end. The female figure seems highly mystified. More often than not, she turns out to be "invented," imagined.

The woman, a muse incognito, usually turns up in the protagonist's life unexpectedly and under strange circumstances. Alma surprises Zimmer by waiting for him at the front of his house in the middle of the night. Martin Frost wakes up one morning to find a strange woman lying next to him in his bed. Auster's writer-protagonists constantly have to question not only whether these female characters are "real," but also whether they can trust *anything* they experience and perceive as real. In *The Inner Life of Martin Frost*, Claire is reading aloud to Martin excerpts from works by David Hume and George Berkeley, two philosophers of human perception, who question whether what we see and experience is "really there," or only exists in our minds.

"[E]verything is in our head," Claire tells Martin, referring to Berkeley.[140] In *Lulu on the Bridge*, it is Izzy who asks Celia: "Are you a real person ... or a spirit?"[141] Later, towards the end of the film, when Izzy's friend, a film producer named Philip, informs him about Celia's sudden disappearance from the film set in Dublin, he says: "The whole thing's like a dream, like she was never really there."[142] In another episode, the agent/angel interrogating Izzy, Dr Van Horn (played by Willem Defoe), specu-lates about Celia's name, which originates from Latin and means both "heaven" and "blind." "Celia," suggests Dr Van Horn, by spelling out her name on a piece of paper, could perhaps reveal something about the untrustworthy nature of one's perception and epistemological beliefs: "Celia—Celia—Ce-li-a—S'il y a." The last phrase has a significant double meaning in French: "If there is ...," or "if she exists ..." (Auster has obviously borrowed this pun from Samuel Beckett's solipsistic novel *Murphy*).[143]

Ultimately, as Auster himself has admitted, "to a large degree, the film [*Lulu on the Bridge*] is about how men invent women."[144] This invention and re-invention (in the manner of Auster) of the female is done through both the story of Celia and her relationship with Izzy on one level, and through the *mise en abyme* of Celia playing Lulu in a film production on another.[145] In either case, the ongoing epistemological uncertainty surrounding the female character and the events related to her are maintained throughout the film. Yet there is no doubt that, regardless of her provenance, she is to a great extent responsible for the writer's creative and existential recovery. Apart from her ability to inspire, she often *is*, in fact—like the typewriter— the voice that is dictating to the writer his text. Or, perhaps (as Auster himself believes), she is the text itself.[146]

When Auster was asked in an interview with Larry McCaffery and Sinda Gregory about the origins of his novel *In the Country of Last Things* (his only text featuring a female protagonist and narrator), he confessed that he felt that the whole text was being "dictated" to him by a strange female voice: "I *heard* her voice speaking to me, and that voice was utterly distinct from my own"[147] (my emphasis). This is the voice of the protagonist Anna Blume, who towards the end of the book presents herself to the addressee as "your old friend from another world."[148] What is more, this female voice dictating to Auster, like the typewriter, seems to be functioning as the agency of truth. Rheindorf has also noted that

> Auster ascribes—or follows others in ascribing—almost mystical (and certainly mythical) qualities to 'a woman'. In *The Invention of Solitude*, one of these qualities is the power of storytelling, another that of speaking the truth—'[f]or it is his belief that if there was a voice of truth … it comes from the mouth of a woman' … —and, in particular, speaking to a man the truth of himself.[149]

As soon as the writer-character has recovered from his "crisis" and "the truth" has been attained (it gets typed up as a new story) the woman-character must disappear, or die. Yet the writer hardly ever wants to take the blame for their deaths, even though he is clearly implicated in the crime. Auster's women are simply made to accept their fate and embrace their own end. At the end of *The Book of Illusions*, Alma commits suicide. As she explains to Zimmer in her farewell letter, "It's good that it's ending before you find out who I really am"—a phrase that, like her whole letter, is laden with interpretive ambiguity. Celia likewise vanishes at the end of *Lulu on the Bridge* by jumping off a bridge into a canal. Her fate is left unknown. A third mysterious woman, Claire from *The Inner Life of Martin Frost*, nearly dies at the protagonist's completion of his story. "Nearly"—because in this text Auster suspends the usual course of action, and eventually brings her back to "life." In that way he leaves his musings on (type)writing open-ended. Either way, if we want to understand the co-relation between the female figure and writing—between a muse and a (type)writer, in other words—we should look at *The Inner Life of Martin Frost* more closely.

Within the writing-assemblage, set up early on in the film, the typewriter, as always, is a primary agent in production of the story. Yet before it begins, Martin Frost is hit by inspiration: "A few hours of silence, a few gulps of fresh air, and all of a sudden an idea for a story was turning around in his head. That's how it always seems to work with stories. One minute, there's nothing. And the next minute it's there. Already sitting inside you."[150] As sudden as the appearance of an idea is the ensuing materialization of a strange woman, Claire, whom he finds lying beside him next morning. As the two become close, Martin feels inspired to write, and sits down at a fifty-year old Olympia typewriter he has discovered stored away in a closet.

The film, which explores the work of imagination in writing, pays little attention to the contents or form of Martin's story. That story is simply a creative abstraction that gets materialized. The text merely exposes the process of writing, foregrounding the objects from the writer-assemblage which confirm and verify this process of writing. The act of writing becomes objectivized, its materiality emphasized through the camera's focus on close-up views of "things" used in writing, and sounds made by them. There is the writer sitting at a desk, the insistent clacking of the typewriter keys and the tinkle of the carriage return, the rustle of paper and the squeaking of a pencil as the hand slides over sheets of paper. Occasionally, there is a shot of Martin's typewriter, rotating or hovering isolated in black limbo. As Martin later says to the resurrected Claire about his freshly-written, freshly-destroyed manuscript (he throws it into the fire once he understands the connection between writing and Claire): "You see, Claire? It's only words. Thirty-seven pages—and nothing but words."[151]

Objects are shown to signify the physical effort involved in "real" writing: the camera shows Martin typing, throwing a fresh draft in a wastebasket, and editing the typewritten text with a pencil. In addition, we are given commentary about what Rheindorf calls the "interior representations of things," the elusive form and transient nature of the story that is being built in the writer's mind.[152] This meta-fictional commentary provided by the narrator (whose voice in the film belongs to Auster himself) is supplemented by suggestive visual metaphors set against a black background. A "puff of cigarette smoke waft[ing] into the frame"; "steam … pouring from the spout" of a kettle on the stove; a pair of "thin white curtains fluttering in the embrasure of a half-open window"—all formless, insubstantial things with no fixed form.[153] Together with the narrator's off-screen voice, they inform us that

> [e]very story has a shape … and the shape of every story is different … from the shape of every other story. Some stories move in straight lines. Others make circles … or zig-zags … or pirouettes. Rather than go in one general direction, Martin's story seemed to be looping back around itself—or veering off in a series of sharp, right-angled turns—or spiraling in toward some invisible point at the center.[154]

Yet as Martin's story gradually starts to materialize through typewriting ("every day he added a few more pages to the pile"),[155] the woman who turns out to be Martin's muse falls sick, becoming weaker and weaker until she "dies." Significantly, she is never close to the typewriter or Martin when he is (type)writing. It is either her or the typewriter that Martin engages with. The writing-assemblage can only incorporate either the female element or the typing machine. In a writing situation, the two are incompatible.

An inscription on the cover of the film's American DVD release states that the film explores "[w]hat bearing … this mysterious muse has on Martin's work and what consequences … Martin's writing have on her …"[156] Yet a more appropriate phrasing would be: what consequences Martin's "typewriting" has on his muse, since it is the typewriter, above any other thing, which kills her. The more it materializes the story, the more it dematerializes her. In the film, the shots that show the writer's fingers in a synthesis with the typewriter, forcefully striking its keys, interchange with shots that show Claire lying in her bed next door in obvious agony, and the correlation between the two is made apparent by the use of parallel montage. Each tap on a key seems to cause her pain, killing her at the moment that Martin types a period to end his story.

At this point, the typewriter has become a dangerous weapon.[157] It reminds me of David Cronenberg's visions of talking typewriters in his adaptation of William S. Burroughs' novel *Naked Lunch*. In Cronenberg's film, the various half-mechanical, half-biological typewriters become "metaphors for the varying and often contradictory mental states of the film's characters, almost all of them writers,"[158] while the organization controlling the machines appears as "a symbol of [the protagonist's] own internal muses."[159] In both Cronenberg's film and Burroughs' novel, the female-typewriter combination is an equally impossible assemblage, and the writer-protagonist Lee has to shoot his wife Joan before he can actually start typing.

As Wershler-Henry puts it, "in the discursive universe of Cronenberg's *Naked Lunch*, operating a typewriter and operating a pistol [become] equivalent acts."[160] Although this act of murdering a spouse is interpreted by Wershler-Henry as "the moment where authorship begins"[161]—and in Auster's texts there are no "spouses," only "muses"—this relationship between a female and a typewriter is telling of the kind of tensions and complicated or contradictory relays that have always existed between the female gender and writing technology. If one replaces the other, then maybe the two are the same? What if the typewriter in essence is not so different from the female muse?

McHale expresses a similar thought—he equates the typewriter with the construct of the female muse, and with one's internal imagination. Whether it is a muse inspiring the writer, or whether it is the typewriter itself, "machine composition reinvigorates the traditional assumption that [writing] involves collaborations between [writers] and something beyond or outside themselves."[162] For McHale, there are several "sources" that can be attributed to the dictating voice:

> Before the onset of Romanticism, that sense of poetry as collaboration was captured in the figure of the Muse; the Romantics psychologised the Muse, internalizing it as the imagination, or the power lodged in the poet's unconscious. Postmodernist prosthetic poetry returns to pre-Romantic assumptions, in a sense, externalizing the Muse again, projecting "her" outside the poet, into the machine; [Charles O.] Hartman's book on computer-poetry experiments is titled *Virtual Muse*, with reason.[163]

That makes the typewriter and the female twin agencies of inspiration and dictation that are used interchangeably in Auster's work. Both are tools of writing and the materialized text itself. As intermediate things in-between, both are also mediators between the imaginary and the real. Claire (who comes to Martin from "there," sent by "them"), like the typewriter, essentially is "a thing" that is "trapped between here and there," as the story tells us.[164]

Perhaps, it is in the nature of the inspiring voice to find its expression through double—no, multiple—actants. Writing itself is schizophrenic. It comes with the unavoidable split of the "I." And tools of dictation and writing, such as the typewriter or the muse, seem to further intensify this schism in the self that happens at the writer's desk. "*Je est un autre*," wrote Auster, here doubling Rimbaud. Auster finds it almost impossible to write about himself in the first person. His two "autobiographical" pieces, "The Book of Memory" (from *The Invention of Solitude*) and the recent *Winter Journal*, are written in the third-person (referring to himself as "A.") and in the second-person voice (referring to himself as "you"), respectively. For "[t]hat is how you see yourself," says Paul Auster to himself in the book about himself.[165] To write this sentence, he used a doppelgänger. In fact, he so frequently relies on the idea of the double to expose this process of (self)writing that, in his intratext, it has become yet another "type." A phantom-like, often invisible tool of writing, it is, nevertheless, entirely responsible not only for the schismed nature of his texts but also for the mutual doubling that occurs between them all.

Doubles and Disappearances

This is how I see it. The parting of the self that happens in the act of writing is not always obvious. Writing often starts with a focus on the other, a distant object of detection. But that other is a double, in fact, a sort of doppelgänger, needed so that the process of investigation at some point can shift toward the detective himself. The quest gets turned inward, as the other (*un autre*) becomes "I" (*je*). The writer's self gets explored through writing—for Auster, writing (doubling) is a self-conscious, self-reflexive act. It is an ongoing conversation between the self in the writer's mind and the (type)written self that has already split from that mind. That conversation often gets impeded by the limits of the postlapsarian language that itself falls apart, shattering into endlessly reflecting fragments.

So, while trying to solve his existential identity crisis, Auster's lonesome writer-figure also explores meta-fictional questions related to the essence of writing, authorship, and meaning. This process can be traced in *City of Glass*, *Ghosts*, *The Locked Room*, *In the Country of Last Things*, *Leviathan*, *The Inner Life of Martin Frost*, *The Book of Illusions*, and *Smoke*, among other works. These texts abound with doubles—from characters doubling other characters, to the "Paul Auster" character in *City of Glass* and Auster's "lookalike" Paul Benjamin in the film *Smoke*, as well as the "doppelgänger in the other sex," artist Sophie Calle in a collaborative project between the two.[1] In Auster's life-work, which is full of writers writing about other writers, detached selves (doubles) proliferate.

In fact, through the use of adaptation, collaboration, intratextuality and *mises en abyme*, Auster's texts themselves become each other's doubles. After all, the postmodern double not only works on different levels (character, linguistic, narrative and intra- or intertextual), but is also always a multiple. Instead of one mirror, in Auster's oeuvre the double functions as an assemblage of multi-faceted, fractured mirrors that reflect each other, *ad infinitum*. The question is: how to read such an assemblage of doubles, and how to read the double itself? Throughout history, this concept has accumulated layers of associations and principles that all are set to work as soon as a double appears in a text.

Even in its simplest, most traditional sense, the double has what Andrew J. Webber in his monograph on the doppelgänger calls a "programmed ambiguity" that resists sustained and unified interpretation.[2] The ambivalence of the double first of all lies in the fact that the term "doppelgänger" itself can be read in two ways. It literally translates from German as "doublewalker" (from "*doppel-*"—"double" and

"-*gänger*"—"goer"), and is usually read as the double of someone. A doppelgänger is perceived as the other—the uncanny, the ghostly, the repressed version of the original. But the term's earliest definition is thought to appear in a footnote to Jean Paul Richter's late 18th-century novel *Siebenkäs*.[3] There Richter describes doppelgängers as "*Leute, die sich selber sehen*" or "people who see themselves." This explanation overturns the dominant view that the doppelgänger is the "other," the one who doubles the "original" self. "From the start," writes Webber, "it seems that the subject may not so much have as actually be the *Doppelgänger* by seeing itself."[4] That means that the only doppelgänger in Paul Auster's life-work is Paul Auster himself. Because of this contradiction in terms, from the very beginning there has been uncertainty as to whether the doppelgänger in question is the original self or its alter ego. The doppelgänger has a "doppel" meaning.

As Webber points out, in an autoscopic situation, where one sees one's own body in extrapersonal space, the "subject beholds its other self as another, as visual object, or alternatively is beheld as object by its other self."[5] ("For that is how you see yourself," says Auster.) This shows, as noted in *The Oxford Companion to the Body*, "the fundamental level at which the phenomenon challenges conventions of identity, by making the self see itself double (or, more precisely, see itself going double, as a duplicate body which may go its own way)."[6] The fact that the apparition of the double is not static, but characterized by movement (as "goer"), further problematizes the sense of certainty and fixedness we may want to attribute to it, and to the related concept of identity. The doppelgänger is always on the move, fluid, in the process of becoming and transforming, but the starting and ending points of its "going" often remain obscure. In such a way, the slippery doppelgänger defies origins and genealogical readings.

And it gets even trickier. As Webber explains, in the doppelgänger situation, there is no "original" self that then has a double, or a copy of itself. There is just the splitting of the self into two doubles (think of monozygotic twins), both of whom often "see themselves," and both of whom, to a varying degree, are affected by the consequences of this act. The double, therefore, possesses a somewhat lenticular quality, which, depending on the angle of viewing, foregrounds one or another of the doubles, and one or another of its features.

This description of the double as a lenticular image is probably what Gordon E. Slethaug had in mind when he called the double "hologramatic." He points out, in his *The Play of the Double in Postmodern American Fiction*, that any attempt to conduct a historical reading of the double implies "a blending of the evasive and direct, occluding and clarifying, self-differing and analytically categorical."[7] This seems compatible with the uncertain nature of the double itself. And there is no other way to speak about the double than in somewhat schizophrenic terms. Such an approach, he continues, is

> implicitly self-contradictory, a strategy that [nevertheless] is in keeping with *the flickering, hologramatic presentation of the double in literature.* The double is constituted upon difference, and despite … anyone's … attempts to categorize, elucidate, resolve differences, and validate categories through well-poised examples, will always remain *duplicitous, dialogic, and relativized.*[8] (my emphasis)

That poses a challenge to me, a problem that cannot be resolved. For I can say nothing definitive about Auster's doubles that could not be contradicted. Both fractured and multiplied, the double can never present itself as a complete image. As the concept itself suggests, it is "a part of" something (because it is generated through splitting) and yet "a multiplicity" (because it always embodies more than itself—it is also "the other" that it reflects). So, as we attempt to follow the associations the concept has acquired throughout history, the double appears to us as a stream of continuous, flickering and fragmentary reflections.

For example, the same fractured multiplicity can also be attributed to the many functions that the double as actant carries out on the narrative, meta-fictional and intertextual levels. The double here is not a derivation of the writing self but a narrative function that generates rhizomatic structures in Auster's intratext. The double, after all, as both Friedrich A. Kittler and Gilles Deleuze suggest, may be more than a ghostly alter ego to be read in psychoanalytic terms. Rather, it is a "messenger" of the medium within which it appears. In Auster's case, it is an adaptation, a collaboration, or a rhizomatically generated doppelgänger of another cross-disciplinary text. In other words, doubles proliferate in Auster's texts exactly because the texts themselves are doublings of one another. We will get to this point soon. But first—how did the concept of the double emerge? What is its story? What are its associations?

It seems that the ghost of the double has always haunted literature and mythology, from the Ancient Greek myth of Narcissus to Aristophanes' gender creation myth as retold by Plato in his *Symposium*, through to Shakespeare's twins in *The Comedy of Errors* and *Twelfth Night* and the fearsome Gothic doubles of Lord Byron. However, the most significant point of reference in the history of this discourse can be traced in late eighteenth-century German Romanticism and its birthing of the doppelgänger as a transformed and more frightful version of the double, which then gradually spread throughout Europe. The doppelgänger of Romanticism above all is both fear-evoking and fascinating, reflecting Europe's increasing interest in the emerging science of psychology at the time. It unquestionably has an eerie quality about it.

The obsession with the idea that someone could all of a sudden acquire a doppelgänger, and the fears related to this predicament, emerged at a time when interest in hypnosis, mesmerism and animal magnetism was on the increase. In fact, both the literature and psychology (and later psychoanalysis) of the time used the early practices of mesmerism and hypnosis, as well as theories of animal magnetism, as their basis for explaining the fantastic and, later, Freudian concepts (such as the conscious and unconscious mind and the uncanny).[9] It means that the history of the double and the early history of psychology are "in some senses the same."[10] The two are so entwined that for critics like Kittler, Webber, and Lexey Anne Bartlett, psychoanalysis, which has become the predominant mode of explaining the uncanny nature of the double, fails as a satisfactory method of analysis precisely because of this reason. As Webber puts it, "[i]n the case of the Doppelgänger, theory and creative writing are engaged in a complex and highly ambivalent exchange of reciprocal readings and representations."[11] The two discourses are therefore to an extent inseparable.

While literary texts such as E. T. A. Hoffmann's doppelgänger tale "The Sand-Man" offered a psychological explanation for the protagonist's hallucinations of an evil phantom and its controlling power, psychology and psychoanalysis used these texts as case studies (e.g., Otto Rank's and Sigmund Freud's seminal readings of the theme of the double in "The Sand-Man"). The double, in other words, became one of the dominant motifs in both Romantic literature and early psychoanalysis. For Kittler this means that "certain basic assumptions [about the double] remain unquestioned in the psychoanalytic verification of the fantastic, precisely because it transfers poetry into science"[12] without actually questioning "why the figure of the Double populates the literary record since [the nineteenth century] and only since then," and "why the Double turns up at the writing desk, of all places."[13] This leads us to an ironic conclusion—the history of the literature of the double and the history of early psychology are themselves but doubles, each one reflecting and exploiting the other in an attempt to understand the double.

The greatest impact that psychoanalysis has had on the literary double is this: it liberated the concept of the double from the tyranny of blood-freezing horror that the literature of the double initially evoked. The turning point in the literary discourse of the double happened at the beginning of the twentieth century, when psychoanalysis, psychology, and clinical psychiatry were already flourishing throughout Europe. With the publication of Joseph Conrad's short story "The Secret Sharer" in 1910, for the first time the double was portrayed as not evoking fear in the original self.[14] Perhaps slight uneasiness but no sense of terror is created any longer in the reader who witnesses the confrontation. In Conrad's story, the protagonist (an unnamed captain on a ship) and the mysterious stranger (Legatt, his doppelgänger), whom the captain rescues from drowning, act to save each other. While the captain hides Legatt, a fleeing murderer, from the crew and helps him escape to a secluded island, the latter helps the captain come to terms with his self-doubt and discover a new sense of confidence.

This liberation from the fear of seeing oneself "going double, as a duplicate body which [goes] its own way," is best epitomized by a curious and marginal collaborative project between Paul Auster and French artist Jacques de Loustal, "The Day I Disappeared." This is Auster's first original comic book story and it deals directly with the doppelgänger motif. In this story for children, published in Art Spiegelman's *Strange Stories for Strange Kids* (*Little Lit, Book 2*) in 2001, the protagonist wakes up one morning to discover that he cannot see his reflection in the mirror. Immediately after this discovery, he sees, through the window, himself walking down the street, and decides to follow.

This discovery evokes no fear in the protagonist. Rather, it is a strange curiosity that prompts him to rush out into the street after his other self. He makes an observation that he "looked sad" and "seemed lonely."[15] He follows himself through the empty city streets down to a lake, where he saves himself from accidental drowning (very much like in Conrad's tale). In the evening, he lies next to himself in bed, and wakes up next morning to discover he has his reflection back and is wholly himself again. The story ends with the protagonist going to his place of work, which, predictably, is "The Bureau of Missing Persons." The Austerian trope that equates writing and detecting

Figure 3.1 The ultimate doppelgänger situation: the self sees itself going double. A frame from "The Day I Disappeared," by Jacques de Loustal and Paul Auster.

in order to investigate identity is also at work in this text. To sum it up, our detective could report: "this is how you see yourself."

Here is what I find interesting: the double the protagonist encounters in this story is not a phantom of himself. It is not a doppelgänger that could be defined as "a ghostly double of a living person, especially one that haunts its fleshly counterpart."[16] It is the protagonist himself that has become a phantasm, unperceivable to the "original" self, as well as the rest of the world. Nobody out in the streets can see him or hear him. Which one of the two is the disappearing "I" that the title refers to? One has already disappeared (is invisible); the other one is disappearing (drowning). Webber, after all, has warned that the "doppelgänger" possesses a "doppel" nature. It goes in both directions at once.

In either case, the Romantic horror and shock from encountering one's double (whether classified as the alleged original seeing its ghostly double, or *vice versa*), is gone. Yet a sense of uncanniness remains, which in postmodern fiction finds its expression in *mises en scène* and the "strangeness" of the text itself, with unexpected narrative twists and ambiguous ontological closure. Although the psychological theories of the twentieth century led to general acceptance of the inherent duality, and later fragmentariness and multiplicity, of both human identity and the world itself, the effect of this primeval, irrational fear that the apparition of the double evoked can certainly still be sensed. It continues haunting the concept up to the present.

And I think that is why many of Auster's texts, like the above-mentioned "The Day I Disappeared," are set in a noir-like diegesis (which is a descendant of Gothic urban spaces). These texts have lost the highly intense, horror-inducing language of Romantic literature, but can be described as having an "austere," "bizarre" or simply "clinical" quality (the setting of *Travels in the Scriptorium*, in which the amnesiac protagonist is trapped, for example, resembles a psychiatric ward).

Figure 3.2 The doppelgänger generates a noir chronotope. Frames from "The Day I Disappeared."

However, there is a fundamental difference between the sensations of horror sparked by the pre-psychological Romantic doppelgänger and the split of the self it causes, between the way that psychoanalysis regards the double, and what could be described as the postmodern curiosity about fragmentariness of the self, language, and the world. The Romantic literature of the double most often relied on binary oppositions within the self, where the other side of the personality, revealed through the materialized figure of the doppelgänger, appeared as evil, immoral, repugnant, and phantasmal. As horrifying, in other words. It belonged to the realm of the unknown and the inexplicable, and often lent itself to superstitious beliefs (the doppelgänger as an omen of impending death, a harbinger of bad luck). This horror associated with the apparition of the double has now been dispersed. But we should not turn away from the historical discourse surrounding it as yet. For it is clear that some of its early associations have found their way into the post-Romantic and post-psychoanalytical literature, including Auster's texts.

The birth of the double

What evoked the horror? The social history of the doppelgänger tells us that the origins of the fears associated with it are closely related to the emergence of hypnosis, mesmerism, and the idea of animal magnetism in early nineteenth-century society. First, there was the fear that there might be an unconscious side of the self that is repugnant to the real, "waking" self (as evidenced by actual cases of hypnosis at the time). Second, that it was possible for the self to be remotely controlled by (an evil) outsider, as manifested by the puppet-puppeteer situation in Hoffmann's "The Sand-Man" (1816), one of the central doppelgänger stories that was later subjected to psychoanalytical study to explain the workings of the double.

Hoffman's short story goes like this: the protagonist Nathaniel falls in love with a "woman" named Olimpia who turns out to be an automaton, produced by a certain Spalanzani (Olimpia's "father") and controlled by an evil force expressed through the multiple/schizophrenic figure of a mythical "Sand-Man," "the repulsive vendor of weather-glasses, Coppola," and "the diabolical Coppelius."[17] Obsessed by Olimpia, and haunted throughout by this evil power, Nathaniel in the end falls into a state of insanity and plunges to his death from a high tower, while Coppelius looks on laughing. What are we to make of this story? Psychoanalysis has one kind of answer. With the three analyses of "The Sand-Man" by Ernst Jentsch, Freud, and Rank nearly a hundred years after its publication,[18] it became the dominant mode for explaining the psychology of uncanny sensations evoked by texts like Hoffmann's, and the reason why, gradually, the doppelgänger gets freed from the effects of shock and terror its appearance initially induced.

What does Freud say? He takes as his starting point Jentsch's argument that uncanny effects are produced by the mind's inability to determine whether "an apparently animate object really is alive and, conversely, whether a lifeless object might not perhaps be animate."[19] And he rejects this claim, by saying that the fear and uncanniness is evoked by another element altogether: "the Sand-Man, who tears out children's eyes."[20] Freud offers part literary criticism, part psychoanalytic study of Nathaniel's (and Hoffmann's) suppressed childhood trauma in relation to the father figure, and the Freudian concept of the fear of castration (epitomized in the story as the recurrent threat of losing one's eyes).

For Freud, the uncanny (in the form of Sand-Man, Coppelius, and Coppola) arises due to the return of repressed traumatic infantile material. The motif of the double is explained (in one way) as the return of the primary narcissism of the child—the self-love. The Jentschian uncertainty as to "whether an object is animate or inanimate, which we were bound to acknowledge in the case of the doll Olimpia" for Freud is "quite irrelevant in the case of this more potent example of the uncanny."[21] Olimpia, this automatic doll, "cannot be anything other than a materialization of Nathaniel's feminine attitude to his father in his early childhood," as well as "a complex that has been detached from Nathaniel and now confronts him as a person."[22] The control that this complex exercises over him "finds expression in his senseless, compulsive love for Olimpia," says Freud.[23]

Auster is undoubtedly familiar with Freud's writing on the uncanny. In "The Book of Memory" part of *The Invention of Solitude*, he devotes a passage to the discussion of the Freudian concept of "homelessness" (the central trope for the uncanny, *das Unheimliche*).[24] Auster also toys with Freudian concepts and the associations established by psychoanalysis between the sense of uncanny self-estrangement, suppressed childhood trauma, and the father-son relationship in his *The New York Trilogy*. Especially so in *City of Glass*, where in a twisted way, the puppet–puppeteer relationship between an evil father and his traumatized son gets played out by the figures of the mad Peter Stillman Sr. and Peter Stillman Jr. (who is described as "machine-like, fitful," "rigid and yet expressive," "like … a marionette … without strings").[25]

As a result, many critics feel inclined to perform a psychoanalytical reading of *City of Glass* (and of the other two parts of *The New York Trilogy*). Roberta Rubenstein, for example, highlights Auster's discussion of the absence of his father figure in *The Invention of Solitude*, and picks up on such aspects of the uncanny in *City of Glass* as the recurrent "imagery of eyes and automatons,"[26] as well as the similarities between the figures of Peter Stillman Jr., Hoffmann's Olimpia, and the protagonist Quinn himself. The latter, according to her, at the end of the story becomes a homeless "'no-*body*'—an automaton, a 'still man.'"[27] Yet saying that Quinn is "obsessed with eyes and vision"[28] by reading the element of detection (Quinn as "the private eye" or "private I") in exclusively psychoanalytical terms does not have the same persuasive strength when applied to the wider context of Auster's intra-connected work, where it is a recurrent motif. And where the double—the multiple!—assumes functions beyond the mere expression of the protagonist's psychological state by becoming, instead, a structuring principle of the entire Auster intratext.

In fact, I have several possible objections to an exclusively psychoanalytical interpretation of texts such as Auster's. Psychoanalysis assumes that the reader perceives all external events through the perspective of the protagonist as mere projections of the character's (and the author's) psyche. While such readings are possible, as Rubenstein also illustrates, they cannot account for other possible readings of (especially collaborative) texts that have multiple main characters and multiple perspectives. Auster's texts do not yield themselves to unitary readings. Psychoanalysis, unlike rhizomatics, is reluctant to acknowledge the co-existence of a plurality of meanings.

Psychoanalysis has also impetuously turned its back on the relation between uncanniness and the emergence of new technology, as described by Jentsch, the pioneer in exploring the uncanny. Like Freud himself, psychoanalysis discards as irrelevant the claim that new technologies and mechanical devices that bear an uncanny resemblance to life can become a source of simultaneous fear and fascination. But the period between the mid-nineteenth century and the first decade of the twentieth century is known as "the Golden Age of automata" in Europe (predominantly in France), and was marked by society's obsession with life-like mechanical devices and the exploration of their limits and possibilities. And Nathaniel's friends in Hoffmann's "The Sand-Man," although praising Olimpia's singing and piano-playing skills as "disagreeably perfect," feel an uncanny anxiety towards her.[29] They sense that, although in all respects she appears human-like, she seems "to be only acting *like* a living creature, and as if there was some secret at the bottom of it all."[30] (his emphasis) In fact, they admit to be feeling "quite afraid of this Olimpia," and would rather not "have anything to do with her."[31]

Nathaniel, on the other hand, feels captivated and inspired by Olimpia's "divine charms." Although she can only repeatedly sigh ("Ach! Ach! Ach!") in response to her admirer, for Nathaniel, "[t]he glance of her heavenly eyes says more than any tongue of earth."[32] She is "such an exemplary listener" that, in her presence, he feels compelled not only to return to all his previously written work ("poems, fancy sketches, visions, romances, tales …") but also generate new texts.[33] In other words, Olimpia becomes Nathaniel's muse. In this sense, Olimpia is not that different from Olympia, the SM9 model typewriter that Auster regards as his talking muse, and whose eerie qualities and capacity to be possessed while possessing the one who uses it we have already witnessed.

A machine (or medium) that works on our thoughts through inspiration has the ability to simultaneously fascinate and scare us because it makes us question the autonomy of our thoughts, which the machine appears to be co-generating. I sense it whenever I involve things in the process of assembling a book—whenever I let a cigarette, a typewriter, an image of Auster pinned to the wall in front of me do its part in the thinking and writing for me. And so it is not me writing anymore, but things with me and through me. Any inconsistencies, fissures, and non-synchronicity in the written text arise due to the polyphony of voices and forces involved in the writing process.

The double, as Kittler maintains, is "the ghost of poetry"[34]—of the medium itself. The double of classical Romanticism "essentially emerge[d] from books",[35] books being the only medium or "machine" for reading at the time. Kittler relates the emergence of the ghostly double to the prescribed way of reading literary texts in the given culture, which on the reader's part presupposed a strong use of imagination and instant visualization of the written word. He points to the early German Romantic author and philosopher Novalis, who instructed the reader: "If one reads correctly, then a real, visible world unfolds itself in us internally according to the words."[36] Kittler concludes: "The printed word was skipped and the book forgotten, until somewhere between the lines a hallucination appeared—the pure signified of the printed sign. In other words, Doubles in the era of classical Romanticism originated in the classroom where we learn to read correctly."[37] Hence, the doppelgänger predominantly haunts the writers of the Romantic and pre-Romantic era (Johann Wolfgang von Goethe, Guy de Maupassant, Percy Bysshe Shelley), while those following the Industrial Revolution have to settle for the oddities and quirks produced by the capricious muse of the typewriter, and other technologies.

A book that generates hallucinations, a typewriter that appears to have a dictating voice, and a lifelike automaton which seems to imitate (to double) human actions in a seemingly autonomous way all generate uncanny sensations in those who experience them. While each period in history has been marked by a different type of emerging new technology or medium (what Kittler would call "a discourse network"), this fear of the new technology "becoming alive" by talking to us, haunting us, doubling us, and "writing" us has always been present throughout the times. That is why, for Deleuze, as Jan Harris points out, the doppelgänger is above all "an encounter with the horror of the non-organic."[38] It renders, continues Harris, "'anthropomorphic urban surroundings [as] devils no less real than the golems of Nordic legends'—a realm uncovered but not created by the convulsions of the individual or collective mind."[39] When it comes to the uncanniness of doubles, "things are much simpler than psycho-analysis imagines," concludes Kittler.[40]

The double functions of the double

Psychoanalysis fails to deal with the double in yet another respect—it ignores the multiple levels on which the double (that has become the multiple) acts in postmodern discourse. Auster's *City of Glass*, which so often is read from a psychoanalytical perspective, is the epitome of the postmodern multiple that is always in flux, threatening to disintegrate and disrupt its own (supposed) genealogy.

The entangled network of mutual character doublings in *City of Glass*, where a double mirrors another double who mirrors yet another double *ad infinitum*, corresponds to what critics have noted as the rhizomatic relationship between the characters.[41] The image is captured by Bernstein: "the characters of the trilogy collapse into one another through their own labyrinthine (but illogical) interrelationships and then, finally, into multiple images of the author himself."[42] Rubenstein herself comes to a similar conclusion:

> As each character in *City of Glass* splits and disintegrates into fragmentary doubles of himself and/or disappears, as impersonators become the figures they impersonate, the narrative virtually doubles back on itself, threatening to cancel itself out. The title image thus suggests not so much a transparent surface as an opaque glass or the glass of a distorting mirror; alternatively, glass connotes a fragile material, susceptible to shattering into multiple pieces, all of which reflect the same (multiplied) image.[43]

And so "there is no 'master key' to *The New York Trilogy*—even at the end, the locked room remains locked."[44] What the reader who "perseveres" until the conclusion of the final story does encounter is "deliberate patterns of repetition that provide a kind of coherence in Auster's interlocking, overlapping tales: each thematically mirrors, narratively 'doubles,' and even threatens to cancel out, the other versions."[45] A structure of doubling patterns characterizes *The New York Trilogy*—a structure that, of course, applies to the entire Auster oeuvre. His life-work builds and extends itself through characters, themes, and narratives perpetually doubling each other. So, with the remark above, even Rubenstein herself inadvertently liberates the concept of the double from the burden of psychoanalytical representation and its singular focus on the psychology of the self.

But there is, as we saw, a new "comfort with the uncertainty" of one's identity, and the lack of interest in psychoanalytical unveilings of its construction.[46] We may as well explain it, as Bartlett suggests, using Brian McHale's distinction between what he calls the epistemological and ontological dominants of modernist and postmodernist fictions. Although in postmodernism the interest in identities and doubles (multiples) continues, the epistemological questions have long since been replaced by ontological curiosity. There is a move, says McHale, from questioning the limitations of human knowledge about the world, and our ability to interpret it, towards questions that Dick Higgins calls "post-cognitive": "Which world is this? What is to be done in it? Which of my selves is to do it?" And, no less importantly, there are questions of another kind that relate to "the ontology of the literary text itself," or "the ontology of the world which it projects":

What is a world? What kinds of world are there, how are they constituted, and how do they differ? What happens when different kinds of world are placed in confrontation, or when boundaries between worlds are violated? What is the mode of existence of a text, and what is the mode of existence of the world (or worlds) it projects?; How is a projected world structured? And so on.[47]

The twentieth century required "a new double" that would help it, in Bartlett's words, "imagine the implications of new realities and new ideas of subjectivity, rather than the psychoanalytic theories so grounded in Romantic psychology."[48] This quest, which is an exploration at once of the postmodern identity, world, text, its authorship and language, is constantly rehearsed in Auster's texts with the help of the double. The double is not only a phantom, a mystery, an ambiguity. It is the very opportunity to pose a question, to challenge a norm, to go in an alternative direction. It is a chance to receive several answers, not just one (assuming there are any). Although it is always attached to some other entity, which it then doubles and mimics (and hence is a "part of"), the double as doppelgänger also seems to act on its own, to go its own way. This is a liberating movement, mobility, multiplicity and dynamics itself, an essential driving force of the rhizome. That is why I think that, instead of reading the double in psychoanalytical terms, we should view it as a function, an actant, a tool used to ask and explore such post-cognitive questions, all in the wider scope of Auster's intratext.

Figure 3.3 Curiosity has replaced the fear of the double. A frame from "The Day I Disappeared," by Jacques de Loustal and Paul Auster.

I have observed, for example, that in Auster texts one of the functions that the double takes on is to split the narrative into two, and in that way inscribe the possibility of a simultaneous alternative narrative. This vaguely echoes the Borgesian idea of the "forking paths,"[49] which presupposes a world where multiple narratives with different outcomes of events are allowed to co-exist simultaneously. Each one, furthermore, leads to new rhizome-like proliferations of possibilities. For that reason in *City of Glass*, the Stillman Sr. figure appears as a double—to remind us that the text is a rhizome, and to mark a node which has the potential to produce a new narrative offshoot.

Quinn, who in the novel is supposed to follow a certain Peter Stillman Sr. from the moment of the latter's arrival at the train station, sees emerging from the train two almost identical men who both correspond to the description of Stillman Sr., the only difference between them being that one looks respectable and poised while the other

Figure 3.4 The doppelgänger creates a Borgesian "forking path." A frame from *City of Glass: The Graphic Novel*, by Auster, Paul Karasik and David Mazzucchelli.

appears shabby and slightly demented. This doubling results in a forking situation as each goes away in a different direction. At this point, Quinn must make a choice—which of the two "Stillmans" to follow?

Regardless of which one he chooses to follow (he eventually goes after the shabby-looking man), the ontological foundations of the narrative are shaken, since, from this very moment, it has acquired a ghostly alternative double. A shadow of doubt is cast over the story that does not disappear with the last pages of the book. As the "detective story" progresses, making less and less sense to both the reader and "detective" Quinn, I cannot help but start wondering if, by some chance, the wrong man was being followed all along. This question never gets answered, and the narrative obtains an aura of ambiguity. That creates in the reader an uncanny feeling that there might be several versions of the story existing, and that, possibly, the reader has been given the wrong one. The double places a question mark over the entire story: "What if ...?" That question, as Dennis Barone has noted, persists throughout Auster's life-work.

The uncertainty caused by the appearance of the double stirs in the reader another eerie feeling—that the characters, situations, and stories might actually exist beyond the pages of the given book, in other books, other worlds, where they live through alternative experiences. You get such sensations when reading *Moon Palace*, *The Book of Illusions*, or *Travels in the Scriptorium*, which arouse a *déjà vu* feeling in the reader. The characters there bear names familiar to the reader from other Auster texts. Yet there is no coherent link between them. They seem to be somehow different, as alternative versions or doppelgängers of their namesakes in the other texts.[50] And, as long as these doubles keep wandering through Auster's texts, none of his stories will ever appear as a single finished story. Instead, there will be at least two versions.

The double generates not only surrogate versions of the narratives, but also *mises en abyme*. This vaguely resonates with the psychoanalytical take on the double. If the figure of the doppelgänger turns out to be an imaginary construct projected by the protagonist's mind (as in *The Book of Illusions*, *Lulu on the Bridge*, *The Inner Life of Martin Frost*, *Travels in the Scriptorium*, *Man in the Dark*, etc.), it acts to create embedded narratives, or stories within stories. Webber notes that doppelgänger stories are

> rife in the effects of *mise-en-abyme*, whereby figures or structures are reflected within each other ... The *mise-en-abyme* of emblematic figures at once serves to repeat and so affirm *ad infinitum* the identity for which they stand, and yet to cast the sign of identity into abysmal or groundless non-identity.[51]

Or I could say: the doppelgänger emerges to challenge the constructions of reality by transcending the borders between the real and the imaginary, and by introducing instances of alternative diegesis. In this way, the doppelgänger or the double is directly involved in the construction of the story, and is to be held responsible for the narrative multi-layeredness of Auster's texts.

If such a method for generating stories seems mechanical, it has its explanation in the nature of objects that work to assemble the story-making situation in Auster's life-work. Like the typewriter, the double/doppelgänger is a machinic tool of writing. Just look at one of the earliest narratives about the double—the myth of the creation of sexes and genders that, attributed to Aristophanes, is retold by Plato in his *Symposium*. It depicts the creation of the two sexes and three genders[52] as a purely automated process. The gods, threatened by the growing strength of people (who roll about as round, eight-limbed creatures), decide to "cut those human beings in two," "the way people cut sorb-apples before they dry them"; they cut them one by one, so that they "lose their strength" and also "increase in their number."[53]

And so, if one of the abilities of the typewriter (whose early predecessor was a copying device) is to multiply by copying, then the double multiplies by splitting. These mechanical and seemingly autonomous processes at the same time allow the author to inscribe himself in the text. If typewriting allows Auster to leave a lasting imprint on a tangible page, then doubling addresses his desire to create an imperishable double; that is what André Bazin in relation to the cinema called "the mummy complex."[54] But the result is unexpected: through surrendering himself to the seemingly infinite, mechanical process of self-splitting and multiplication, the author loses himself in the machinery of text and its numerous doubles.

It only makes sense that, in an early interview, Auster refers to his writing process as "the machinery of the book,"[55] and talks about his desire to implicate himself in it—a human using a prosthetic writing machine to produce texts. Encapsulated by our chosen image of Sam Messer's Auster-machine, this resembles the Deleuzian spiritual automaton, which puts into play "the distinctions between inside [the author's mind] and outside [the writing machine], human and technics."[56] David Norman Rodowick describes the concept of the spiritual automaton as "machinic thought"[57]—at once spiritual, immaterial (as the flow of writer's imagination) and automatic (as determined by the dictates of external laws of the writing tools, such as the typewriter, or the double). In Auster, the spiritual automaton is most readily traceable as the assemblage of the writer and his typewriter, or the writer and the figure of his double: two semi-automatons that are simultaneously the sources of dictation/inspiration and threats to the author's authority and control over the text.

The doppelgänger in the other sex

Aristophanes' myth of the splitting and multiplication of man also makes one think of the gender question, which sits at the margins of Auster criticism. You might have noticed that at the center of Auster's assemblage of the smoking-typing-detective writer investigating a double is always a male character. Male as in writer, male as in double, male as in its many offshoots. That is simply determined by the logic of splitting, says Plato: by cutting a hermaphrodite into two, one gets a female and a male; by splitting a female, one gets two females, and by dividing a male, two males.[58] So it is only natural that the doubles that reflect the protagonist should always be male.

This formula may not convince you. But the very concept of the doppelgänger itself has evolved as a male construct. The "maleness" is inherent in its nature, as Webber points out. One of the nine premises that Webber has used to define the double states: "the *Doppelgänger* host and visitant are axiomatically gendered as male."[59] It simply is the "axiomatic property of male gender."[60] In German, there is no term that denotes a female doppelgänger; there is no "*doppelgängerin*." Whenever the doppelgänger appears as female, the transgender double can only be framed as "*Doppelgänger im anderen Geschlecht*," or the "*Doppelgänger* in the other sex."[61]

More significantly, in cases where "forms of female doubling are indeed effected," they have "little to do with altered or divided states of female subjectivity."[62] Instead, "the female *Doppelgänger* are typically in the service of male fantasies of the other,"[63] even more so since the male protagonist is chronically lonesome—"sex-less, even if [he is] racked by sexuality."[64] That is exactly how the female doubles are rendered in Auster's body of work, from Virginia Stillman, the over-sexualized *femme fatale* apparition that Quinn encounters in *City of Glass*, to the imagined muse figures, Claire and Celia, as projections of male imagination and desire in the films *The Inner Life of Martin Frost* and *Lulu on the Bridge*. Recall Auster's words—the latter is a story about "how men invent women"—and this invention is based on imaginary constructs not unlike those of the female Hollywood stars whose photos decorate the male bathroom in the opening sequence of the film.

Either way, the feminine in Auster seems to belong solely to the realm of the imaginary, or rather the spiritual. And yet, the female doppelgänger, this source of inspiration and self-reflection for the character, like its counterpart the typewriter, turns out to be equally capable of manifesting uncanny autonomy and authority. With her invasive force, this female double is able to not only copycat and double the original but also deprive it of its authorial power. The best example I can give you is the curious case of Auster's ultimate double and "doppelgänger in the other sex," French artist Sophie Calle.

Like Hoffmann's Olimpia and Auster's Olympia typewriter, the double in Auster's work that is gendered as female and epitomized by Calle turns out to be not only spiritual but also ruthlessly machinic. She is another kind of "spiritual automaton" that holds the potential to reverse Auster's text-generation process and turn it against the author himself. Recall McHale's muse of automatic writing. A writer's muse performs similar functions to a prosthetic writing tool (such as the typewriter) as both imply the writer's collaboration with "something beyond or outside [himself]."[65] Perhaps, Auster's text-generating process, which, regardless of his humanist concerns, appears rhizomatic and mechanical, is best revealed through the intervention of this female double that is both machinic and spiritual. It seems it is exactly her spirituality ("museness," or muse-driven imagination) that, in combination with prosthetic writing tools such as typewriters or doubles, generates Auster's intratext.

Like typewriting, writing that involves doppelgängers is never a straightforward process. The doppelgänger threatens to destroy the supposed division between itself as a double and the origin it copies, and between its text (as a copy of an alleged original) and other texts, undermining the author's position and, in fact, overtaking it. The doubles that are constructed and projected by Auster are capable of reversing the process of text-generation at some point by turning it against the author himself. And so it happens that Auster becomes manipulated by his own fictional doubles. The more Paul Auster implicates himself in the "machinery of the text," and the more he lets himself be copied and repeated, the more Paul Auster becomes dispersed in and subjected to his own doubles.

This process of reversing subordination is best revealed by female doubles because the female-gendered spiritual automaton appears to be the most "truthful" doppelgänger—a doppelgänger that, in Webber's words, "operates as … a phantasm which enters into and challenges the constructions of realism,"[66] and destabilizes the notions of the work's authorship and origins. While Auster's female doubles often fulfill Webber's premise by yielding themselves to "male fantasies of the other [sex]," and are therefore "invariably bound up" with "the question of gendering,"[67] their presence and the impact of their performance on the text are more powerful than that of male doubles. Auster's female doppelgängers function at the core of text-creation as one of the sources of the dictating voice.

At this point, let me bring you back to some of the thoughts that opened this book. Auster's texts are inseparable from each other. Each is a part of, and yet a multiplicity of, his other texts and together they form a complex facto-fictional rhizomatic structure which I have named Auster's intratext. Narratively or thematically reflecting each other, these texts often overlap, becoming different sides of the same image, resembling fragments of a cubist painting, such as those by French artist Fernand Léger, where each plane, while presenting a slightly different perspective, is part of the same larger mosaic. As we noted, Auster's *Leviathan* (1992), for example, is seen by Varvogli and Shiloh as another version of his early novel *The Locked Room* (1986), due to the conspicuous parallels in the narrative, character, and plot constructions. It is a textual overlap.

But *Leviathan* is more than an illustration of Auster's haunting repetitions of a set of textual assemblages. This novel, which became part of an early collaboration between Auster and Calle, stands out in Auster's textual rhizome as a strange node, an anomaly. It brings together two authors' intratexts whose boundaries in relation to one another are indefinable. *Leviathan* becomes an intersection, an entry point, or "a hole" (to use Briggs' term) in Auster's intratext through which connection is made to another author's work. In a peculiar way, a part of Auster's life-work merges with that of Calle's. Two spider-webs intersecting, then creating a bizarre "third space" that can be claimed by no one and yet both, a sort of shared gray area. So, unavoidably, as we inspect *Leviathan*, we are going to wander into Calle's life-work, too, but there we will pick out threads of text that lead us back to Paul Auster. We have chosen to read Calle's work as the intruding other. But the angle that we take could, of course, be reversed. Such is the nature of the double.

The collaborative project with Calle, resulting in a book compiled by her (*Double Game*, 1999), is a kind of textual mutation. It has evolved from bits and pieces of earlier texts written by Auster and Calle separately, and a new text that they worked on together.[68] As the book's title suggests, the textual game has two participants— the project's author is Sophie Calle "with participation of Paul Auster." It also has a two-way development, where both authors in turn claim and reclaim authorship over each other's work by rewriting it. It confirms one of the main premises of the doppelgänger situation—the staging of a power play that, in Webber's words, is "always caught up in exchange, never to be simply possessed as mastery of the self, of the other, or of the other self."[69]

But let us imagine that the game starts when Auster decides to create a doppelgänger for Calle. In his novel *Leviathan*, he introduces a character named Maria Turner, an eccentric American artist whose "work ... had nothing to do with creating objects commonly defined as art."[70] This artist, whose creative activities resist categorization ("some people called her a photographer, others referred to her as a conceptualist, still others considered her a writer, but none of these descriptions was accurate"),[71] is a prototype of Calle. This is acknowledged in the front matter of *Leviathan*, which states that "the author extends special thanks to Sophie Calle for permission to mingle fact with fiction." For his novel, Auster borrows from Calle not only her personality and biographical data, but also her artistic projects. Calle's *The Striptease* (1979), for example, appears in *Leviathan* as Maria's project *The Naked Lady*. Among other Maria projects, whose detailed descriptions span nearly ten pages of the novel, we can easily recognize various works by Calle published over more than ten years: *The Wardrobe* (1998), *To Follow ...* (1978–9), *Suite vénitienne* (1980), *The Detective* (1981), *The Hotel* (1981), *The Address Book* (1983) and *The Birthday Ceremony* (1980–93). In addition to these "borrowed" projects, Auster also invents for Maria new ones, such as observing a diet based on foods of a particular color each day, or living each day under a certain letter of the alphabet.

This Maria plays a pivotal role in *Leviathan* and, like any other element in a rhizomatic assemblage, functions at multiple levels. At first she appears, not unlike Lulu and Claire, as "a woman invented by men"—a muse and bed partner of the writer-character Peter Aaron. She is the story's *femme fatale*. Her strong charisma, overwhelming sexuality, and "habit of courting trouble in whatever form she could find it" in the end leads to "catastrophic" consequences—"at least two lives were lost" because of her, the narrator states.[72] The character of Maria then resembles what Webber describes as "[t]he demonically erotic [female] double," a devastating "automaton" and "a sophisticated sex-doll," who "might usefully be called a sort of bachelor machine, a spin off from the prototype of Olimpia in Hoffmann's *Sandmann*."[73] Maria clearly carries within herself traces of outdated connotations of doppelgängers as harbingers of bad luck, and has the potential to become a catalyst for major plot developments. She is the "reigning spirit of chance," "the goddess of the unpredictable."[74] And, as the narrator of *Leviathan* laments, "the whole miserable story" starts when Maria finds a black address book lying on the street: "Maria opened the book, and out flew the devil, out flew a scourge of violence, mayhem and death."[75] Here, an association is established with the story of Lulu and Pandora's box that is embedded in the film *Lulu on the Bridge*. So, the Maria/Calle who appears in *Leviathan* already has a hybrid nature: part fictional character, part "real" person, part fruit of the male imagination, and part mythical construct resembling the Romantic doppelgänger.

And then the situation gets further complicated. Calle asks Auster to continue the double game and to "invent [another] fictive character which [she] would attempt to resemble."[76] She seeks to double a new version of her double that, like the other doppelgänger, would be authored by Auster. As she later recalls in an unpublished brief for an exhibition of the project,

I proposed that he write a story about a fictional character named Sophie. I would borrow events from the life of that character and offer myself, for one year, to fulfil the obligation. I would try to become "his" Sophie and complete the story wherever it would take me.[77]

Calle's fantasy of total submission to Auster and his creation of the double never comes true (but it results in the project "Gotham Handbook," the final part of *Double Game*). Even so, in her determination, Calle confirms the two basic premises of the doppelgänger situation—that the characteristic positions of power and authority, and the total lack of those, are exchangeable, and that there is no "original" to be found among the doubles. Already with the *Leviathan* project, we face the impossibility of telling the two (Calle and Maria) apart. *Leviathan* and *Double Game* allow Calle to merge the boundaries between the fictional and the real, the double and its alleged "original," arriving at an equation of the postmodern multiple: Sophie Calle = Maria Turner = "Sophie Calle" (Auster's Sophie).

Not only Calle but also Auster displays what Maria Lind would call "devotion to intensive self-fictionalizing," a "well-tested method for questioning authorship" as well as identity.[78] We, of course, know that already. And *Leviathan* is no exception. Its protagonist, the writer-figure Peter Aaron, shares with Auster his occupation and initials. The names of his wife and children are similar to those of Auster's.[79] In other words, Aaron is "a writer whose career [and life] suspiciously reflects, or refracts, Paul Auster's own," as one critic proclaims.[80] Meanwhile, the first name of the second most important character in the novel, another writer-turned-detective character called Benjamin Sachs, is Auster's middle name. These two characters become the two faces of Auster. The attempts by the quester (Aaron) to decode the essence of the quest's object (Ben) appear as Auster's own inward journey, and his own quest for identity, so characteristic of his texts.

And when it becomes apparent that the doubling takes place not only between Auster and his fictional characters, or Calle and her fictional stand-ins, but also between the two authors themselves and their individual texts, things become still more complicated. When looking at both Auster's *Leviathan* and its version as rewritten by Calle, we see what Anna Khimasia describes as "the slippage between the characters Auster/Aaron/Sachs and Calle/Maria/Calle" that eventually "makes it particularly hard to establish *who is speaking*"[81] (her emphasis). As a meeting point for two authors and two intratexts, *Leviathan* is full of overlaps, replacements, and doublings of identities, facts, fictions, and authorships. It is an unstable multiplicity—an "unattributable" assemblage, as Deleuze and Guattari would call it.

Some things, however, are more attributable to Auster than Calle, and *vice versa*. In an article written for a Sunday paper on creativity and the pleasures of reading, Auster talks about his work being born through the solitary experience of "sitting alone in a room with a pen in your hand, hour after hour, day after day, year after year, struggling to put words on pieces of paper in order to give birth to what does not exist—except in your head."[82] It would be difficult to imagine Sophie Calle as either "solitary" or "struggling". Calle "lives" out her art and performs it in real-life circumstances through various self-imposed rituals. She is the ultimate postmodern double-player. She documents her fictionalized performances and experiences in diary-style first-person narratives, where descriptions of emotions are supplemented with bare reports of facts and details, and "authentic" documentary photographs.

Calle, says Khimasia, "not only disrupts the binaries of author/subject and fact/fiction, but simultaneously explores the materiality and temporality of identity in such a way that the latter remains ambiguous."[83] Her experiences become "entangled in a series of displacements and supplements of 'Sophie Calle' making it difficult to determine and define the edges of her roles as author and subject."[84] Or, as Aaron puts it in *Leviathan*, "her pieces exhibited the same qualities one found in Maria herself," an observation that suggests Maria/Calle's artistic projects should be called "life-projects" and "life-art" rather than "art." It is Calle, more than Auster, who in a loosely Deleuzian sense can be said to "live her philosophy," or cultivate "practical philosophy" by subjecting her life-art to experimentation, experience and philosophical "encounters." She aspires to "fieldwork" in which "theory and practice seem to be reconciled," as another critic/curator, Jeanine Griffin, observes.[85] There are definitely no solitary rooms in Calle's life-work, and if there are, they are all unlocked. She pulls into the public even the most intimate spaces: for one of her projects, she plants her bed on the top of the Eiffel Tower, and invites willing strangers to share it.

And yet, Calle's and Auster's texts, especially their early "detective" stories, show striking similarities, not least in the ways the double is employed. The doppelgänger, according to another of Webber's premises, recurrently introduces "voyeurism and innuendo" into "the subject's pursuit of a visual and discursive sense of self."[86] This motif, so symptomatic of Auster's whole *New York Trilogy*, is also rehearsed in Calle's "detective" projects, such as *Suite vénitienne*, *The Shadow* (republished in *Double Game* as "The Detective"), *Address Book*, and *The Hotel*, which are all based on the acts of stalking and voyeurism that the double has to carry out in its pursuit of the other. Seen through this lens, the two authors' texts appear as no less than "accidental" doubles of one another.

Consider *Suite vénitienne* and *City of Glass*. After coincidentally meeting a stranger, identified as Henri B., twice on the same day, Calle decides to follow him from Paris to Venice, unaware ("unaware") that her actions would one day constitute a "life-project." She embarks on her quest because she feels "totally lost."[87] *City of Glass* begins with the devastated Quinn feeling lost—"[l]ost, not only in the city, but within himself as well."[88] To him "New York was an inexhaustible space" that "always left him with the feeling of being lost." Yet the city is also his only escape as it allows him to be reduced to "a seeing eye," and "escape the obligation to think," distracting him from what he believes to be an otherwise purposeless existence.[89] Calle says in a *Suite vénitienne* review: "I followed a person to find a direction for myself. I had no energy, so I would absorb someone else's purpose."[90] Later, in the project, she admits: "He [Henri B.] is consuming me."[91] Griffin, one of the few critics to notice Auster and Calle's double games, draws this analogy:

> During this project ... Calle was subsumed in the Other, usurping his impetus just as Auster's 'detective', Quinn, is subsumed in the life of his quarry and of his

assumed role of 'Paul Auster, detective'. Through tracking and documenting the other they lose a grip on their selves.[92]

Calle's Venice, after all, is not unlike Quinn's New York—an urban space that makes one lose oneself and that is, in Baudrillard's words, constructed "like a trap, a maze, a labyrinth that inevitably, however fortuitously, brings back people to the same points."[93]

In Venice, Calle, disguised in a blonde wig and sunglasses, follows Henri B. around the streets and canals of the city for two weeks, photographing the man and documenting his movements. In *Double Game* we read her sleuth-style surveillance reports, complete with black-and-white photographs of the object:

> 11:05 A.M. The woman goes inside the Banco di Roma. I guess that he went in before her. To see him, I approach the front windows of the bank. I can just make out the woman on the other side of the glass. I back away.

> 11:15 A.M. She leaves and heads toward the Ponte di Rialto. She's alone. I rush into the bank. He's not there. I run after the woman. She's disappeared. For the next few minutes, I search for them in all directions in vain.

> [Etc.][94]

At the same time, the text also reflects Calle's own anxieties and doubts when her vigilance fails her and when, like Quinn, she loses control of her task ("I give up"), or experiences sudden flashes of irrational hope ("I have high expectations of him"). Her book also features scanned copies of a map of the city and her tracings of the man's movements. Like Quinn, she seems to believe that drawing a map of her suspect's urban travels will bring her closer to understanding the man. And Quinn, like Calle, in shadowing the suspect, decides "to record every detail about Stillman he possibly could."[95] Later, in the graphic novel version of *City of Glass*, Quinn's observations appear as hand-written records that he has made in his notebook, along with the little hand-drawn maps:

> Continues north to 82 St. Turns left.
> Buys sandwich in deli at corner. Walks along 82 St. to Riverside Park
> Sits on bench in park and reads through notebook
> Searches through bushes—finds discarded coffee cup, puts in bag ...[96]

But then—an unexpected turn of events that almost always occurs in such detective quests. At some point in the works of both authors, the process gets reversed and the follower-detective becomes the center of attention for someone else who surveils and reports on them. The followed one catches the follower in the act, or becomes the follower of his follower. For Baudrillard, this reversal is a crucial element of shadowing. In fact, "[t]he possibility of reversal is necessary," he writes.[97] And so "[t]he objects of surveillance change constantly in both artists' works," as Griffin has also noticed: "viewing subject and viewed object may become viewing object and viewed subject," depending on who is manipulating the relation at any given moment.[98]

This often self-imposed surveillance that we witness in Auster and Calle marks the surveilled object's desire to have its existence affirmed by the Other—even if that other turns out to be "impossible." Note the words that Michel Contat attributes to Auster's relationship with his father as expressed through "Portrait of an Invisible Man" (words that also clearly resonate with Auster's doppelgänger tale "The Day I Disappeared"): "... you write to become visible yourself, to become visible to him; but he is dead, he's not there anymore, so you have to invent him, make a person out of him who would be your witness.[99] Or, as Baudrillard puts it,

> [o]ne must follow in order to be followed, photograph in order to be photo-graphed, wear a mask in order to be unmasked, appear in order to disappear, guess one's intentions in order to have your own guessed—all that is ... the most profound, symbolic requirement. One has to be discovered.[100]

Creating that possibility seems to be a fundamental task of the doppelgänger.

Double Game, and the mingling of texts

You can see this reversal of doppelgänger roles in two other texts by Auster and Calle, *Ghosts* and *The Detective* (or *The Shadow*). In Auster's novel, the trained private eye Blue spies on a man named Black, writing detailed reports about him and submitting those to a client named White. At the end of the novel, Blue learns not only that White is the same person as Black and the request to be spied on was made by White/Black himself, but also that throughout this time, Black had been spying on Blue as well. Black justifies it at the end: "That's the whole point, isn't it? He's got to know [that he is spied on] or else nothing makes sense ... He needs my eyes looking at him. He needs me to prove he's alive."[101]

In 1981, after the *Suite vénitienne* project, Calle asked her mother to go to a detective agency and hire someone who would "follow [her], report on [her] daily activities and ... provide photographic evidence of [her] existence."[102] For several days, the detective, unaware that Calle knew about him, took pictures of her and recorded her movements in a small notebook, "omitting nothing from the account, not even the most banal and transitory events."[103] Later the results are published in *Double Game* as the detective's (yet another "author's") report along with black-and-white photographs:

REPORT

Thursday, April 16, 1981

At 10:00 a.m. I take up position outside the home of the subject, 22 rue Liancourt, Paris 14th.

At 10:20 the subject leaves home. She is dressed in a gray raincoat, gray trousers, and wears black shoes with stockings of the same color. She carries a yellow shoulder bag.

At 10:23 the subject buys some daffodils at the florist's on the corner of rue Froidevaux and rue Gassendi, then enters Montparnasse cemetery at 5 rue Emile-Richard. She lays the flowers on a tomb then leaves the cemetery on the boulevard Edgar-Quinet side …

[Etc.][104]

Calle, it seems to me, follows the rules of the doppelgänger game with great ease. And, I think, there is no way she could have remained a mere intertextual reference in Auster's book. She responds to her double by reversing the process to double her doubling, as well as its creator, directly intervening in Auster's work. And so the front matter of the resulting *Double Game* acknowledges: "The author extends special thanks to Paul Auster for permission to mingle fact with fiction." She further undermines Auster's authorship over his work by including there a copy of the relevant piece of *Leviathan* (the eight pages that deal with the fictional Maria) as (literally) a book-within-a-book. With a red pen she edits the miniature replica of Auster's book by striking out or correcting any words or sentences that, to her mind, are not adequate or factually true. She also adds her own bits of information, along with personal comments:

Some time ~~after~~ **before** that, **she followed** a man ~~tried to pick up Maria~~ on the street. ~~She found him distinctly unattractive and rebuffed him.~~ That same evening, by pure coincidence she ran into him at a gallery opening in ~~SoHo~~ **Paris**. They talked ~~once again,~~ and this time she learned from the man that he was leaving ~~the next morning~~ **soon**.[105]

And this is where we observe that the precision with which Calle mimics her double resembles a sort of writing machinery at work. Calle becomes machinic in copying, editing, and multiplying Auster's work. Besides, she not only re-writes Auster's text but also turns the fictional back into the factual. A fictional text written by Auster, who partly built it on Calle's personality and life, becomes Calle's (auto)biography, written by Auster and edited by Calle. But if the lives of Maria and Calle can be equated, and if Maria = Calle, then the fragments of *Leviathan* that are dedicated to Maria also become part of Calle's fictional autobiography, which in this case has been authored by someone else (Auster).

Some critics describe the conceptual works of Maria/Calle as "autofiction"—a kind of artistic practice "through which authors create new personalities and identities for themselves, while … maintaining their identity (their real name)."[106] Yet there is also another way of reading Calle's "autofictionality." Her work that contains a strong performative element is nevertheless almost always ritualistic and based on her obedience to preset rules. Since Calle's "life-writing" is limited, enhanced, and shaped by a set of prescribed rules, it is, in McHale's sense, prosthetic—an automaton. "Autofiction," for Calle, then, is not only "autobiographical fiction", but also "automatic fiction." Not only her way of rewriting Auster's text but also the way she carries out the tasks and roles ascribed to her are automatic. The mechanical nature of Calle's text-generation makes her a more powerful—more aggressive—doppelgänger than Auster, whose texts are often infused with humanist and existentialist concerns. We will return to this comparison. But so that you notice, at this point what we witness in the Calle-Auster double game is a machine versus a human.

When Calle edits *Leviathan*, she reclaims her authorship over it and over all the facts inscribed in it. But, if Auster's works are inseparable from his life and are two sides of the same Möbius strip, then by doing so Calle rewrites no less than Auster's life. Auster is no longer the sole author of his life, but his life is partly authored by Calle. In this way, Khimasia notes, Auster and Calle problematize not only the distinction between reality and fiction, but even the concept of autofiction, and authorship over that.[107] The borders between two texts, narrators, authors, and their lives are once more demolished by the work of the double, whose intervention overturns all textual conventions.

In a sense, the game of collaboration between Auster and Calle reflects the form and contents of their own creative texts, and what is happening within them; the double becomes a messenger of its medium. Their collaboration becomes another example of surveillance, shadowing, and reporting. A game this time played not between fictional characters created by Auster or Calle, but between the two authors themselves as they become each other's doubles, impersonators, and chroniclers. What Quinn does in *City of Glass* and Calle in *Suite vénitienne* is not so different from what Auster and Calle do to each other. Both Calle and Auster get implicated in a mutual re-writing of the self and the other as their intratexts slowly merge together.[108]

Calle's intervention in Auster's intratext does not stop at including his text in her project and partially re-writing it. Calle equates fact with fiction, and herself with Maria, when she edits with a red pen the "factual mistakes" that appear in the pages of Auster's *Leviathan*. She also reverses this process—from the fictional to the factual—by carrying out in real life the fictional projects that Auster invented for Maria. Published in her *Double Game* as *The Chromatic Diet* and *Days Under the Sign of B, C, & W*, they appear in the first part under the title "The life of Maria and how it influenced the life of Sophie." In the words of Maud Lavin, "[w]hen Calle enacts and lavishly documents Maria's esthetic exercises, they become hers, and when she republishes the art works originally hers that Auster ascribed to Maria, they become hers again."[109] Calle also rewrites Auster's projects by improving the parts she does not like, as in her project *The Chromatic Diet*.[110] And so she acknowledges Auster's authoritative-authorial voice at the same time as she strips him of it.[111]

Calle is clearly a literary murderer. Baudrillard says that following someone's footsteps, with or without reporting on their activities, in itself is already an aggression, compared to which even "murder is more subtle," because following someone step by step means "*erasing his traces* along the way, and no one can live without traces"[112] (his emphasis). And it may be that Baudrillard's commentary on Calle's ability to steal those traces, after losing herself "in the other's traces," and so reclaim her own existence, explains the different outcomes of the quests undertaken by Auster's pseudo-detectives and Calle's stalkers.

For Calle, as for Deleuze, destruction is a part of productive creation. The confidence, even aggression, and submissiveness with which she throws herself at the mercy of the other is most visible in her "attacks" on Auster when she invades his *Leviathan* and literally erases (and at places—replaces) parts of it. She indeed reminds me of Hoffman's inspiring automaton Olimpia—an irresistible comparison. Men are afraid of Calle's work as they are afraid of the Olimpia doll—because, as art dealer Olivier Renaud-Clement puts it, "[s]he pins them down."[113]

When critics address the similarities between Auster's and Calle's projects, they view both authors' work in terms of conceptualism and conceptual art.[114] Charlotte Schoell-Glass calls Auster's writer-characters "art historians," or conceptualists, "figures [who are] situated between scholarship and the active life" (art), and who both "belong[] to the world of art, yet do not belong to it entirely, as artists do."[115] There is definitely art, and especially criticism of it, inhabiting Auster's work. *Moon Palace* features an ekphratic analysis of a Ralph Albert Blakelock painting by the protagonist Marco Fogg. In *The Book of Illusions* and *Man in the Dark*, the characters perform cinematic analysis of movies. And so on.

Yet these works are reflecting not only "an increasing interest in visuality and the image" by Auster's "art historians," but also a fascination with "art form situated between the creation of objects and the enactment of rituals."[116] Or, in other words, with conceptual art. We see the characters "inscribing [their] obsession[s] in the urban space" and in objects and things that surround them.[117] Marco Stanley Fogg makes rearrangeable furniture out of boxes containing books. He consumes—he "eats"— these written texts the same way as Calle eats her color-coordinated meals under her chromatic diet and "consumes" tangible and intangible things as part of her "alphabetic diet" (she spends several days under a different letter of the alphabet each time). Peter Stillman Sr. from *City of Glass* inscribes his messages on New York's urban space through his daily walks. Quinn, meanwhile, tries to decode and interpret them. And Benjamin Sachs from *Leviathan*, whom the Austeresque twists of fate and chance have turned into a terrorist, starts blowing up small Statue of Liberty replicas throughout the United States. According to Schoell-Glass, his actions—carefully planned and performed, with messages left for the public—resemble conceptual art.

Artistic life-projects are often based on performances that grow out of accidents and coincidences (itself two hallmark themes in Auster's life-work). More than motifs, they become narrative devices: the reliance on the coincidence structures most of Calle's projects and many of Auster texts.[118] Both Calle and Auster let their creative practices "depen[d] upon it to a great extent to constitute an aesthetic reality," and, in fact, "rely on coincidences to define 'reality.'"[119] Quinn receives a mistargeted phone call three times; Calle runs into a stranger twice. These contingencies are enough to turn the two characters into self-styled detective heroes, ready to play along in an impromptu game whose rules and purpose might also remain unclear. In a sense, they are conceptual artists who turn a chance encounter into an artistic project and a performance of their life.

A story (a "project") may be born out of a thing that performs alongside the artist. A seemingly ordinary notebook that Sidney Orr in *Oracle Night* buys at a stationery store turns out to have an incredible impact on his life. For Calle, in her *The Address Book*, it is the eponymous object found lying on a street that prompts her to start a new "detective" quest.[120] As Auster describes the origins of Calle's project, "[t]he book had been transformed into a magical object for her ... Chance had led her to it, but now that it was hers, she saw it as an instrument of fate."[121] Pay attention to Auster's remark. Perhaps it reveals to us the main difference between Auster and Calle. If for the former the element of chance is often "an instrument of fate," then for Calle it is merely "the instrument of writing," or creating art. A tool, in other words.

Why is Calle different? She who sees herself as a conceptual artist lets her life, with all its unexpected twists (which Auster would affectedly refer to as "fate"), coalesce with her creative work. Auster seems to insist on dividing life- from -work (a split possibly caused by his writing machine which separates out the written word; he cannot "live out writing"—he "writes"). But for Calle, not only unexpected chance events but also personal tragedies have the capacity to be skillfully turned into a new art project.[122] She refuses to seek for meaning in such "signs of fate," and indeed refuses to interpret any situation she encounters. (She would instead let others do it, as in the project *Take Care of Yourself*, where she asked over a hundred "women," including a parrot and a hand puppet, to interpret a break-up email she had received from her partner.) What matters for her is the process of performance—doppelgänger-ish, investigative, experimental—rather than the purposefulness of its result. As the ultimate doppelgänger, she is, to repeat Webber's premise, the "inveterate performer" of the acts of detection, voyeurism, and exploration, for whom "fate" is but a game. Hence also the title of her book, *Double Game*, and the explanation of "The Rules of the Game" in its beginning.

Here is an illustrative case. When Calle/Maria embarks on her self-imposed quest to follow a strange man in Venice/New Orleans, her intention, says the narrator of *Leviathan*, is to "keep herself hidden, to resist all contact with him, to explore his outward behavior and make no effort to interpret what she saw."[123] In *City of Glass*, Quinn embarks on a never-fulfilling and destructive quest, and is driven to insanity because of his obsession and desire "to ascribe significance to every event or clue" and to always look for signs of fate and meaning, which he, however, is unable to interpret.[124] In *Suite vénitienne*, Calle purposefully throws herself into a seemingly meaningless ritual. In fact, as opposed to Auster, Calle's "quests" are hardly quests at all, since, as Baudrillard puts it, they "have *no* reason"[125] (his emphasis).

Discussing Calle's projects, Baudrillard points out that it is even necessary that her "overture make no sense, in order to have a chance of success in this sphere of strangeness, absurd complicity, fatal consent."[126] The ritualized performances she carries out without questioning their meaning, and the voluntary subjection to the rules of self-imposed games, makes Calle a puppet, a robotic doll, at the mercy of "fate," coincidence, and the other (Auster). She explains "the rules of the game" of her collaboration with Auster:

> I was ... inviting Paul Auster to do what he wanted with me, for a period of up to a year at most. Auster objected that he did not want to take responsibility for what might happen when I acted out the script he had created for me. Instead, he preferred to send me "Personal Instructions for SC on How to Improve Life in New York City (Because she asked ...)". I followed his directives.[127]

And yet in her creative work, Calle manages to steer a chain of coincidental and chance situations "into a system of relationships" that she maintains "under her control."[128] Subjecting herself to arbitrariness and chance, and the "impetus of the other," by giving up her authority and letting "other people decide," is a choice in which she holds the final control.[129] In this sense, Auster loses his authorial control because he does not agree with the principle of the game, and the logics of the doppelgänger: to lose yourself in the other's traces is to steal its traces in return (Baudrillard).

Think of Auster's detective-characters. In the course of their narratives they lose all control over their identity, life, and decisions. They disappear and are swept away by what could be called Auster's fatal coincidences. His writer-figures, unlike Calle and her doubles, seem unable to yield their experiences, emotions, and existential questions to the kind of mechanization, aestheticization, and ritualized repetition that the latter seem to practice. And most of his characters are doomed to perish. Quinn goes mad and vanishes from the story. Ben is literally blown up: "his body burst into dozens of small pieces."[130]

Auster's characters, as some critics would see it, are forever doomed in their quest to find meaning and fight linguistic disintegration, what Schoell-Glass calls "the ultimate and fundamental punishment for being human," being doomed to always "misunderstand, misread and misconstrue each other and the world."[131] Hence their obsession to inscribe themselves in the urban space and in objects to try to make meaning from those, and their futile attempts to re-construct the pristine relationship between language and the world, as staged by Stillman Sr. and Quinn (*City of Glass*), Ben Sachs (*Leviathan*), Anna Blume (*In the Country of Last Things*), or Mr. Blank (*Travels in the Scriptorium*).

It seems that Auster's humanist side traps his characters in an eternal quest for unattainable meaning (existential, linguistic, meta-fictional), while Calle's life-art is liberated from such a burden, since it is acted out in a purely mechanical way. No, there is not much difference between Calle, Hoffmann's Olimpia, or Auster's Olympia typewriter—they are all tools of both inspiration and mechanical generation of art. Calle makes art, the automatic doll Olimpia sings and plays harpsichord, and the typewriter produces writing. Missing in the cases of these "spiritual automatons" are the existential doubts that always manage to find their way into Auster's writing.

"Gotham Handbook"

If you want to see Calle act as a machine, you should look into the final part of the collaborative project between her and Auster—"Gotham Handbook." There, our writer uses a puppet-like Calle to address his humanist concerns. This project differs from most of his other texts in its absence of self-focus and explorations of identity. No more identity quests and stories of personal recovery and redemption. Instead, the focus is on "the moral issue" and one's responsibility towards other people. That resonates and reconnects with Auster's films *Smoke* and *Blue in the Face* and his novel *The Brooklyn Follies*. The specific instructions that Calle must observe are supplemented with Auster's personal moral explanations that justify these tasks. It is, in fact, Auster's call for exercising one's responsibility as a human being through small altruistic acts and emphatic gestures that could boost the city's morale and improve the life of the people in the neighborhood. Auster becomes the dictating voice, the inspirer, the preaching urban poet, while Calle—his messenger—mechanically carries out his instructions, inscribing her acts on the city space.

The set of instructions to Calle consists of four parts, each of which contains a different task for her: *Smiling* (Calle must smile at strangers when the situation does not call for it), *Talking to Strangers* (as there will be people who talk to her after she smiles at them), *Beggars and Homeless People* (she must give out sandwiches and cigarettes to them), and *Cultivating a Spot* (she must choose a spot in New York and beautify it). That is because Auster believes "it's our responsibility as human beings not to harden our hearts. Action is necessary, no matter how small or hopeless our gestures might seem to be."[132]

By following these instructions and carrying out small acts of charity, Calle is to improve life in the neighborhood. However, acts that are supposed to signify genuine kindness and generosity of spirit are rendered into experimental performances that are carried out and documented in an automated way. Calle's notes on the project reveal her unconditional submission to the given orders ("I have a duty to obey. That was the agreement. I have no other choice but to submit"[133]) and her commitment to achieving precise implementation, down to the smallest details. ("The only problem is keeping track of the number of smiles received each day. Paul didn't ask me to count the smiles I give. Unquestionably an oversight."[134])

In his instructions to Calle, Auster repeats what his characters Anne Blume and Quinn had expressed more than 20 years previously in their anti-utopian urban visions: "People are not the only ones neglected in New York. Things are neglected as well … Look closely at the things around you and you'll see that nearly everything is falling apart."[135] Hence the last task for Calle—*Cultivating a Spot*. Auster asks her to pick one spot in the city—"a street corner, a subway entrance, a tree in the park"—and begin to think of it as hers.[136]

You may notice the similarity with Auggie's photo project that was invented for "Auggie Wren's Christmas Story" and later reused in *Smoke*: Auggie is to take a photo of the same spot (the corner of 3rd Street and Seventh Avenue in one version, the corner of Atlantic Avenue and Clinton Street in the other) every day for 13 (12) years. Not only the type of instruction but also the desired outcomes are shared by the two projects. These aspirations are suggested by "Paul," "a writer," in "Auggie Wren's Christmas Story":

> Auggie was photographing time, I realized, both natural time and human time, and he was doing it by planting himself in one tiny corner of the world and willing it to be his own, by standing guard in the space he had chosen for himself.[137]

Calle chooses a fancier site—a public telephone booth located on a street corner in the SoHo neighborhood. And Auster gives her the instructions:

> Go to your spot every day at the same time. Spend an hour watching every-thing that happens to it, keeping track of everyone who passes by or stops or does anything there. Take notes, take photographs. Make a record of these daily

observations and see if you learn anything about the people or the place or yourself.[138]

He asks her to set up a space for prolonged surveillance, and keep track and a record of everything that happens. Yet this is unlike any of the self-detection plots of most projects by Auster/Calle. "Gotham Handbook" takes the direction outward, to the larger social assemblages formed by people, spaces, and objects. To some extent, that seems to be prescribed by the nature of collaboration itself, which implies shared authorship with multiple perspectives and voices. I have already noted this connection before. If two authors are involved, there seems to be a possibility for at least two-fold movement.

On the one hand, the cross-medium collaboration wants to question itself—what happens when the notions of unique authorship get undermined, or one author is allowed to intervene in another author's work, as in the case of Auster-Calle collaboration? On the other hand, the nature of the collaborative rhizome liberates the collaborators from excessive self-centeredness and self-consciousness. And so its content corresponds to its democratic and open form. As González notes in relation to another Auster collaboration, *Blue in the Face*, "[t]his experience of communal artistic production reproduces in fact the main theme of the film: the importance of communities and relationships versus individualism, cold capitalism, and globalization."[139]

When curator Maria Lind, in her essay "The Collaborative Turn," addresses collaboration and collectivism in contemporary art, she refers to artist-writer Gregory Sholette and "art scientist" Blake Stimson, who talk about the emergence of two new types of collaboration.[140] One reflects what is referred to as the growing Islamist desire for an anti-capitalistic, absolute, and idealistic collectivism, while the other turns against *all* ideology or, in Deleuzian terms, the fruit of arborescent thinking (be it the ideals of dogmatic religion, nationalism, or communism, etc.). Deleuze and Guattari would consider this the process of emancipation, as collaborations that operate horizontally and, in Lind's words, give voice to "agents from different fields."[141] And Lind notes the connection: in its structure, a collaborative project "ends up looking very much like the rhizome as described by Gilles Deleuze and Felix Guattari," and "certainly shares some of the characteristics of Michael Hardt's and Antonio Negri's understanding of the 'common.'"[142]

Instead of prioritizing the voice of one author, its preference is the plurality of voices. Benjamin D. Carson points out (quoting Deleuze and Guattari) that the collaborative rhizome, in contrast to arborescent, hierarchical systems, appears as an acentered asignifying system with "finite networks of automata in which communication runs from any neighbor to any other."[143] For Deleuze and Guattari, these "stems or channels," unlike the predetermined paths within the arborescent system (the one-author project), "do not pre-exist, and all individuals are interchangeable, defined only by their *state* at a given moment—such that local operations are coordinated and the final, global result synchronized without a central agency"[144] (their emphasis). In a rhizomatic, asignifying system (collaboration), where hierarchy has been displaced by multiplicity, the individual's location or identity is, as Carson notes, "indeterminate."[145]

You can see this happen not only in "Gotham Handbook," where everyone—any and every stranger who interacts with Calle—has the potential to be heard and documented. Also in "his" *National Story Project*, Auster gives voice to the ordinary American people, "allowing the people to be heard."[146] The hierarchy that exists in the writing of the nation's narrative gets dismantled. After Auster announces the project on the radio, letters start pouring in from all corners of the country: "so many voices coming at [Auster] from so many different directions."[147] And he acknowledges that the *National Story Project*'s "book has been written by people of all ages and from all walks of life."[148] His attempt to "let people be heard" through *Smoke* resembles this, since nearly every character there is given a chance to tell their story.

But a film such as *Blue in the Face* not only further "expand[s] the issues from *Smoke*; it also corrects them to integrate groups and opinions that were excluded in the first film, specifically racial minorities and women."[149] This condition—that voice be given to the others, especially the abused or forgotten ones—goes hand-in-hand with one's moral obligations, underlined by Auster in his letter to Calle, where he writes to her: "Don't ignore the miserable ones."[150] I can only repeat González's observation that Auster's collaborations are "all moral tales."

Such thoughts lead us back to the territories already traversed—spaces of assembled communities, of rhizomatic sharing and of Auster's humanist concerns, epitomized earlier by a shared cigarette. But that should not come to us as any surprise. The notion of novelty, after all, is somewhat problematic in Auster's oeuvre. Even a "new" collaborative project keeps pointing back to other Auster texts. The description of Calle's works, that each "stands by itself, yet echoes the presence of the other,"[151] can be equally attributed to Auster. That makes Auster and Calle two doppelgängers, caught in a never-ending cycle of semi-machinic multiplication, doubling, and repetition. The double that insists on a split, a diversion, always eventually returns to itself. And if the double is implicated in Auster's writing machinery, there is little wonder that his texts through detours, deviations and divergences nevertheless keep leading back to themselves.

A paradox: the double that comes back to what it doubles questions it through the split it has created. I have already said that before. The double may not evoke fear any more, but it certainly generates anxiety. It poses a question when encountered, for the double is, essentially, a question mark. So, even though the double functions as a tool for reading, detecting and writing, it never stops questioning the implications of these very acts. For example, in my attempts to read the "other," must I become like it (its double)? Is it, perhaps, as the very consequence of writing that a double is created to whatever I write about? Does my writing on Paul Auster, then, create more "Paul Austers"?

The problem with the double, as we already know, lies not only in the impossibility of telling it apart from its alleged original. An uncontrollable phantom, it is also always on the move (is "going"). It is not even a thing—tangible—but a fleeting ghost. It slips away from your reach the moment you try to grasp it. And the double, of course, is also the multiple. See it for yourself: the moment I attempt to write about the double, my writing loses its unidirectionality and extends into many directions at once, threatening to disintegrate.

Perhaps the only way to trace the work of the double is through the act of doubling itself. That would make sense, given that any other actant whose work we investigated required a similar means of performative tracing. Hence my smoking of cigars, cigarettes and cigarillos while determining the role of smoking and following its associative work. Hence my typewriting. And so on. In a sense, this research has turned me into a smoking, touch-type-writing writer, and as such "connected" me to Auster and his characters, although I am afraid that eventually, like them, I will have to admit that the quest to capture the life-work of someone else is a hopeless struggle.[152] And yet, for us, there is no other way than to "follow the actors" themselves.

Where does it take us, then? Quinn learns in *City of Glass* that detection requires complete identification with the object of search.[153] It means that the work this book does in dissecting the things that assemble the writer-character and the ways they produce multiple, shifting and sometimes contradictory meanings would likewise require me to identify with it. But identification would become copying, doubling— itself, of course, another element that is part of Auster's writing machine. And so, a scholar's reading of Auster's texts would unavoidably start to turn into a performance of them. Slowly, I would feel, I am starting to take on the role of the double of both Auster and his characters. Slowly, the scholar would transform into a self-styled writer-detective.

This rule of detection would require me to read Auster's texts *in situ* by doubling his characters and literally retracing their routes as inscribed in the space of New York the same way as Auster's writer-detective characters follow their subjects in *City of Glass*, *Leviathan*, and "The Day I Disappeared" (and as Sophie Calle, Auster's female doppelgänger, follows what she interprets as instructions given by his work). But if I doubled an Auster character, I myself would become like a character, and the required intellectual distance would be impossible to retain. The more I became aware of my own agency in reconstituting and expanding Auster's intratext through the process of "reading" it and writing about it, the more pronounced the "I" would become. Any critical distance would collapse the moment that this disruption in perspective occured. For any scholar, this is surely an outrageous prospect.

And there would be consequences, implications to such acts. Would I indeed become yet another actor that "does some work" with(in) Auster's intratext? The addition of "such an ontological ingredient," after all, might deeply modify the network itself (as Latour warns).[154] Through the performative process of my reading of Auster's intratext, and my tracing of the elements that act within it, I would simul- taneously be re-writing these texts in a way that resembles Calle's double-writing of Auster's life-work.

Latour has warnings to give us about the nature of tracing. A network, he says, is not something that gets traced or inscribed by someone else. The actor-network itself is that "entity that does the tracing and the inscribing."[155] Tracing an actor, a "thing" along a network in which it acts and where it forms and re-forms its assemblages is what creates the network itself.[156] It means that my tracing of the Auster-assemblage and its constituent elements across Auster's oeuvre simultaneously creates and illuminates the connections it has rendered, the functions it has assumed, and the different kinds of other assemblages, situations and networks it has constituted. The Auster-assemblage is merely a node within the rhizome that this book has foregrounded. In a sense, it was not there before. And now it is.

For Deleuze and Guattari, writing about a rhizome itself creates a rhizome. In the introduction to *A Thousand Plateaus* they state: "We are writing this book as a rhizome. It is composed of plateaus. We have given it a circular form, but only for laughs …"[157] The process of tracing, describing, and reading a rhizomatic multiplicity of texts itself results in a rhizome. It means this book that I am writing here might also become a bit rhizomatic—it might lack some of the symmetry, linearity, determination, arborescent structure, and conclusiveness characteristic of scholarly works that engage in more "traditional" criticism. But, in fact, it does not want to, and could not possibly, rely on fixed theoretical frameworks, prescribed assumptions, and an *a priori* set order that predicts the ways a text should be read and so "keep it under control." It is possible there is as much madness as there is method in this book. And I cannot justify that in any other way than by saying: it is an attempt to get rid of "the tyranny" of critical distance, and of preset thought (to paraphrase Latour).[158] An attempt to re-read both the writer Paul Auster and the writer's tools, if you please.

I am staring at Sam Messer's portrait of the Auster-machine pinned onto the wall in front of my desk, and it is staring back at me, enigmatic as ever. Have we managed to catch a glimpse of this machinery at work, of the ways that parts of it operate? We have seen, for example, the work of that cigarillo that the writer is holding in his hand. Or the acting performed by his white Olympia in the production of text. There always are, of course, more thing-like suspects to investigate that are equally implicated in the "crime." Like New York, for example—which, strictly speaking, is not even a "thing." Often pushed into the background against which "Paul Auster" is placed, it is nevertheless a forceful actant whose presence is demanding and often devastating. The typing, chain-smoking writer-detective is embedded in its spaces. For there to be a "Paul Auster, the New York writer," we need its urban mazes.

So, it seems, this is what I have to do now: I have to leave my writer's desk and travel to New York. I will devote the next chapter to "Paul Auster's New York" whose associations and acting I will attempt to follow, and report to you. There will be several objects of interest and several objectives to my quest that will, no doubt, lead me into diverse directions. But those will be tied together by the rhizomatic conjunction of "and … and …" The study of the significance of New York marks the final stage of my scholarly quest, whereby I myself travel to this city in search of Paul Auster's New York … and Paul Auster himself.

Since Auster is both the source and the epitome of the "writer-character assemblage," finding and meeting him would let me ask questions about authenticity, truth, the distinction between fact and fiction, and the importance of authorial intent in the interpretation of texts, among other questions. In the end, perhaps, this quest will not only be about New York, or Paul Auster's New York, or even my Paul Auster's New York, but will concern the curious relationship that exists between the text, its author, his critic and the reader in the production of meaning. It will become the site where finally "it all" comes together. As a sort of grand finale, marking the end of this unfinishable book. But, at this stage—there is no way to be sure of any of this.

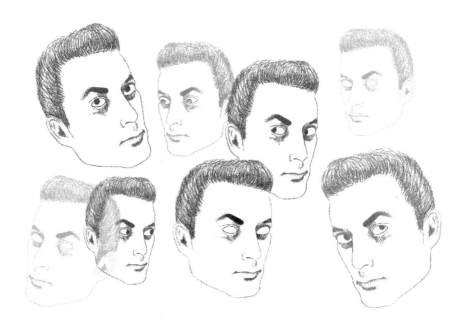

4

New York, Where All Quests Fail

There would be no Paul Auster's writer-character without New York. Such a prospect is simply unimaginable. Sam Messer's paintings most often depict Auster as a writer-assemblage, with its trademark cigarillos and typewriters, set against a view of the Brooklyn Bridge or Manhattan's skyline or its high-rise buildings. Jesús Ángel González opens his article "How I interviewed Paul Auster" with the following note: "Beware! Stop reading now if you don't want to get hooked. Paul Auster is addictive. He smokes and writes. And lives in Brooklyn."[1] In the Sonic Memorial Soundwalk project that took place four years after the 9/11 events, Auster narrates a walking tour around the neighborhood of what is now Ground Zero, introducing himself as "Paul Auster; writer, New Yorker." In an interview with Allon Reich in 1988, Auster declares that "New York is the most important place for me."[2] It is unsurprising that Paul Auster is seen as the quintessential New York writer, his name so synonymous with the city that it recurrently gets included in literary travel guides.[3] Exploring and experiencing New York has become analogous with reading Paul Auster. And the other way round.

With a few exceptions (*The Music of Chance* novel and film, *Travels in the Scriptorium*, and *The Inner Life of Martin Frost* film—although that, too, concludes with the protagonist's return to his home in New York), most of Auster's works are set predominantly in Brooklyn and/or Manhattan. Here are some of them: *Smoke, Blue in the Face, The Brooklyn Follies, The New York Trilogy, Moon Palace, The Invention of Solitude, Auggie Wren's Christmas Story, City of Glass: The Graphic Novel, Oracle Night, Lulu on the Bridge, Leviathan, The Red Notebook*, the recent novel *Sunset Park*, Sophie Calle/Paul Auster's project "Gotham Handbook," etc.

Alternatively, a Paul Auster story is set in an unnamed big city that carries within itself the same characteristics that are often attributed to metropolitan New York—its vastness and the overwhelming size of its architecture, its maze-like streets that can consume an individual and make one feel lost, the consequent sense of threat and confusion, and the illusion that the city is constantly changing, so that things and buildings are either disappearing or transforming before one's own eyes (as *In the Country of Last Things*). For Mark Brown, the critic who has most extensively explored the significance of a variety of spaces in these texts (rooms, streets, downtown, dystopian city), Auster has "consistently taken the city of New York as a central feature in his work."[4] Brown notes that the city, which "inhabits [Auster's] essays, novels and films," is both "a backdrop against which the plots unfold," as well as "*an active agent* in their outcomes"[5] (my emphasis). In other words, New York is not just a place of action for Auster's characters—New York itself "acts" along with them.

The urban spaces that Paul Auster, his fictional surrogates and his other characters inhabit—the spaces that themselves are assemblages of people, objects and "things"— are distinctively "New York." The other recurrent space in Auster's work—the writer's bare study room—has no geographical boundaries and could be located almost anywhere. But the street, a markedly urban locale, is suffused with experiences that would, among big cities, be possible first and foremost in New York. As Phillip Lopate points out, "New York's essence—literary or otherwise, grows out of the street experience ... New York has from the start been an extroverted, not a covert, place..."[6]

In this sense, at least at the very first glance, it appears to be opposite to the writer's isolated studio, which more than any other space generates his solipsistic worldviews. Lopate lists some of the experiences that emerge from the streets of New York: random encounters, impressions of the city's contradictory faces of glamour and squalor, sensations of being overwhelmed that derive from the man-made quality of the gigantic built environment, its labyrinthine streets with the threat (or the opportunity) of losing oneself, its crowds with their offer of anonymity, its large, dense population that provides space for the immigrant and the nonconformist, *et cetera*.[7]

In a book entitled *Paul Auster's New York*, the writer's city is expressed through Auster's texts that are classified according to the following categories of experience, each of which become a separate "chapter": Impressions, Encounters, Maze, Vanishing Points, Transformations, Babel.[8] Luc Sante, who wrote the preface to this compilation, has another list of "things" associated with the New York of Paul Auster: "coincidence, synchronicity, bilocation, and other matters that brush metaphysics, as well as ciphers, games, displays, apparently impromptu sidewalk performances—the city's inside jokes."[9]

Yet, there is a problem. Although we notice certain associations that stem from the urban experience, tracing the multiple meanings of the city in the same way one traces the associations of the cigarette, the typewriter, and even the concept of the double seems impossible. We could see New York as an anthropomorphized character in relation to other characters (the city as a non-human actor, a "thing that things" or "acts"). But New York is, above all, a spatial concept, and, as such, it is an assemblage in itself.

To Bruno Latour, any spatial construct—a bank, for example—would imply a whole network assembled by both human and non-human actors (tellers, bank clients, safes, cash machines, money, security, and so on). All these are components whose agency is required for the bank to function. As such a network, New York is simply too big, too uncontainable, too multiple. It also has manifold faces, each of which is read in different terms. The name itself can denote many "things"—a geographic locale, a cultural venue, a socio-political space, and so on.

The concept gets further complicated when one realizes that New York is both a fictional realm and an actual geographical location. It is also very "real"—at the corner of Fifth Avenue and 42nd Street, for example, one finds the New York Public

Library, whose Berg Collection contains three archives of Paul Auster manuscripts and "papers." That space of the manuscript library, where an intimate, raw text gets objectified for the public's ruthless scrutiny and where "pure writing" (unverified, imaginary) meets "critical reflection" ("objective," worldly), is a sort of a meta-place. And, of course, New York is also the place where the empirical author, the "real" Paul Auster, lives, and smokes, and writes in his studio in Brooklyn's Park Slope neighborhood. Perhaps he is there as you read these very lines.

So I am struggling: how to even start a discussion on this facto-fictional New York? How to introduce this city? The place resists any introduction, quite apart from its physical skyline, which becomes visible as one approaches Manhattan from a distance. But even the physicality of the city is deceptive. Like Colson Whitehead's character in *The Colossus of New York*, I cannot help but question its authenticity: "Maybe you recognize it from the posters and television. Looks like a movie set, a false front of industry. Behind those gleaming *façades*, plywood and paint cans. Against it we are all extras."[10]

In the opening scene of *Manhattan*, Woody Allen's impersonated narrator struggles to encapsulate his feelings towards the city: it is a place he adores, idolizes and romanticizes out of proportion, a place that, to him, still exists "in black and white, and pulsate[s] to the great tunes of George Gershwin."[11] Yet it is also a metaphor for the decay of contemporary culture and society, "desensitized by drugs, loud music, television, crime, garbage."[12] Paul Auster, too, in one interview calls New York a city that he is both attached to and hates.[13] As Woody Allen's narrator reiterates variations of the first sentence to a "Chapter 1," looking for the right words to introduce the city (New York in this case opening both the film and the *mise en abyme* book that the character is writing), all his descriptions, to his frustration, come across as either "too corny," or "too angry," or not "profound" enough.[14] As he eventually proclaims his love for the city, combining both romantic and embittered attitudes, the accompanying music of *Rhapsody in Blue* reaches its culmination, and the camera captures fireworks exploding over the black-and-white Manhattan skyline. As a site of contradictions, and the tensions these produce, New York perhaps is always on the verge of exploding.

Lopate notes in the introduction to his anthology of New York texts that "[f]ew cities have inspired as much great writing as New York, or indeed as much writing: the literature of the city is extraordinary for its variety and sheer volume."[15] The numbers of texts written by "legions of minor authors" and "countless distinguished visitors" are, indeed, uncountable.[16] Yet New York as city simply resists being epitomized in the same way as, for example, James Joyce has encapsulated the essence of Dublin. Early on, from the beginning of the nineteenth century, New York started taking on its literary and cinematic qualities with the first notable texts devoted to the city (Washington Irving's *A History of New York*, Charles Dickens' *American Notes for General Circulation*, Henry David Thoreau's *Letters from Staten Island*). Two centuries later, New York is still "too big, too complex to be served by any one writer."[17] There is a certain "too-muchness" of everything that characterizes New York.[18] At best, any writer can "only offer his little tribute to something he loves, but which is beyond him," as New York's city planner Robert Moses concludes.[19]

In the end, the only way for the narrator of Woody Allen's film to faithfully introduce the city is to present it as "his own"—"New York was his town. And it always would be."[20] To avoid the overwhelming, uncontainable too-muchness of this place, one has to select a more limited number of elements, from which one can then construct and assemble one's personal "town." Whitehead's New York, too, although expressed through the voices of anonymous others, becomes "his own" the moment he breaks the city down into 13 specific "parts," each of which fills and also names a chapter: City Limits, The Port Authority, Morning, Central Park, Subway, Rain, Broadway, Coney Island, Brooklyn Bridge, Rush Hour, Downtown, Times Square, JFK. Yet his book also suggests that New York is a never fully readable and never containable colossal assemblage, woven from an infinite thread of things as well as "things."

Recall the assemblage of Brooklyn from Auster's *Blue in the Face*, which we stumbled across earlier in our tracing of the work of the cigarette. That Brooklyn was made up not only of places and spaces (Chinatown and street corners) or sites (1,500 churches, synagogues and mosques), but also of innumerable, intangible elements (Tahitian music and salsa dances) and measurements and statistics (1,600 miles of streets, 50 miles of shoreline, and 39,973 robberies). It becomes apparent not only that this list could be infinite, but that each of the "things" that assemble the Brooklyn borough in themselves carry layers of meanings and associations.

Infinite quantity is one reason behind New York's uncontainability, but there are others: New York is a network of heterogeneous multiplicity, and this multiplicity is alive. Latour says that recognizing the city as such a network helps us "lift the tyranny of geographers in defining space," and offers a notion which is "neither social, nor 'real' space, but associations."[21] The network of "multiple and overlapping enactments that constitute urban life" in New York derives from the operation of tangible objects, abstract notions, human beings, and other things.[22] All of which are agents in establishing connections, generating associations and proliferating meanings in a massive, ever-expanding network of urban assemblages.

New York is an infinite site of such associations and relations between all actors. *Actants*, after all, are not only people and objects, but also things and spaces, ideas and concepts, norms and practices, customs and technologies, and so on. As a rule, a city like New York becomes characterized by a particular complexity and openness to change, and is itself always contingent. This multiplicity of New York is always changing, makeshift, "intermezzo" and in the state of "becoming." MS Fogg in *Moon Palace* describes the dynamics of "things" that fill up and assemble his city:

> A fire hydrant, a taxi cab, a rush of steam pouring up from the pavement—they were deeply familiar to me, and I felt I knew them by heart. But that did not take into account the mutability of those things, the way they changed according to the force and angle of the light, the way their aspect could be altered by what was happening around them: a person walking by, a sudden gust of wind, an odd reflection. Everything was constantly in flux, and though two bricks in a wall might strongly resemble each other, they could never be construed as identical. More to the point, the same brick was never really the same.[23]

And the sub-titles given to the "chapters" of *Paul Auster's New York* express its dynamic, instable and rhizome-like character, which results in the impossibility of ascribing any sort of stable "reading" or interpretation to the city. New York there is associated with a "maze," "vanishing points," "Babel," "transformations."

When compared to object-like things, such as a cigarette or a typewriter, New York as a thing-like agent, as a city, is not only uncontainable (can "New York" be restricted to its physical boundaries, and, if not, where does "New York" end?), but is also inexhaustible in its significance. An early poem by Paul Auster, "Disappearances" (from his collection of the same title), describes "a city / of the undeciphered event," a "monstrous sum / of particulars."[24] The only way to cope with this monstrous sum, as already suggested by Woody Allen and Whitehead, is to try to "grasp" and "contain" bits of it by "constructing" one's own city.

This construction of one's private New York starts the moment one lays one's eyes on it for the first time.[25] Consequently, there is no single New York, but rather a multiplicity of private and shared New Yorks. Talking about fellow New Yorkers, Whitehead remarks that "[t]here are eight million naked cities in this naked city," which, furthermore, "dispute and disagree" between themselves.[26] "The New York City you live in is not my New York City; how could it be?" he asks rhetorically, and explains:

> This place multiplies when you're not looking. We move over here, we move over there. Over a lifetime, that adds up to a lot of neighborhoods, the motley construction material of your jerry-built metropolis. Your favorite newsstands, restaurants, movie theatres, subway stations and barbershops are replaced by your next neighborhood's favorites. It gets to be quite a sum. Before you know it, you have your own personal skyline.[27]

Besides, the city, whose land territory alone spreads over nearly eight hundred square kilometers, accumulates not only vast numbers of "things" located in its geographical space, and over eight million personal impressions of these, but also transcends temporal boundaries, accumulating experiences from both past and present that all overlap. After his return to New York from Florida, Miles Heller from Auster's 2010 novel *Sunset Park* is unable to recognize the city anymore. What he encounters is a different New York, and "even if he is home again, this New York is not his New York, not the New York of his memory."[28] So Heller finds himself in the city that is both his home but also someplace else, a place he fails to recognize. One remembers New York both as it was and is, its past and present simultaneously coexisting, in the same way that New York carries in its places and spaces memories of one's old selves.[29] Whitehead explains again:

> Go back to your old haunts in your old neighborhoods and what do you find: they remain and have disappeared. The greasy spoon, the deli, the dry cleaner you scouted out when you first arrived and tried to make those new streets yours: they are gone. But look past the windows of the travel agency that replaced your pizza parlor. Beyond the desks and computers and promo posters for tropical adventure,

you can still see Neapolitan slices cooling, the pizza cutter lying next to half a pie, the map of Sicily on the wall. It is all still there, I assure you.[30]

New York, then, not only contains millions of different personal "New Yorks"—a multiplicity in itself—but also layers and layers of its own past: "[t]housands of people pass that storefront [or that tobacco shop, or that beggar sitting on the sidewalk, or...] every day, each one haunting the streets of his or her own New York, not one of them seeing the same thing."[31] These traits of New York—that it is "indefinable," that its essence behind its façades remains deceptive and impenetrable, and that everyone is only able to see their own skyline of the city—are best summed up by Auster himself in an early handwritten and unpublished draft of a story called "Invasions":

> New York, a city of impenetrable facades ... Everywhere it eludes the grasp, sealing itself off from the mind, forbidding the secret knowledge that would allow it to be defined. The redundancy of its parallels and intersections. ... I move through it like a somnambulist. Faces might appear, large crowds might grow, but they cannot alter or penetrate the facades that surround them. The city ... reduces its inhabitants to objects. Each person, entitled to just a single perspective, creates a city which is merely a function of his imagination. Properly speaking, New York does not exist.[32]

"Façade" is a telling word. Brought into English from French, through Italian "*facciata*" and "*faccia*," it comes from Latin, "*facia*," which means—"face." But this "face of a building" is not the Lévinasian "face" that provides access to the essence of Being, unveiling its "defenceless interior."[33] Quite the opposite. It suggests the superficial or artificial appearance of a thing, its false "frontage," a "simulacrum of the interior."[34] What one first sees in New York is the dominating physicality of urban layout, the skyline of skyscrapers, and the façades of towering buildings—those are the city's many faces, all of which are potentially deceptive (masked).

So, there is the "public" New York, with its simple physicality, visible surfaces, geometries, shared cultural codes and signs, and many common conceptions that have become associated with the city. Yet beyond these façades and the surface of simple exteriors and myths lies something that resists definition and that for every individual has its own meaning. Perhaps that which Auster refers to as "imagined" corresponds to his solipsistic worldview, but, in the words of Whitehead, could be described as "private" or "personal."

Either way, New York is multi-dimensional and mixes the public with the personal, the actual with the imagined, the physical with the psychological. Like the other things whose associations I have attempted to follow in this book, it may be as much characterized as an emotional state, a process, or an event, as by its own tangible physicality. We could call New York "a complex"—as both an architectural and a psychological concept.

Besides, because of its frequent representation in literature, film and the arts, New York seems to be both cinematic and literary *and* "real," the fictional suffusing the voracious physicality of the city, and *vice versa*, so that in New York, one is always somehow also in a book, or a film. Its literary and cinematic particularity—the fictionalized "New Yorkness," and the overwhelming presence of it, sets it apart from other contemporary metropolises (Shanghai, London, Rio de Janeiro, Mexico City) that each, equally uncontainable (unmappable), are laden with their own sets of associations. New York is one of the most heavily fictionalized cities in the world, like Paris or Rome. It simply lends itself to the idea that the fictional and the factual have always belonged to the same realm—allegedly two sides of a Möbius strip, embedded in the same surface. New York is that territory in which the factual overlaps with the fictional, and which is inhabited both by Paul Auster and "Paul Auster."

What does that imply for the critic, the reader? Because Paul Auster constantly interweaves fiction and fact, reading his life-work, which is predominantly set in this city, requires one to both read the fictional as well as the factual dimensions of New York. Tracing the associations of Auster's texts set in New York instructs the reader to go to the city and do the reading *in situ*, a reading that takes on performative elements on the reader's part. As that passage from Whitehead's book implies, one needs to be physically present—immersed—in the city, in order to be able to see the many layers of spatial narratives that its façades hide. One has to actually be there to be able to look past the windows of the travel agency that stands in the place of the old pizza parlor, and, beyond its office interior, see those "Neapolitan slices cooling, the pizza cutter lying next to half a pie."

In search of Auster's city

And that was another reason for my trip. To see beyond the façades of Auster's New York, I had to go there myself, and to identify with his characters in order to try to catch glimpses, however brief, of what Luc Sante has named "Austeralia." That place has, as he deftly identifies, "the same geographical coordinates as New York City in the same way that the nervous system occupies the space of the body."[35]

To uncover episodic fragments of Austeralia was all I could hope for. And yet, from the moment I set my mind to this task, I was overcome by what seemed to be an unreasonable, unacceptable, clearly unscholarly urge—to find signs and signatures of the writer encrypted in the city's walls and streets, to discover hermeneutic clues left there by his characters, to find their traces, to follow them, until they lead me if not to some sort of a revelation then at least to the empirical author himself, who, after all, is bound to have some answers to his own textual riddles. The growing excitement I felt was also accompanied by a sense of looming failure (for I knew of the fates of Auster's "detectives"). But at that point, of course, I had no other choice but to follow in their tracks.

To assist on the scholarly quest of discovering Paul Auster's New York, I took with me *Paul Auster's New York*, to serve as a sort of travel guide to Austeralia.[36] Compiled and classified in titled sections by Thomas Überhoff,[37] with a preface by Luc Sante, the "book" consists of fragments recounting various experiences of New York from Auster's prose writings, both fictional and nonfictional, that were published up to 1997. It is also complemented by photographs of New York scenes by German photographer Frieder Blickle.[38] Since the compilation is incomplete—it not only excludes Auster's texts written in later periods, but also his films and collaborations (an exception is "Auggie Wren's Christmas Story")—whenever additional travel directions and information were necessary, I had to consult the respective filmic and literary texts by Auster, and use the knowledge about his life that I had acquired over time.

This "book," *Paul Auster's New York*, is a curious thing that in itself deserves more attention. And not only because, as an anthology of fragments of his texts associated with the city, it can serve as a handy travel guide to Austeralia, outlining the major locations, routes and urban experiences featured in and expressed through Paul Auster's texts. An ambiguous "non-book" itself, for a critic this hybrid text also provokes questions about its status, genre, and, most importantly, its authorship. Who is the author of *Paul Auster's New York*? Were it officially published, could it be seen as part of Auster's oeuvre? This "book," after all, consists of fragments from copyrighted Auster texts that were, nevertheless, selected, classified and arranged in a particular order under new titles by Überhoff. Simultaneously "a part of" and "yet a multiplicity," it contains excerpts from selected works by Auster, while assembling together a larger narrative, a story of Paul Auster's city, which has now become visible and foregrounded, its associations traced horizontally throughout Auster's body of work. It contains both literary and "real" encounters that Auster or his fictional surrogates have taken from the city. They are reflections on New York as well as on "New York." It can also be seen as a quadripartite collaboration between Auster, Überhoff, Sante and Blickle, whose black-and-white photos of the city complement the writer's texts and add another layer of significance to the (re)constructed Auster's New York. That book essentially reminds us about the Foucauldian impossibility of ever comprehending one author's oeuvre as a complete whole.

To some extent, *Paul Auster's New York* illustrates the rhizomatic approach to reading texts through the tracing of particular recurrent motifs and elements across one author's body of work. It is similar to Rheindorf's suggested methodology of choosing a given element in Auster's life-work and following its expression over years of writing, offering a reading of New York that does not necessarily have to start from the beginning and move chronologically. That reading can start somewhere in the middle and uncover the movement of a particular strand extending in all directions across time. Sante, who, like Rheindorf, recognizes the interconnectedness and internal associations that have formed within Auster's network of texts, speaks of the writer's New York experiences as "seemingly random elements" linked "as if by tunnels or alleys."[39] Auster's work is like the city itself (and the other way round)—a network of crossing paths, a rhizome. Hence the parallels between the map of the city and the mapping of the rhizome, and the analogy between "reading" the city and reading a literary text.

But this also reminds me of another association that Auster himself often invokes in his texts: the correspondence between the "inner" and "outer" terrains, the inside of a mind and the outside surrounding it, or the way that one's thoughts rhizomatically move as one traverses, or so one imagines, the rhizome-like city:

> But just as one step will inevitably lead to the next step, so it is that one thought inevitably follows from the previous thought, and in the event that a thought should engender more than a single thought (say two or three thoughts, equal to each other in all their consequences), it will be necessary not only to follow the first thought to its conclusion, but also to backtrack to the original position of that thought … if we were to try to make an image of this process in our minds, a network of paths begins to be drawn, as in the image of the human blood-stream (heart, arteries, veins, capillaries), or as in the image of a map (of city streets … preferably a large city … of roads that stretch, bisect, and meander across a continent), so that what we are really doing when we walk through the city is thinking … in such a way that our thoughts compose a journey, and this journey is no more or less than the steps we have taken, so that, in the end, we might safely say that we have been on a journey … even if we do not leave our room … we have been somewhere, even if we don't know where…[40]

There are two types of travel, then: the movement of thoughts, the interior journey, which happens to the writer in his bare room, and the exterior movement, the travel through the streets of the city—the streets, which, as Rheindorf points out, alongside objects and things, are sites where the exterior merges with the interior through association.[41] An analogy that Auster loves to draw equates thinking ("writing") to walking. It is exactly the experience of walking through the city that, because of its associations with the ways that thoughts travel, "acts" to encourage thinking, and the other way round.

In this sense, the role of "acting" that a city like New York plays for the writer-character is equal to smoking cigarettes or typing on a manual typewriter, which both encourage thinking—writing—by opening up the dimension of the imaginary, and by allowing the writer to feel "connected" with whichever other smoking and typewriting writers he finds inspiring. That means the streets can also be a "covert place," after all. So New York is more than its physicality reveals; it is always also somehow a state "within," and the "within" is that personal platform from which one starts to build one's own New York. That might be, as I had come to fear, the main obstacle in my task of locating Auster's New York. I knew, from the beginning, that this project was going to fail.

In Austeralia

On the night of June 1, 2011, I stepped off the plane at JFK Airport and set my foot on what I hoped would turn out to be Austeralia. I had no exact plan as to where to begin, although I felt I was well-prepared, and could start my exploration from any point, tracing its sites and routes rhizomatically, and letting chance determine my choice.

I had gathered every single important fragment from Auster's literary and visual texts that had anything to do with the spaces of New York, and compiled them in several large documents, with additional descriptions and my commentary attached, so as to distinguish actual places from fictional ones and, in the case of the former, to expand my knowledge. I had marked down all the major locations, both existing and invented, from Auster's books, films, collaborations and his life, on detailed colorful maps of Brooklyn and Manhattan that I had bought specifically for this purpose. On some other maps, I had traced the routes made by Auster's writer-characters in a similar fashion as Quinn from *City of Glass* outlined on paper the Manhattan walks of his suspect Peter Stillman Sr.

A week before leaving, I had acquired a used Olympus dictaphone to record my impressions, experiences and findings as I followed in the footsteps of Auster's characters; and I was delighted with the idea that the name of this voice-recording machine resembled the name of Auster's recorder, the Olympia typewriter. I bought a fountain pen and a good-quality pink notebook (Emilio Braga, hand-made in Portugal), hoping that, coincidentally, it might turn out to be the same brand of notebooks that Paul Auster himself favored.[42] I had also secured two cameras for my trip, a semi-professional Minolta DiMAGE and a pocket-size Panasonic for taking impressionistic snapshots.

From Auster's body of work, I had taken with me only a select few books to read on location, but I planned to buy more once I got to Brooklyn's Park Slope, in a shop that would resemble "Brightman's Attic," the crammed, badly-organized second-hand bookstore that one finds in *The Brooklyn Follies*. With regards to Auster's manuscripts, which I had also intended to study, the night before I left for New York I received an email from the New York Public Library, informing me that the boxes with the requested "Auster papers" had all been delivered, and were awaiting my arrival at the Berg Collection.

The two weeks after my arrival in New York I spent trying, as much as I could, to duplicate the actions of Auster characters, reading about their experiences on location—I walked the same routes they did, I visited the locations where they lived, ate, worked and rested, and I was always on the move, reminding myself that, in Auster's New York, the journey itself often was the destination. At times, when I wanted to rest, I would sit down in a park or a café, smoke a cigarillo, and scribble in my notebook, knowing that, perhaps, at that very same moment, Paul Auster was doing the same in his Park Slope studio.

"When I left my [hotel at the corner of 7th Avenue and 33rd Street] on the first morning, I simply started walking, going wherever my steps decided to take me. If I had any thought at all, it was to let chance determine what happened, to follow the path of impulse and arbitrary events."[43] There, within the giant walls of towering skyscrapers that engulfed every block, I felt that New York, indeed, was "an inexhaustible space, a labyrinth of endless steps," and "no matter how far [I] walked, no matter how well [I] came to know its neighborhoods and streets [in the next few days], it always left [me] with the feeling of being lost."[44] Yet, unlike Quinn, I failed to feel lost "not only in the city, but within [myself] as well"; New York for me did not become "the nowhere [that Quinn] had built around himself."[45] No matter how hard I tried to "lose myself," to catch that moment of transformation into inwardness that walking the streets seems to initiate, the city kept interrupting, reminding me of its overwhelming presence through oncoming crowds and noise and heat, all of which were too distracting.

One day, I wandered down to Chinatown, to see how the city alienates itself, its façades even more impenetrable and its face, all of a sudden, transformed into something unrecognizable. There,

> ... I was overwhelmed by a sense of dislocation and confusion. This was America, but I could not understand what anyone said, could not penetrate the meanings of the things I saw ... I could not gain entrance past the mute surfaces of things, and there were times when this exclusion made me feel as though I were living in a dream world, moving through crowds of spectral people who all wore masks on their faces.[46]

For days, I walked up and down Broadway, always starting from Times Square and moving up past Columbus Circle, as far as the Upper West Side. I was on the lookout for chance encounters with strangers whose incomprehensible, bizarre actions would resemble those that MS Fogg and the young Paul Auster witnessed along this particular route—the story of the man with the broken umbrella (*Moon Palace*), or the story of Effing and, in another case, H. L. Humes or "Doc," handing out fifty-dollar bills to passers-by, a "spectacular show" on Broadway (*Moon Palace and Hand to Mouth*).

I visited several apartment buildings on West 107th Street, looking for that "run-down, nine-story affair," in which Auster used to live for a while and which, as he claims, like most places on the Upper West Side, "housed a motley collection of people,"[47] among whom was a rabbi and a homeless man, from whom Auster received a strange proposal one night, recounted later in *Hand to Mouth*. Near Broadway, at 262 West 107th Street, I found a brown brick nine-story building, and, then, further eastwards on the same block, at 203 West 107th Street, a more pleasant-looking white brick tower of the same height. But the gray building that was the site for Auster's encounters remained hidden from me, and I never found it.

I spent another day wandering through the streets of Manhattan, to observe, "as never before: the tramps, the down-and-outs, the shopping bag ladies, the drifters and drunks" that supposedly inhabited both "good neighborhoods and bad."[48] But I failed to record any "wretched brokenness," and nothing of interest ever happened to me. So far, my records of the city were dull—report-like lists of facts, numbers, addresses and descriptions, and uninspired, static photographs of the same.

I soon came to realize that, as Auster probably already knew, one cannot walk out into the street with the expectation of experiencing what Henri Cartier-Bresson calls "the decisive moment"—that unexpected encounter, or an instant of inspiration and revelation that allows an artist to transform the street experience into a poem or photograph. Yet, as Auster reminds us in *The Art of Hunger*, one must be prepared to embrace that moment "whenever the opportunity presents itself."[49] And as I thought of the ways I could weigh the probability of unexpected things ever happening to me in this city, I wondered how many weeks, if not years, or even lives, one must spend here, to ever experience the unusual chance encounters and coincidences that abound in Auster's life-work.

When eventually I felt worn out by the city, I took the subway No. 6 from Midtown up to 86th Street station, got off, "continued uptown for several more blocks, then turned left, crossed Fifth Avenue, and walked along the wall of Central Park. At 96th Street [I] entered the park," expecting to be "glad to be among the grass and trees."[50] Unlike Quinn, I did not find the park's environment "miraculous and beautiful"; the surroundings were green, but its greenness was of dull and grayish shade, and noting all the dirty undergrowth around, I could not imagine myself, like Quinn, lying down under an oak tree, using the notebook as my pillow. I cut my way through the thicket back to the street and kept walking down 5th Avenue towards the Metropolitan Museum. I was now looking for the spot where MS Fogg "entered the park ... trekked out toward the interior for several minutes, and then crawled under a bush."[51] I hoped to find that place that could become "a sanctuary for me, a refuge of inwardness against the grinding demands of the streets," but as I approached the museum, I saw that a part of the park around it had been fenced off.

Another day, I became Quinn, who had himself become "Paul Auster, the detective." I visited Quinn's house at West 107th Street (I presumed it to be the same nine-story building, where Auster himself lived for a while), as well as that of Virginia Stillman, which was likewise located in upper Manhattan, but at the east side of Central Park, between Madison Avenue and Park Avenue.

As I stood there, head tilted up, looking at Virginia Stillman's six-story residence, Number 25 at East 69th Street, which is the same house where Auster worked for eight months after his return to New York from Paris in 1974, I could not help but feel disappointed at its modest simplicity in size and decor, and the lack of enigma and faded grandeur I had come to associate with the home of the noir-like *femme fatale* Virginia Stillman and her Kaspar Hauser-like husband, Peter Stillman Jr. On my way back to the subway station, at the corner of East 69th Street and Park Avenue, I encountered what I believed to be the real house of the Stillmans—a massive white *art nouveau* style building with the Roman numeral MCMXXXII inscribed at the bottom. I took a photo and recorded a note that Paul Auster had, obviously, made a factual mistake in the novel. I also realized, for the first time, that I had unwittingly started to create my own New York/Austeralia, with no clue as to how far or close its borders stood to those of Auster's New York.

I then moved on to Grand Central Terminal—that awful, dirty and crowded place where "a man determined to disappear could do so without much trouble," and where one is likewise likely to run into someone's doppelgänger.[52] Quinn "wandered through the station ... as if inside the body of Paul Auster, waiting for Stillman to appear"—a move I tried to imitate, but the unrecognizable interior, which looked so different from *City of Glass*, made it difficult to retain the connection with the text, and with its protagonist, narrator, author.[53]

The giant Kodak Colorama photos that used to occupy the station's east wall, reminding Quinn of his visit to Nantucket with his pregnant wife, were gone, and there was nothing much I could relate to the book, nothing I could use to extract memories from; no gateways for tracing those old associations that appear in Auster's early texts. I failed to find the waiting room, "generally a grim place, filled with dust and people with nowhere to go," where Quinn had spotted someone reading a book by him, only to learn that she did not really like it. That place had disappeared for good during the station's renovation at the end of last century, and has been replaced by what is now known as Vanderbilt Hall, a new kind of space that, like other renovated parts of the station, adds a feel of grandeur, luxury, and opulence to Grand Central.[54]

Back in the years when *The New York Trilogy* was written, more than 30 years ago, perhaps the station, like the whole city, was a dark labyrinth, a maze in which to lose yourself and others, or, conversely, encounter one's doubles—to become lost, come to dead-ends and crossroads, and, from then on, to encounter uncertainty, as Quinn does when confronted with two Stillman Seniors, each walking in the opposite direction:

> Quinn froze. There was nothing he could do that would not be a mistake. Whatever choice he made … would be arbitrary, a submission to chance. Uncertainty would haunt him to the end.[55]

What I encountered was a different New York to Auster's—cleaner, safer and brighter, and it made Austeralia an even more inaccessible realm—too hard to relate to, and too hard to imagine.

The same sense of failure to connect to someone else's experience and memories, and through those to gain access to particular spaces and places that carry some significance in their narration, overtook me when, walking up Broadway near Columbus Circle one day, I noticed the house in which Auster's grandfather lived, and which Auster himself used to visit as a child, "that tall, squat, oddly shaped building" on the corner of Columbus Circle and Central Park South.[56]

In "The Book of Memory," the second part of *The Invention of Solitude*, A. talks about his return to his grandfather's house as an adult, to look after the place for a few weeks while his grandfather is in the hospital. For Auster, the place had not changed—"[i]t was the same place he had been visiting since earliest childhood," with its "Chinese telephone table, his grandmother's glass menagerie, and the old humidor," and, "surrounded by this place again," he felt he had "walked straight back into his childhood."[57] Auster connects with the New York of his past, when, looking through "those same sixth floor windows," he sees the statue of Christopher Columbus and wonders how many hours he had spent as a boy watching "the traffic as it wove around [it]." The memories are triggered by recognizable objects, but other associations with the past derive not from what is familiar, but rather from what has changed. Beyond the urban scenery that he sees, A. evokes the New York of the past, and how he had "watched the Thanksgiving Day parades," and "seen the construction of the Colosseum."

As I was standing on the street in front of that house, at the south-west entrance to Central Park, I tried to imagine not only how this place had looked in Auster's childhood, but also how it was when Auster reminisced about it 30 years ago. The building itself had vanished: the New York Coliseum that was built from 1954 to 1956 was demolished in 2000 to give way to the Time Warner Center. Columbus Circle was changing, but I could not note the change because its former appearance evaded me.

The city never showed more than its façades to me, the surface of its visible geometry, its buildings, and streets. They all seemed blank and indifferent, and very soon, I realized again, the only New York I could talk about was my personal New York and my personal Auster's New York, which I had slowly started building from scratch. That place I was constructing lay somewhere in-between all those other related New Yorks—it was both real and imaginary, private and yet shared, both historic and literary, not entirely a city of the present, but neither one of the past, not mine, really, yet neither his.

The same day I visited Grand Central Terminal, I went on following Quinn following Peter Stillman Sr., from the platform No. 24 of the station to the Times Square Shuttle that brought me to the West Side, where I changed to the Broadway express and travelled up to 96th Street, after which I walked up Broadway to 99th Street, turned left and there, halfway up the block, supposedly found "a small fleabag for down-and-outs, the Hotel Harmony," in which Stillman had settled.[58] For the next few days—or weeks maybe—Quinn, who had posted himself on the traffic island at the intersection of 99th Street and Broadway, would watch Stillman leave the hotel every morning, and follow him on his walks as he scavenged for old discarded objects on his way:

> What Stillman did on these walks remained something of a mystery to Quinn. He could … see with his own eyes what happened, and all these things he dutifully recorded in his red notebook. But the meaning of these things continued to elude him. Stillman never seemed to be going anywhere in particular … [a]nd yet, as if by conscious design, he kept to a narrowly circumscribed area, bounded on the north by 110th Street, on the south by 72nd Street, on the west by Riverside Park, and on the east by Amsterdam Avenue.[59]

I spent half a day wandering around the west side of the Upper West Side, taking photographs of places that seemed suitable for the novel, dutifully recording everything in my voice recorder, or else in my pink notebook. But, like Quinn, I soon became "deeply disillusioned" with the results of my efforts:

> He had always imagined that the key to good detective work was a close observation of details. The more accurate the scrutiny, the more successful the results. The implication was that human behavior could be understood, that beneath the infinite facade … there was finally a coherence, an order … But after struggling to take in all these surface effects, Quinn felt no closer to Stillman than when he first started following him. He had lived Stillman's life, walked at his pace, seen what he had seen, and the only thing he felt now was the man's impenetrability. Instead of narrowing the distance that lay between [them], he had seen the old man slip away from him, even as he remained before his eyes.[60]

At times, I told myself that I had to try harder and actually follow someone; I randomly picked people on the streets, as Maria Turner/Sophie Calle had done in her "detective projects," and, within a distance of some 30 feet, I started following them. More often than not, people would almost immediately notice me—loaded with a big backpack, and cameras, notebooks, and voice recorders, I instantly drew attention to myself; the streets were also wide and empty, with hardly anything else to take note of. I did not dare take any pictures of them.

Having failed as a detective, I decided to retrace Quinn's famous walk from Upper Manhattan to its bottom, and back—after all, that is what Quinn did when he felt he had lost his case. The route that resembles a big "V," as in "victory," comes all the way down from the Upper West Side, through the heart of the city to the bottom of Manhattan, and then up again, ending in the Upper East Side. The distance of the walk was intolerably long for the hot, humid summer weather of June, and the original intention of focusing on Quinn's walking experience soon gave way to feelings of thirst, hunger, tiredness, and the never-ending search for even the smallest spots of shade that, with the sun high in the zenith, the skyscrapers were reluctant to provide. The movement along the streets of Midtown was dominated by crowds, whose flow was, in turn, determined by the traffic lights and the rows of honking cars that constantly jammed the way. Everywhere around me were loud people and billboards, and, as a stranger in New York, I could not help but let them distract me.

I failed to reach the state of "inwardness" that so many of Auster's characters achieve among the crowded streets. As I lost belief in the prospect of ever achieving this task, I started to question the motive and value behind my endeavor. Could it ever be possible to understand the significance of someone else's place? "The essential thing [was] to stay involved," I reminded myself.[61] Yet, "[l]ittle by little [I] began to feel cut off from [my] original intentions, and [I] wondered [again] if [I] had not embarked on a meaningless project."[62] Perhaps, I was slowly going insane, like Quinn himself, or like Peter Stillman.

Of all the Manhattan-based Auster texts, I had deliberately chosen to focus on *City of Glass*, as it was the most abundant in naming specific locations, visiting which, I had hoped, would bring me closer to understanding Paul Auster and his life-work. (A pity, I can now say in retrospect, that all of this took place before Auster's *Winter Journal* came out in 2012. In great detail it catalogues the 20 or so houses in which the writer has lived over years, including their exact addresses.[63])

Yet it started to appear to me that the map of Manhattan that Auster draws in his texts is maybe but a string of streets and numbers, devoid of any particular significance, or else their significance is too personal for an outsider to be able to see behind their façades. Perhaps, as one reviewer suggests, Auster's Manhattan is indeed empty of signification other than its function for meta-fictional purposes. The grid-like structure of the streets allows Stillman in *City of Glass* to spell out words like "THE TOWER OF BABEL," while Auster's choice of Orange Street as one location in *Ghosts* is simply "in line with the rest of the novella's use of colors."[64] Manhattan appeared to me distant, empty and flat, without any specific signification. Nothing of interest ever happened to me there, no "unexpected things" that seem "almost impossible"—it was as if Auster's city was simply refusing to open up for me.[65] Austeralia and Paul Auster were both evading me.

Yet there were rare moments when my own
experience in the city seemed to cut into the fictional
realm of Auster's texts, my own personal New York
overlapping with Austeralia, and in those instances I
could not help but feel that I was inhabiting Auster's
texts, that, somehow, these places had been invented
by Auster, and that whatever was happening to me
right then was the result of what one chain-smoking
writer in Brooklyn was jotting down in his notebook.
Luc Sante, who, like me, found himself in Austeralia
upon arriving in New York, years before any of
Auster's books were published, gives the following
explanation:

> These incidents [that happened to me], variously
> amusing or puzzling, or oddly lyrical, appeared
> bereft of context ... Now, however, I recognize
> them as lying within Paul Auster's imaginative
> territory, as being his productions. It is worth
> noting that all of them occurred before any of
> Auster's works in prose had been written. But
> then, if Borges could submit that Kafka ... was the
> predecessor of Hawthorne, it is equally possible for
> Auster's signature to appear on events that took
> place when his novelistic oeuvre was barely a glint
> in his eye.[66]

I had got my first taste of Auster's New York on the
night I arrived in the city; Manhattan was as hostile
to me as it was to both MS Fogg from *Moon Palace*
and the young Paul Auster himself (*The Invention of
Solitude*). I was taken from the airport straight to my
hotel on 7th Avenue between 32nd and 33rd Streets, a dingy and derelict monster of
a hotel with 22 floors of nightmare. This historic landmark, once a grandiose hotel,
one of the largest in New York, was now slowly disintegrating and facing the threat
of demolition.

At night, the place was eerily empty. The only sounds apart from one's own
breathing came from air conditioning ducts and turbines, punctuated occasionally by
the nightly sirens. Its labyrinthine corridors were a place of gloomy foreboding. The
place acquired the cinematic qualities of films set in grotesque hotel environments
(*Four Rooms, The Shining, Barton Fink* ...). During the day, the lounge was flooded
with tourists, keen to claim their share of New York's glamour. The crowds and the
constant draught caused by the hotel's many rotating doors, gave the place the air of a
filthy train station. One could not help but feel lost there.

Room Nr 1693 on the 16th Floor became my cell for the next five days, no more than a pigeonhole, "a small fleabag for down-and-outs."[67] Formally a non-smoker's room, "[t]he place stank of cockroach repellant and dead cigarettes."[68] Its Spartan setup consisted of a bed, a chair, a pair of bedside cabinets, a desk and a large mirror, all in the same pale color of what once used to be light green, or gray, or, perhaps, even blue. It all made the room look bare, "[t]he place seemed blank, a hell of stale thoughts."[69]

That first night, I could not sleep because the horror evoked by the place was too overwhelming; the next day I fell sick, and the following few days I spent in a sort of delirium that alternated between sudden attacks of fever and long hours of insomnia, too weak to go outside, too scared to stay where I was. I had nightmares, and the brief moments I managed to fall asleep never brought much rest. The isolation and misery increased with every minute and every thought.

And then I realized: I was, in fact, reliving an Austeresque experience. The possibility of seeing myself as someone else, a fictional character living a life authored by someone else, gave me the same sense of comfort as inhabiting "Paul Auster" gave to Quinn:

> Although he still had the same body, the same mind, the same thoughts, he felt as though he had somehow been taken out of himself, as if he no longer had to walk around with the burden of his own consciousness ... he felt incomparably lighter and freer ... he knew it was all an illusion. But there was a certain comfort in that. He had not really lost himself; he was merely pretending ...[70]

I was, at that point, becoming Marco Stanley Fogg, as much as I was becoming A., Auster's facto-fictional surrogate. The "blankness" and bleakness of the place, and its "hell of stale thoughts," not only recalled the hotel room in which Peter Stillman Sr. stays (*City of Glass*)—it was the same shabby, filthy, but bare-looking room in which the young struggling writer is forced to live, both as MS Fogg in *Moon Palace* and A. in *The Invention of Solitude*.

When MS Fogg moves into the small, dim apartment on West 112th Street above Central Park, he feels "some pangs at first, small thumps of fear" about inhabiting this horrific space. But then he makes a discovery that helps him "to warm up to the place and settle in."[71] It is a neon sign visible from his window, "a vivid torch of pink and blue letters" that spells out the words "MOON PALACE," advertising a Chinese restaurant.[72] Fogg invests these letters with his own meaning, the associations varying from his Uncle Victor and his jazz band, to a sign of good fate. "They were magic letters," he says.[73] They opened an imaginary realm that gradually filled the place. "A bare and grubby room had been transformed into a site of inwardness, and intersection point of strange omens and mysterious, arbitrary events."[74]

A. meanwhile is left alone in his apartment at 6 Varick Street in Lower West side of Manhattan. It is Christmas Eve, 1979, and he has recently divorced his first wife Lydia. The place he lives in on his own is grim:

> He cannot call it a home, but for the past nine months it is all he has had. A few dozen books, a mattress on the floor, a table, three chairs, a hot plate, and a

corroded cold water sink. The toilet is down the hall, but he uses it only when he has to shit ... For the past three days the elevator has been out of service, and since this is the top floor, it has made him reluctant to go out.[75]

By staying in his room for longer stretches of time, A. has nothing but his own thoughts to fill and transform the place,

> and this in turn seems to dispel the dreariness, or at least make him unaware of it. Each time he goes out, he takes his thoughts with him, and during his absence the room gradually empties of his efforts to inhabit it. When he returns, he has to begin the process all over again, and that takes work, real spiritual work.[76]

Lying in bed in my dreary room, I too was not there anymore—I was someplace between my own life and the life that comes from Auster's books, not entirely myself anymore, but playing, pretending to be someone else, and, above all, I knew it was not my bad luck, but, somehow, it was all meant to be this way, and my only task was to live through it. On the fifth day, as soon as I felt better, I gathered my strength and went out into the streets. I found the nearest internet cafe and booked myself into the first hotel I could find. I came back, packed my bags and left, never to return again. The new hotel, as it turned out, happened to be located in Park Slope, the neighborhood where Paul Auster lives. That was the first coincidence that came to me directly from Auster's universe.

Discovering the notebooks

Having failed to reach beyond the façades of Austeralia after a week-long quest of following the footsteps of Auster and his characters, having failed to access those points of convergence where the exterior meets the interior and where the streets of the city merge into the pathways of thought and imagination that belong to the subject of my search, I felt I needed to find a different approach to get closer to the author's mind. In the words of Ian Hamilton, who once embarked on a similar quest in his search for J. D. Salinger, "missing from our search for [the subject] was any vivid sense of presence. What we needed was the first person, off-the-record voice of [the author] himself."[77]

I needed somehow to get into the "locked room"—that writer's studio in which Paul Auster and his fictional stand-ins (in texts such as *The Locked Room*, *Ghosts*, *Moon Palace*, *The Invention of Solitude*, *Travels in the Scriptorium*, *The Inner Life of Martin Frost*, etc.) generate their texts while "perfect[ing] [their] narrative[s] of solipsism",[78] a room that is the place where life and writing meet—that is, in a way, "the room that is the book."[79] It is in the solitary room that the smoking, typewriting writer's mind generates the world of its own; it is the site where the entire world "rush[es] in on him at a dizzying speed"[80]—whole worlds, in fact, "a plenitude of worlds within worlds," as *Moon Palace* tells us.[81]

On my first day in Brooklyn, I therefore found Paul Auster's studio apartment, which is situated on a quiet street in a beautiful Park Slope neighborhood. This is where he spends his days, writing down stories in notebooks and typing them up on his Olympia. I walked past the building a few times, not even daring to stop and take a proper look at it, let alone knocking at its door, which I felt would always remain locked for me—too scared to be seen by the writer himself, and too ashamed of my sudden realization that I might have just crossed that thin line that separates a scholar from a stalker. I returned back to my hotel, and on the same day, having changed my plans, visited the New York Public Library in Manhattan, at Fifth Avenue and 42nd Street.

My rationale for this move was simple: I needed to get as close to the writer's mind as possible. The closest one can get to that—the closest expression of that mind—should be found in the writer's notes, sketches, drafts, and manuscripts, in this case all held at a special collection in the New York Public Library. As Marco Stanley Fogg says in *Moon Palace*, "Libraries aren't in the real world, after all. They're places apart, sanctuaries of pure thought."[82] A sanctuary like that might even contain materials that would allow me to make conclusions about the arborescent notions of origin and order in Auster's work, and the rhizomatic expansion of his texts. Perhaps his manuscripts would confirm the suspicions I had been harboring from studying his published texts.

I was also determined to find the red notebook there—the "real" red notebook, which through Auster's fictional and nonfictional texts has acquired almost mythical dimensions, the promise of some sort of key or clue for understanding the meaning of his texts. From the beginning, of course, I was skeptical about the allegations regarding the contents of the notebook, yet I had to find it and read it, because that would be what an Auster character would do. Although I kept reminding myself that scholars often study manuscripts in order to better situate the given text in the cultural and documentary context in which it was produced, and so to move closer to finding, for example, the author's intended meaning, I could not really believe in such a prospect. That would be too simple. Still, it was worth trying, and I did not have any other choice but to follow all possible leads to the end in this quest for meaning.

The New York Public Library's Berg Collection contains three separate archives with "Paul Auster papers"—holographic and typed manuscripts, notes, and correspondences, altogether hundreds of boxes of materials dated from 1963 to 2005. And, as I sat there, waiting for the librarian to bring in the boxes with the contents I had requested, I admit I felt a growing sense of excitement and privilege to be able to witness, if not the genesis, then the evolution, the growth, the "becoming" of Auster's stories. There is something special about a manuscript—not only the authorial intimacy with which it is presumed to be invested, but also the alleged truthfulness of its contents—as if it were somehow more "authentic," more sincere than the final product. I recalled what has been said about the modern manuscript: it has about it

> what Walter Benjamin calls an "aura"—a numinous quality of "authenticity." [Manuscripts] seem to reveal the workings of the author's mind, taking us as it were behind the scenes of literary creation. Perhaps because it is marked as the

beginning of a process of mechanical reproduction, we perceive the modern manuscript as carrying greater ontological weight than its copies.[83]

These associations of the manuscript with truthfulness and authenticity partly derive from the modern understanding of the process of publishing. The creation of the original text is believed to be "corrupted" by the intervention of other "authors"— editors, proofreaders and publishers. A manuscript, on the other hand, gives the most direct access to the writer's mind, or such is the assumption. For, as Auster puts it, the manuscript is "a very private material" that is "still attached to you."[84] It is the opposite of a published book that is "a public object" and contains only "what you are willing to show to the world."[85]

At the same time, this does not eliminate the tension we can observe in the sometimes contradictory perception of the manuscript versus the published version of a text, the original versus the refined. This paradox is also noted by Brandon Hopkins, who points out that, while sometimes the manuscript is viewed as the closest reflection of the author's intent, at other times it is the final version that is prioritized as the ultimate expression of that same mind. He says:

> A modern manuscript often seems to us to be the individual and relatively unmediated expression of its author. Yet we always wrestle with a contradiction between regarding a manuscript as "the genuine article" (next to which certain printed versions may be corruptions) and the final work as the authority (of which the manuscript was a mere prototype).[86]

But manuscripts also have unique value as objects that are then turned into artifacts. Auster uses these associations in *The Brooklyn Follies* to create a subplot that deals with the sale of a counterfeited manuscript of Nathaniel Hawthorne's *The Scarlet Letter*. Manuscript by definition, "written by hand" (from Latin *manu* and *scriptus*), is almost always "the original" and therefore the most valuable, while printed sets of the same text are viewed as merely "copies."[87] This gap in value between the original text and its copies was further increased by the advent of mass-produced books, which, in Hopkins' words, "are not themselves seen as individual objects."[88] It is their manuscripts that are unique. And so, as the Sartrean manuscript scholar Michel Contat concludes in a conversation with Paul Auster, the manuscript "itself has an undecided status: it is in between fetishism and aesthetic object" and is also used for "scientific purposes."[89]

It was these sorts of associations that I felt resided in Auster's holographic and typewritten manuscripts. And, as such, these materials seemed to hold the promise of letting me discover some more authentic meaning in his texts and get closer to "the writer's mind." As I went through the contents of the boxes of Auster papers, I discovered the famous notebooks that Auster favors, which came in a variety of sizes, types and colors, and some of which fitted the description given by the protagonist of *Oracle Night* (except that, as I found out, Paul Auster uses a different brand, the French Clairefontaine):

> The Portuguese notebooks were especially attractive to me, and with their hard

covers, quadrille lines, and stitched-in signatures of sturdy, unblottable paper, I knew I was going to buy one the moment I picked it up and held it in my hands. There was nothing fancy or ostentatious about it. It was a practical piece of equipment—stolid, homely, serviceable, not at all the kind of blank book you'd think of offering someone as a gift. But I liked the fact that it was cloth-bound, and I also liked the shape: nine and a quarter by seven and a quarter inches, which made it slightly shorter and wider than most notebooks. I can't explain why it should have been so, but I found those dimensions deeply satisfying ... There were ... four notebooks left on the pile, and each one came in a different color: black, red, brown and blue. I chose the blue, which happened to be the one lying on the top.[90]

I picked from one of the boxes a blue holograph notebook containing the draft to *Oracle Night*, and "when I held the notebook in my hands for the first time, I felt something akin to physical pleasure, a rush of sudden, incomprehensible well-being."[91] It also felt eerie, as if again I was inside an Auster text; I was holding in my hands a blue notebook, that mysterious object which for Sidney Orr from *Oracle Night* sets in motion a chain of strange, unexpected events. Characteristic of Auster's oeuvre, I soon found myself trapped in a loop of self-referentiality, in which one thing or object points to another, and yet another, *ad infinitum*, without ever disclosing its actual meaning. It was as Anne Garner, the archivist of the Auster papers at the New York Public Library, had pointed out: "Looking at [this] manuscript creates a kind of Russian doll effect where the viewer opens one blue notebook only to read about another, where a miraculous story involving yet another manuscript unfolds."[92] The sensation of discovering this significant artifact was overwhelming to me, but it was not helpful for my investigation. Like Sidney Orr, who does not know how to begin writing in his yet blank notebook, "I had no idea how to begin" my reading of the text and the thing I saw before my eyes.[93] I closed the blue notebook, put it aside and turned to inspect other notebooks.

While in some of these notebooks the paper was held together by a spiral, most of them were sewn-bound; with the exception of a few lined ones, most had a grid of pink or blue squares that appeared to better control Auster's tiny handwriting, produced in black ink from a fountain pen. At times his handwriting was so unintelligible that I had difficulty deciphering the text, and had to ask for the librarian's help. And as I was sitting there, bent over the notebooks with a magnifying glass, I felt, like so many times before, that I was following the deceptive guidance of an Auster protagonist, who suggests that truth and meaning are discoverable if the reader agrees to assume the role of detective.

From the large collection of the Auster "papers" that the archives contain, I was mostly interested in the author's preliminary drafts because I believed them to be most intimate and personal, the rawest and purest expression of thoughts, and, therefore, the closest link to his mind and the "locked" space within which it works. In most of these notebooks containing the first drafts of Auster texts, pages were often divided into sections, separated by a line break, sometimes numbered, at other times not, and there would be several repetitions of the same sentence, or of a whole paragraph, with slight variations introduced with each repeated version. These non-linearly arranged fragments more resembled brief sketches and notes than a coherent narrative in development. In some cases, a few sentences or words or a whole section would be crossed out or amended, corrections done with a fountain pen, or, alternatively with a pencil. In other cases, the repeated bits of text would be left untouched on the pages of the notebook—three, five, or even more repetitions of seemingly the same idea.

Looking at Auster's handwritten manuscripts, it seemed to me that through this process of repetition Auster was comparing the sound and looks of words, trying them out for their rhythm and rhyme, and all the other nuances that create his idiosyncratic style of writing. His way of writing resembled building a brick wall or putting together a jigsaw puzzle; it was a process of assembling a text from fragments selected and polished through repetition. For example, the first draft of *The Book of Illusions*, which started with the section on "The Inner Life of Martin Frost" (one of the "written films" in the novel),[94] contained reiterations of the same thought, repeated with slight variation. These were either listed in succession, or, separated out by a line break or a number, reappeared later on in the draft. This is how they looked:

> The Inner Life of Martin Frost runs a little over eighty minutes. It is the shortest and most [?][95] of Hector's late films.

> The Inner Life of Martin Frost was a little over eighty minutes. It was the shortest of the films and [?] ...

> The Inner Life of Martin Frost runs a little over eighty minutes ...[96]

Other similar passages attempted to introduce Martin Frost, the protagonist of this film-within-the-novel:

> Martin Frost is a writer. A smallish [?] man in his early thirties, he is entering the home [house?] as the film begins.

> Martin Frost is a writer in his early thirties ...[97]

This same introduction of the writer-character later reappeared in more variations in Part 5 of Draft 1 to the novel, which was laid out in a different notebook:

> Martin Frost is a writer. A smallish man in his early thirties, he is seen entering the home as the film begins, carrying a suitcase in one hand and a bag of groceries in the other. The home belongs to his friends, Josh and Ruth McRemult, he explains, and he has been offered the use of it while [ends abruptly]

> Martin Frost is a writer. A smallish man in his early thirties, he is seen entering the home as the film begins, carrying a suitcase in one hand and a bag of groceries in the other. The home, he tells us, belongs to his friends, Josh and Ruth McRemult, who are travelling/they[98] are travelling abroad until the end of the year and have offered him the use of their place for as long as he would care to stay there. Martin has just spent [ends abruptly]

> Martin Frost is a writer. A smallish man in his early thirties, he is seen entering

the home [house?] as the film begins, carrying a suitcase in one hand and a bag of groceries in the other. The home, he tells us, belongs to his friends, Josh and Ruth McRemult, who are travelling around. Martin has been invited to stay there while they are gone. He has just spent <u>three</u> [?] years working on a novel, and because he is feeling exhausted and in need of a rest [ends abruptly]

Martin Frost is a writer …[99]

The resulting impression was of a writer composing a text in a back-and-forth movement marked by a re-iteration, or stuttering, of thought, until he found, even if in an entirely different notebook, the "right" segment of text that would eventually make its way to the typewriting stage. This is how one fragment containing the description of the silent "Martin Frost" film from the draft to *The Book of Illusions* appeared:

> The picture fades to black. We are approximately ninety [?] seconds into the film at this point …
>
> The picture fades to black. When we see Martin again, it is morning [?] and he is fast asleep in bed.
>
> The picture
>
> The picture fades to black. We are approximately ninety [?] seconds into the film at this point …
>
> The picture fades to black. When the [?] resumes, it is morning [?].[100]

Auster once described to Contat his process of hand-writing as "build[ing] up the manuscript," a process that involves writing in the notebook, "go[ing] over and over the paragraph," "writ[ing] and rewrit[ing] that paragraph" by hand, and then "typ[ing] it up."[101]

> Michel Contat: "Which means you can write ten or more drafts of the same paragraph."
> Paul Auster: "Yes. Over and over and over again."[102]

Most days he would only write one or two paragraphs, rewriting them by hand "from the start, from scratch," until they began to feel "indestructible" (like typescript) and ready to be typed up.[103] After all, typewriting, unlike notebook-writing, would not tolerate such repetition and backward-forward movement.[104] It would want to impose linearity and order, to tame the chaos.

For Auster's writing on those pages indeed appeared untamed, as if the thoughts of his mind had been directly channeled through the handwriting fountain pen—the hand inextricable from the word, and the word from the hand, as Heidegger has put it, and the pen as the writing tool that acts to make this channeling of the writer's thoughts possible. Rosamary Fernandez in her article on handwriting suggests it is "[t]he speed with which words flow from the pen at the behest of the hand" that has given rise to metaphors that "reveal a sense of streaming and flowing associated with the generative act."[105] Roland Barthes once declared that "the pleasure of the text is that moment when [his] body pursues its own ideas."[106] Media theorist Daniel Chandler in "The Phenomenology of Writing by Hand" talks about writing as an act that "fuses physical and intellectual processes," where writing by hand in particular implies "bodily thinking" and is a pure expression of thought that comes straight from one's body.[107] That is exactly how Auster describes his own attachment to this writing tool: "I can say this, I've never been able to compose on a keyboard. I need a pen or a pencil in my hand, [to] feel that it's a very physical activity. When I write, words are literally coming out of my body."[108]

Auster always writes his texts in longhand, and then types them up on his typewriter. Yet it does not mean that the work of the typewriter has not been present since the beginning of the process. The typewriter acts on the writer's thoughts through associations, and its work is invisible yet intense. That is why—as I discovered in the archives—although the first draft to *The Story of My Typewriter* was written by hand on a few squared pages torn out from a small notebook, Auster still claims that the text was produced by his Olympia typewriter, while he himself was sitting there, his hands on its keyboard, watching it "[l]etter by letter … write these words."[109] He handwrote those very words.

Yet, when looking at these early drafts (I chose to inspect in particular detail the ones related to *The Book of Illusions* and *The Brooklyn Follies*), it was hard to follow the development of Auster's thought. Contat experienced a similar frustration: "for each [book] there is a lot of material. And the question of course for scholars is to know the exact genetic progression," which—as Auster admitted—is "not clear."[110] There were no remarks or clues or notes, hinting at why within this rhizomatic map of thoughts one path was chosen over the others and why the text got shaped in one particular way. Among all the repetitions of textual fragments that were laid out in the notebooks, there was no way of telling the "original" one. In the "original" manuscripts, there was no single point of origin, making it close to impossible to establish any sort of genealogy. Instead, there was a multiplicity of text, a pool of countless possibilities for each word, and, consequently, each sentence and story, to develop further.

These repetitions, I think, reflect more than mere stylistic choices. Each divergence represents subtle ontological differences and possibilities, dozens of versions for beginnings, each with their own potential. It fits the explanation of the multiplicity of the book, as given by the Jewish writer and poet Edmond Jabès in a conversation with Auster:

> When I say there are many books in the book, it is because there are many words in the word. Obviously, if you change the word, the context of the sentence changes completely. In this way another sentence is born from this word, and a completely different book begins … I think of this in terms of the sea, in the image of the sea as it breaks upon the shore. It is not the wave that comes, it is the whole sea that comes each time and the whole sea that draws back. It is never just a wave, it is always everything that comes and everything that goes. This is really the fundamental movement in all my books. Everything is connected to everything

else ... At each moment, in the least question, it is the *whole* book which returns and the *whole* book which draws back.[111] (his emphasis)

Apart from the repetitions of textual fragments that appeared throughout the notebooks, these early holographs also contained something that resembled outlines, or indexes for the ways a text could be assembled. They were sketching out possible developments for a story, naming its parts and sub-parts, and arranging those in a particular order. The first draft to *The Brooklyn Follies* started with an outline that Auster had named "The Ten Lives of Otto Gutmann." It was followed by several other versions of the outline, with initial chapter titles and their numbers in mixed order.

Likewise, the first pages of the notebook, containing what is identified as Draft 2 of *The Brooklyn Follies*, were all filled out with similar outlines—29 possible sections for the novel with some preliminary titles, or 30 sections, or 28, or 32, as on yet another page. Notes providing details of characters, listing their possible name, age, occupation, background and role in the story, likewise recurred throughout the notebooks. The notebook containing the holograph outline and early draft entitled "Dream Days at the Hotel Existence"[112] was, again, symptomatic of this kind of writing. An assemblage of short sketches, ideas, lists, names and outlines, it diagrammed all the possibilities for a book, out of which eventually *The Brooklyn Follies* grew, but what captivated me most at that moment was the thought of how that growth happened, as well as the thought of all those books that did not grow out of these sketches.

Auster himself thinks of arranging his thoughts on paper "in terms of music ... more than in terms of painting," but he also sometimes "think[s] in terms of maps."[113] Interviewed by Contat, Auster talks about the "natural boundaries" of an imaginary world by comparing it to a painting: "It's a page, or a canvas ... That painting [he points to a painting on the wall] does not extend over here; it's in a limited space."[114] Yet, when he talks about "a particular mental space" that he believes every book is "limited to,"[115] like a framed painting, it provokes a string of questions: Who and what would mark these boundaries, and how, for whom?

Here is what I find interesting. Auster himself said in the interview with Contat that he has "somehow always treated the finished text as the choice of the author."[116] Yet, when asked if an author might ever be mistaken by choosing not "the most interesting one" among the many manuscript versions, Auster replied: "I think that's possible."[117] That places these manuscripts in "a strange twilight world," a sort of no-man's land of abandoned contingencies.[118] Those are the same alternative universes that I talked about earlier, whose many textual doubles and phantoms often emerge among his published work to challenge its authenticity.

And yet, these outlines failed to reveal any significant information that would help me to deepen my understanding of Auster's rhizomatic work: like his published works, Auster's notebooks seemed to suggest almost a state of entrapment for his texts in cycles of their own intra- and self-referentiality.[119] The same holograph notebooks containing early drafts of Auster's novels (e.g., Draft 1 of *The Book of Illusions*, or the first drafts to *The Brooklyn Follies*) exposed the rhizomatic structure of his oeuvre through the mutual intertextual references that tie his texts together. Character names and titles were especially telling of this connectivity. For example, in the draft to *The Book of Illusions*, the following films were attributed to its director-character Hector Mann, all of which are titles of other Auster texts:

The Inner Life of Martin Frost (1947) (filmed at ranch)
Travels in the Scriptorium (ranch—NY – KC)
Oracle Night (1971) (ranch—SF)[120]

Within the same draft, a list of something marked as "Stories" appeared:

Oracle Night
Travels in the Scriptorium
The Brooklyn Follies[121]

In the first draft of "Dream Days at the Hotel Existence,"[122] which is an early version of *The Brooklyn Follies*, Auster had listed the possible titles, among which were "The Further Adventures of Martin Frost" and "Report from the Anti-World." Martin Frost is one of Auster's writer-characters, while the other title is mentioned in *The Book of Illusions* as one of Hector Mann's films. An untitled holograph notebook that features another outline for "Dream Days at the Hotel Existence" likewise featured among its section titles already familiar names:

Mr. Vertigo
Pret-falls [?]: Scenes from the Life of Hector Mann
The Red Notebook

It also included—noted separately—"True Stories," followed by a list of story titles. Further on in the draft, other recognizable titles and names from Auster texts reappeared:

Timbuktu
The Brooklyn Follies
Hector Mann

Meanwhile, the character list for the planned novel included "Fogg" (as in *Moon Palace* and *Travels in the Scriptorium*), "Nashe and Juliette" (Nashe appears in *The Music of Chance*), "Quinn (?)" (*City of Glass*, *Travels in the Scriptorium*) and—unsurprisingly—"Auster."

These are just a few examples of the kind of intertextuality and repetition I found to be symptomatic of Auster's unpublished texts. One way of explaining this would be through Auster's own confession that, at least in his mind, he is "always working on two, or even three, books at the same time," even if at the time he is only (type) writing one.[123] But that would not explain why the same intratextual references also keep appearing in his published texts. Later, in the draft to *The Red Notebook*, Auster makes a different observation—"Some stories won't let go of you," a sentence separated out and written on the top corner of an otherwise half-filled page. An Auster text, it seems, can never be entirely finished. Like MS Fogg's life (his name itself a reference to "manuscript"), it is always in development, writing itself as long as

Paul Auster/"Paul Auster" writes. I suddenly felt like the character Blue from Auster's novel *Ghosts*,

> like a man who has been condemned to sit in a room and go on reading a book for the rest of his life ... But how to get out? How to get out of the room that is the book that will go on being written for as long as he stays in the room?[124]

Perhaps, as Stephen Fredman suggests, for a writer whose writing explores the process of writing (or for a reader who attempts to read such writing), to walk out of the room of the book would be simply impossible. "[I]t would mean to stop writing," or, as in my case, to stop reading entirely.[125] I felt my quest was about to end where it had begun—somewhere inside the maze of Auster's texts—cyclical, repetitive and self-referential, without an identifiable beginning, center, or end, and with no possibility of assigning any kind of stable meaning.

Yet before I was ready to give up on my investigation of "Auster papers," I had to examine one final item—the holographic notebook that I believed to be the often-referenced "red notebook." After all, in Auster's texts, the reader is never given a chance to glimpse its contents, while constantly being teased to do so, as in this fragment from *The Locked Room*:

> "Behind you ... A red notebook."
> I turned around, opened the closet door, and picked up the notebook. It was a standard spiral affair with two hundred ruled pages. I gave a quick glance at the contents and saw that all the pages had been filled: the same familiar writing, the same black ink, the same small letters ...
> "What now?" I asked.
> "Take it home with you. Read it ... It was written for you ... It's all in the notebook. Whatever I managed to say now would only distort the truth."
> "Is there anything else?"
> "No, I don't think so. We've probably come to the end."[126]

And as I located the "red notebook," squeezed in among other notebooks in an archival folder named "Notebooks," I became "enormously excited by this discovery,"[127] not unlike Sidney Orr, who discovers in *Oracle Night* that the object of his search, John Trause (note the anagram of the surname), uses the same kind of notebook as himself. Yet the hard-cover A4 Clairefontaine notebook with 192 pages/96 sheets and a red fabric pattern cover turned out to be as deceptive as it appears in Auster's texts themselves. Entitled by Auster "Stories," it listed the following material as its contents:

> Translations—preface
> Meditations on a Cardboard Box
> Clastres—Translator's note[128]
> Lulu on the Bridge—interview
> Why Write?
> The Red Notebook

The first 50 pages or so of the notebook, which amount to approximately one quarter of the entire notebook, were left blank. The handwritten material that appeared in the next few pages was all crossed out. Among other bits and pieces, the ink-filled pages that followed, in which the text had not been struck through, contained references to Philippe Petit and his sky-walking, a random telephone number, and notes on translations, essays and stories, including what one would recognize as draft versions of the "true stories" from *The Red Notebook*.

In the end, it was the question of truth that lay at the heart of my only revelation at the library archives. The discovery came in the form of some subversive material that the red notebook contained, which seemed to suggest that, for Auster, truth and invention indeed are inseparable and suffused with each other. Paul Auster, as the holograph revealed, had invented an interview with himself. The pages filled with his tiny handwriting in black ink contained what appeared to be the first draft to both questions and answers of a conversation that later was published and republished, and became widely cited among scholars.

But if notions of truth and fiction can be so easily overturned, then statements, facts and details that one would otherwise presume to be "truthful" also lose their credibility. After this little discovery, I started questioning how one is supposed to read the following sentence written by Auster, a sentence that opens one of the "true stories" of *The Red Notebook* and that appears in a draft version in the same red notebook as the invented interview: "If anyone should think I'm making it up; think again. Stories like this one are solely the promise of the truth."[129]

When scholars, critics and a general readership seek to increase their knowledge and understanding of a writer's work, the established practice is to turn to additional reading material, such as the available criticism, or the author's other published and unpublished texts, such as manuscripts and notes. Or to study the author's life. Or, sometimes, to look for more direct expression from the author in the form of his personal letters, public interviews and statements.

Yet what happens when one finds out that facts are infused with fiction and the other way round, so that fictional details not only point back to facts, but what one takes to be a reliable fact itself turns out to be fictionalized, invented? For a split second, I felt like Ian Hamilton after an occasion of "unfruitful" study of J. D. Salinger's unpublished material: the data and bits of information that I had just managed to accumulate did not reveal to me anything meaningful about "the subject of [my] study," or else, they turned out to be, "in the main, performances," and as such were unreliable material.[130] I closed the red notebook and placed it back where it belonged, among the hundreds of boxes of Auster materials that are held in the archives of the library. I had no choice now but to find Paul Auster himself and talk to him directly.

Encountering the writer

Having settled in the new hotel in Park Slope, I decided to stay in Brooklyn and look for Paul Auster there. Brooklyn felt more accessible, more open and somehow also more "real" than the distanced, sterile and geometrical spaces of Manhattan and its anonymous crowds. With "a hundred potential scenes to capture, vivid colors all around," it seemed to invite exploration and engagement, an invitation that both I myself and Auster characters (Milles Heller, Ellen and Bing Nathan from *Sunset Park*, Nathan Glass and Lucy from *The Brooklyn Follies*, etc.) responded to after settling in. Both the borough and its people had a certain "character" that one could not only observe from a distance but also engage with on a personal level.

The sense that Brooklyn is more colorful, more accessible, more open and more "real" is also suggested by the particular details attributed to it through specific and often tangible "things" that gather together the Austerlian neighborhoods—namely, Park Slope, Prospect Park and Sunset Park. That is how Auster's Brooklyn-assemblages differ from those of Manhattan, which are characterized largely by emotions and sensations, a certain level of abstraction and something that could be best described as a lack of solid substance (mazes, deceptions, vanishing points, impenetrable façades, blandly numerical street names, the feeling of being lost).

Things in Brooklyn, on the other hand, seem to encourage their naming—but you know that already. In Brooklyn, one notices "things." The architecture and urban planning of Brooklyn draw attention to the heterogeneity of elements scattered along its long, wide avenues, so that what one sees when walking down 7th Avenue, from Grand Army Plaza to Prospect Park, as I did after my arrival, are "hybrid chains of actants"[131]—its many cafés and restaurants, the bookshops and barber shops, the laundromats and repair shops, the old people and young people, the people with children in strollers or dogs on a leash, ice creams and pizzas, music and chatter, kids playing basketball, and so on and so forth, until these strings of things disappear at length into the vanishing point.

For the first few days after my arrival, I acted like Nathan Glass from *The Brooklyn Follies*, and "filled my time by exploring the neighborhood," mainly Park Slope and Prospect Park, while, later on, following Bing and Ellen from Auster's *Sunset Park*, I walked down to Sunset Park, "to explore the territory between Fifteenth and Sixty-fifth streets in western Brooklyn."[132] That "extensive hodgepodge of an area that runs from Upper New York Bay to Ninth Avenue" was "home to more than a hundred thousand people, including Mexicans, Dominicans, Poles, Chinese, Jordanians, Vietnamese, American whites, American blacks, and a settlement of Christians from Gujarat, India."[133] It consisted of

[w]arehouses, factories, abandoned waterfront facilities, a view of the Statue of Liberty, the shut-down Army Terminal where ten thousand people once worked, a basilica named Our Lady of Perpetual Help, biker cars, check-cashing places, Hispanic restaurants, the third-largest Chinatown in New York, and the four hundred and seventy-eight acres of Green-Wood Cemetery, where six hundred thousand bodies are buried, including those of [the famous historical figures] Boss Tweed, Lola Montez, Currier and Ives, Henry Ward Beecher, F. A. O. Schwarz, Lorenzo Da Ponte, Horace Greeley, Louis Comfort Tiffany, Samuel F.

B. Morse, Albert Anastasia, Joey Gallo, and Frank Morgan—the wizard in *The Wizard of Oz*.[134]

In Brooklyn, everything and everyone seems to be given a voice of their own, or else they themselves get voiced, acknowledged and named, as in the case of the dead people and the things they have come to be associated with.[135]

Auster's Brooklyn, which seems to be a communal space, is made up of smaller and larger communities, and as such it encourages participation and engagement, and expression of its polyphony, all of which becomes manifested in Auster's later texts set in this borough. It is clearly also the effect of the place that to a large extent is responsible for the shift that occurs in Auster's texts from a singular focus on one isolated individual and his writer's identity quest (*City of Glass, Ghosts, The Locked Room, Leviathan*, "The Day I Disappeared," *Moon Palace*, etc.) to a larger group of characters that are all assembled by the space they inhabit (*Man in the Dark, The Brooklyn Follies, Smoke, Blue in the Face, Sunset Park*). One of Auster's most recent novels, *Sunset Park*, even includes multiple narrative voices—and, like in the film *Smoke*, each chapter there is assigned to and named after a different character.

Brooklyn, itself a network of assemblages, acts in a similar way as the "thinging" cigarette that draws people together, encouraging mutual sharing and tolerance. It somehow seems less likely that a place like Manhattan could exert the same effect. Brooklyn, the largest and most populous of the New York boroughs, paradoxically feels like a small place, a community and a home—even if to a "hundred thousand people." Brooklyn, in Nathan Glass' words, is both "New York and yet not New York," it is the "ancient kingdom of ... New York,"[136] a home that one returns to (*Sunset Park*) and a place where one comes "to die" (*The Brooklyn Follies*). As the place of "home" and "end," I thought it would also be a perfect site to find some closure to my scholarly quest.

More things happened to me in Brooklyn than ever did in Manhattan, more encounters and more coincidences, and I felt that, wherever I turned, there were signs marking Paul Auster's presence, reassuring me that I was on the right track. The first time I travelled from Brooklyn to the New York Public Library's Berg Collection, I was told upon arrival that the previous day Auster's wife Siri Hustvedt had visited them; the next time I returned there, after just a few days, I was told that Auster himself had come just the day before. Later, in Park Slope, I had lunch in one of the Italian restaurants that are scattered along 7th Avenue; after I told them about my quest for Paul Auster, and showed them his photograph from the back cover of his book, they told me that he had dined there just the previous night.

Then, one day I visited the Prospect Park neighborhood, to see what stands in the location of Auggie Wren's Tobacco Shop (The Brooklyn Cigar Co.) from Auster's films *Smoke* and *Blue in the Face*. I found there a New Zealand pie shop selling pies, Anzac biscuits and New Zealand Breakfast Tea, and the fact that I had travelled all the way from that country at the other end of the world, only to encounter a reflection of my home, appeared to me a promising sign that I was simply meant to be there.[137]

In Brooklyn I also realized that, perhaps, it was time to update *Paul Auster's New York*, since the book that was published—and immediately retracted—in 1997 excludes not only fragments from his films but also from books published after this date—such as *Man in the Dark, Sunset Park, Invisible, The Brooklyn Follies, The Book of Illusions*, and *Oracle Night*. I decided to spend my evenings back in the Park Slope hotel going through these texts, looking for fragments that were related to the city, and working to update Überhoff's original compilation.

Tracing the associations of Auster's New York, finding their expressions and aligning them would allow a new narrative of its own to emerge, which would expose, I believed, the transformation of the alienated and often menacing Australian city, epitomized predominantly by Manhattan, into something more familiar and nameable, mainly manifested by Brooklyn, a site that forms and defines itself through an abundance of details rather than abstract sensations. An updated version of *Paul Auster's New York* would mean an updated travel guide and map of Auster's city, a place that has become more concrete and graphic through his ever-expanding canon. However, as soon as I had started my work on assembling Auster's Brooklyn and "more recent" Manhattan, something happened that interrupted this project and marked the end of my exploration of New York.

I was contacted one day to be informed that Mr Auster had agreed to meet with me.[138] We arranged a date—he picked the time and venue—and on June 10, 2011, I finally came face to face with the object of my search (or was it the subject of my search?). What I encountered was a tangible version of an idea of "Paul Auster" that was now materializing before my eyes—his recognizable posture in a physical presence, the low voice that I had heard before and that was now emerging from this figure standing in front of me, the Schimmelpenninck cigars that were continually lit, consumed and extinguished, and whose aroma and smoke soon surrounded us, his trademark writer's tool—a fountain pen (which he later pulled out of the chest pocket of his shirt to demonstrate on a page in my notebook the kind of imprint of ink it leaves), and other things that assemble a general impression of what "Paul Auster" is.

And so, on a hot Friday afternoon, we found ourselves sitting in the back yard of a French patisserie on 7th Avenue in Park Slope, undisturbed by any other visitors, drinking white wine, conversing and laughing, and, in spite of the new smoking ban, enjoying our cigarillos. The smoke of tobacco was slowly rising from our hands and mouths, or at times from the ashtray in the middle of the table, curling in the air into a variety of shapes, incessantly reinventing and transforming itself until it vanished altogether. I recalled then that human thoughts often had the same structure and shape as smoke, and I felt that our smoking, too, perhaps, was a bit like our conversation, which, although generally tamed by the questions that I had prepared for Auster, at times took unexpected turns and wandered off in other directions.

The occasion also evoked associations of smoking with ancient rites, where tobacco served as the unifying thread of communication between humans and spiritual powers. The act of sharing a cigar with Auster seemed as meaningful to me as the opportunity to talk to the author in person, and the entire experience of meeting him acquired a sort of transcendental value. I felt that, whatever there was to be known about Auster's life-work would be illuminated to me by the end of our conversation, and I remember thinking to myself—"this is it, we have finally come to the conclusion, and nothing could ever be more meaningful than this."

Inconclusion

The sense of euphoria and epiphany that enveloped me during my meeting with Paul Auster vanished as quickly as tobacco smoke disperses in the open air. In retrospect, I never felt any strong sense of achievement when I finally found him and got to meet him. It had been his kindness, not my effort, that brought us together for that conversation. Likewise, it was obvious that the significance of the event and its details, such as the time spent smoking together or discussing the role of cigarettes in film, resided solely in my perception and/or imagination. If there had been anything in that situation suggesting a sort of climactic conclusion, transcendental revelation, or a solution to an interpretative quest, then it had been there only because I myself had wanted it to be there from the very start.

Paul Auster himself, too, did not turn out to be entirely what I had hoped him to be, and the answers he gave to my questions seemed to complicate rather than support the argumentative work of my study. Generous with his time and attention, polite and friendly to me, he nevertheless rejected almost every claim about his work that I have proposed in this book, which is the product of years of research and thought. His responses did not so much refute or argue against my propositions as simply dismiss them as wrong or absurd with a single wave of his hand.

Auster does not believe that his writing tools and machines, such as fountain pens and typewriters, play any meaningful role for him in his process of writing; he also rejected my idea about the work carried out by other "things" (such as cigarettes, doubles, and notebooks) in the creative process. No, his Olympia never "talked" to him; it only "talked" to Sam Messer. For Auster, the typewriter was just a tool that he used without ever thinking about it. He told me that technology, whether used to produce a film, a photograph, or a literary text, would have no significant impact on the result—while some technologies could make things go faster, they did not make them any better, he said.

Equally swiftly he dismissed my suggestions about the overlooked functions and meanings of objects in forming social networks with humans, assembling specific settings for action, or stimulating particular actions. No, although objects sometimes *seemed* to act, they never actually *did*; and one did not require a thing, like a lit cigarette in hand, in order to tell a story.

To my question about the importance of New York in his life and writing he responded succinctly—"no significance." It was simply where he happened to live and a place he knew best; he could easily live and write anywhere else, it was just that he did not want to.

When I asked him about the projects he had co-authored, and whether he would see them as a part of his oeuvre, to be read and interpreted in the light of his other texts, he responded that he had simply stumbled into most of these projects and that, in fact, he had nothing much to do with them.

Auster did not like the idea that one could question the authenticity of his non-fiction, and, conversely, the fictionality of his fiction, and that perhaps, as some suggest, no borderlines separate the two.

As soon as I mentioned the theme of identity, which for the majority of his critics (Carsten Springer, Aliki Varvogli, Mark Brown, Brendan Martin, James Peacock, Madeleine Sorapure, etc.) appears central to his narratives, he cut me short and interjected that he did not understand what they meant by that, and what the concept of "identity" itself was supposed to mean. None of his characters had an identity crisis, and they all knew who they were, he said. Even if occasionally someone like Quinn (in *City of Glass*) took over someone else's identity, that was "just a game" and an act of self-conscious pretense.

And when I pointed to the similarities that many critics note between Auster and his characters, especially the smoking writer-figure that is customarily read as his fictional surrogate, he reminded me that his characters were never really him—ever.

At that point, I was overcome with a sinking feeling that Auster would most certainly disapprove of the book I was writing about him, and that I had failed in my task to say anything meaningful or truthful about his work. I felt I had arrived at a dead end; my detection had not resulted in getting closer to the object of my search; instead, as in Auster's early texts, it had been flipped around and turned against me, turned inwards, so that in the end, as in Hamilton's case, this study does not say as much about the intended subject as it does about my struggle to comprehend it, to interpret what resists interpretation.

Because of Auster's blunt rejections of everything that I had taken to be true of his work, I started questioning the validity, strength, and soundness of my arguments. Perhaps my conviction that there is a particular set of things which through their own synergy constitute what we recognize as "Paul Auster" and his facto-fictional universe, with all its inclusive texts, both literary and audio-visual, is but the product of my imagination. Perhaps, there really is no need for cigarettes, New York, bare study rooms, spiral notebooks, or typewriters in order to, along with other things, create "a Paul Auster story." It is possible, after all, that the image associated with a writer that I share with Sam Messer, and the description of him by Jesús Ángel González that he is "addictive," that he "smokes and writes," and "lives in Brooklyn" are only to be taken as a commentary on Auster's "public persona."[1] It could be merely a set of associations and aspirations that critics along with the public have projected onto him, and which, furthermore, have nothing to do with the underlying structures and deeper meanings of his work.

Hamilton experienced similar doubts during his search for Salinger, and recurrently felt he had to stop to question the connections he had established between Salinger's life and work, the public and the private, the real and the fictional:

And what about the life/work line of scrutiny? We had been able to dig up a few "real-life models," and there *was* some interest in seeing young Salinger foreshadowing young Caulfield. Or was it that this was what we wanted to find? We wanted there to be, from the start, some near-intolerable strain between the "anxious to be loved" side of Salinger and the other, darker side, the need to be untouchably superior. This was our reading of him as he had become, but was it really there ...?[2] (his emphasis)

Perhaps, then, the significance of the objects and things whose associative and connective work this book explores has been overrated and imagined, made possible only by my desire to see them in every text I came across. Hamilton's self-reflective observations on this matter are as harsh as they are acute:

My [alter-ego] companion was looking shrewdly diagnostic. Indeed, for days now there had been something distasteful in the smug, scientific way he'd set about rearranging his file cards. It was as if, having located the malignant source, he could simply sit back and watch the poison spread. All would be "symptomatic" from now on. It didn't seem to matter to him that we hadn't, even in his terms, proved anything that ought to have surprised us. After all, we had to some extent *created* a brash young Salinger who, if he went to war, would almost certainly crack up. But just as we liked the idea of casting our man as an undercover agent, so we warmed to the notion that he might, if only for a moment, have been mad. We liked the idea of him as a mysterious controller of his fate, but we also wanted to see him as maimed by some glamorously dreadful trauma.[3] (his emphasis)

Could it be then that in the end the only result of this whole project of reading Auster's texts rhizomatically is the creation of my own alternative version of "Paul Auster" and his work?

Hamilton describes the deceptive sense of triumph that overwhelms biographers or scholars as they come across what they believe to be a major discovery in their research—data, facts, and opinions which often get extracted from direct or indirect expression of the author's thoughts: "We felt, I suppose, just for a moment, rather as policemen do, or torturers, when the confession finally gets signed."[4] This remark rather bluntly suggests that what critics and scholars are truly interested in when given an opportunity to hear the author's voice, whether in a form of a written text (such as publications, manuscripts, letters, and notes) or the spoken word (such as public and private interviews and speeches), is essentially the author's confession that the critics have been correct about their interpretation of his work.[5]

Was it not the reason why I had, after all, wanted to meet with Paul Auster—to receive an approval for what I was doing, to confront him with questions that already sounded more like statements? Quite possibly, that was the true source of the constant discomfort that I felt throughout the process of my research and the reason why I had to adopt a critical persona in order to distance myself from it.

And yet, I cannot help but mistrust also the author himself. There seems to be a tension, an underlying contradiction that Auster might be unaware of, in his attitude towards criticism of his work, an observation I also made during our interview. Auster's thoughts about the importance of the reader's personal experience in creating the meaning of a text are in agreement with the poststructuralist discourse of "the death of the author" established by Roland Barthes and Michel Foucault. (Of course, it is not always easy to pronounce an author dead, especially if that author is sitting in front of you, discussing with you his own work.) As Auster admitted during our interview, books, once they have been published, belong to the readers' minds. Or, as he said in another interview: "The one thing I try to do in all my books is to leave enough room in the prose for the reader to inhabit it ... I finally believe that it's the reader who writes the book and not the writer."⁶ Being primarily a writer and not a literary theorist, he rather conventionally either displays a light resentment towards what critics have to say about his work, or remains altogether indifferent to it.

At the same time, Auster, who once sold three archives of his manuscripts and papers to the New York Public Library's Berg Collection, expressed his support for the availability of such materials for research. Most of what critics were doing, he said, was uninteresting, but once in a while there was some brilliant person who managed to discover something really illuminating, and the materials at the library were there to aid in this task.

Auster's categorical denial of what the majority of his critics have said about his work (in particular, those who portray his works as examples of the tenets of postmodernism), together with his apparent anticipation of a "better" and more understanding critic, recreated him in my eyes as the traditional, "innocent" writer figure who spends his days at his desk in the solitary room, writing in longhand (with a fountain pen), pounding away on the keys of his typewriter, chain-smoking, and producing texts infused with sentiment, nostalgia, existentialism and humanist values.

What am I to think of my conversation with the author? After I had confronted him about my discovery of the invented interview, Auster confessed to me that the interviewer's original questions had not seemed particularly interesting to him, and since he had known exactly what he wanted to say, he came up with his own version of it. Interviews, he told me, were a whole different art form. Writing interviews was like writing a play—one made them up, while trying to make them sound like natural conversations. Never once during our interview did Auster remove his dark sunglasses. Somehow, I am still not entirely sure whether I got to meet Paul Auster or "Paul Auster," and whether, after the scholarly quest that this book embodies, I have managed to get any closer to understanding his texts.

Perhaps this smoking, typing writer *has been*, in the end, truthful to his life-long project. Whether something is "true" or "false" is irrelevant as long as it makes a "good" story. As we were sitting there, puffing away on our cigars, engulfed in a tranquil cloud of smoke that slowly rose from our hands and mouths, vanishing into the summer air, I remembered that final scene from *Smoke*. Once Auggie and Paul Benjamin have shared a smoke together, and Auggie has shared his "true" Christmas story, the writer-figure Paul reacts: "Bullshit is a real talent, Auggie ... it's a good story."⁷ Perhaps, then, that is all that mattered—a shared cigar and a story, SMOKING that means "FICTIONING" that means STORYTELLING. And, as long as the writer keeps on smoking, his writing machine will keep producing stories. Stories that are born from other stories, and stories whose meanings are never fixed but are constantly changing shape—unsubstantial, ephemeral, and transient as the smoke itself.

That was, after all, also proved by our meeting. To Auster, stories, either "true" or "false," are about being human and sharing human values (freedom, equality, mutual tolerance and respect), and "the unpredictable, utterly bewildering nature of human experience."[8] Yet stories are also about gathering and sharing, and they function like the things themselves, whose acting makes these stories possible in the first place. That is something that, quite possibly, the writer has not noticed. The conversation we shared that afternoon would not have been possible without the "thinging" of "things" that surrounded us and interacted with us, such as cigars, wine, a café, my notepad, Auster's fountain pen, a book on New York, and New York itself.

There once was a real conversation that took place between Paul Auster and Michel Contat, in which the existential mind of the writer refused to give credit to his writing machine:

> MC: So you wouldn't say, like Chateaubriand quoted by Sartre: "Je sais bien que je ne suis qu'une machine à faire des livres [I know that I am only a book-making machine]"?
> PA: No.
> MC: You are not making books, you are writing. But what are you writing if it isn't your life?
> PA: That's a very hard question. What am I writing? The story of my inner life, I suppose.[9]

But the writing machine is there—you have seen it. It works as solidly as mine, which has produced this story through my collaboration with typewriters, laptops, cigarettes, solitude, detection, Paul Auster's books, as well as films, manuscripts, and portraits of Auster done by other artists, among many other (in)tangible things.

At this point, I do not think it is possible to produce any finite conclusions. I can only end with an Inconclusion, combining what is "in conclusion" and what is "inconclusive." But there are new questions that our investigation of Auster's intratext has opened up. Questions, for example, to do with the significance of concepts such as "truth," "originality," or "authenticity." Or questions about the relationship between the author, his critic, and the reader in producing meanings for texts. Or questions about the relationship between contemporary fiction and its criticism, and the efficacy of conventional methods of critical reading—ones that rely on, for example, consulting the author's manuscripts, notes, and personal correspondence, or even the historical author himself. In the end, it is only possible for me to say this: there are things and spaces, concepts and ideas, bundles of values and functions and associations that all work together to assemble a story, and in amongst all that there is a smoking, typewriting writer, whose cigarette emits a cloud of smoke. What lies behind that smoke screen—that I can only try to imagine.

Notes

Preface

1   John Updike, "Introduction," in Jill Krementz, *The Writer's Desk* (New York: Random House, 1996), viii.

Introduction: Paul Auster's Intratext

1   Michel Foucault, *The Archaeology of Knowledge & The Discourse on Language* (New York: Vintage, 1982).
2   See Franco Moretti, *Graphs, Maps, Trees* (London and New York: Verso, 2005), 1.
3   Moretti, *Graphs, Maps, Trees*, 1.
4   Paul Kincaid, "'Travels in the Scriptorium' by Paul Auster," review of *Travels in the Scriptorium*, by Paul Auster, *Strange Horizons*, December 19, 2006, http://www.strangehorizons.com/reviews/2006/12/travels_in_the_.shtml
5   See Barry Lewis, "The Strange Case of Paul Auster," *The Review of Contemporary Fiction* 14.1 (1994), 53; and Rüdiger Heinze, *Ethics of Literary Forms in Contemporary American Literature* (Münster: LIT Verlag, 2005), 41–2.
6   There is also the nameless protagonist in *The Locked Room*, David Zimmer in *The Book of Illusions*, Sidney Orr in *Oracle Night*, and so on.
7   M. Rheindorf, "'Where Everything is Connected to Everything Else': Interior and Exterior Landscape in the Poetry, Essays, and fiction of Paul Auster" (MA diss., University of Vienna, 2001); Dennis Barone, "Introduction: Paul Auster and the Postmodern Novel," in *Beyond the Red Notebook: Essays on Paul Auster*, ed. Dennis Barone (Philadelphia: University of Pennsylvania Press, 1995); Aliki Varvogli, *World That Is the Book* (Liverpool: Liverpool University Press, 2001).
8   Paul Auster, *The Invention of Solitude* (New York: Penguin Books, 2007), 89.
9   These are references to Paul Auster's memoir *The Invention of Solitude*, the collection of essays *The Art of Hunger*, the novel *The Music of Chance* and the collection of poetry *Disappearances: Selected Poems*. See Rheindorf, "Where Everything is Connected," 5.
10 Michelle Banks in the notes to her essay "The Connection Exists: Hermeneutics and Authority in Paul Auster's Fictional Worlds," in *The Invention of Illusions: International Perspectives on Paul Auster*, ed. Stefania Ciocia and Jesús A. González (Newcastle upon Tyne: Cambridge Scholars Publishing, 2011), 170.
11 Banks asks a similar question when she writes: "Wide-ranging ontologically suggestive projects like Auster's bring to the fore key questions of reception order and knowledge influence. What effects will such potentially (or inevitably) unpredictable ordering exert over the reader's understanding of the larger fictional

world being projected? ... The [reader's] production of the *world* will be affected" (her emphasis). See Banks, "Connection Exists," 162.

12   Auster, "The Locked Room," in Paul Auster, *The New York Trilogy* (New York: Penguin Books, 1990), 256. The possibilities for reading an Auster "world" in terms of either components or connections are also weighed by Rheindorf, "Where Everything is Connected," 21.

13   Paul Auster, *Winter Journal* (London: Faber and Faber, 2012), 5.

14   Paul Auster, *In the Country of Last Things* (New York: Penguin Books, 2004), 143.

15   Auster, *Invention of Solitude*, 18.

16   Auster in an interview with Mark Irwin, originally published as "Memory's Escape: Inventing the Music of Chance—A Conversation with Paul Auster," in *Denver Quarterly* 28:3 (Winter 1994): 111–22. Hereafter I will quote from it as republished in the recently released collection of interviews, *Conversations with Paul Auster*, ed. James M. Hutchisson (Jackson: University Press of Mississippi, 2013). See Irwin, "Memory's Escape," 43.

17   Interview with Irwin, "Memory's Escape," 43.

18   Deleuze and Guattari use two concepts borrowed from botany—arborescence and rhizomatics—to show two different ways of thinking. One is based in origins, genealogy and interpretation (and therefore Deleuze and Guattari call it the "root-tree"), the other in connections, dynamics and openness (that is the "canal rhizome"). See Gilles Deleuze and Félix Guattari, *A Thousand Plateaus: Capitalism and Schizophrenia*, transl. Brian Massumi (London: Continuum International Publishing Group, 2004).

19   Deleuze and Guattari, *Thousand Plateaus*, 4–5.

20   Foucault, *Archaeology of Knowledge*, 23.

21   Auster, *Invention of Solitude*, 161.

22   See Varvogli, *World That Is Book*; Roberta Rubenstein, "Doubling, Intertextuality, and the Postmodern Uncanny: Paul Auster's 'New York Trilogy'," *Lit: Literature Interpretation Theory* 9.3 (1998): 245–62; and Kifah (Moh'd Khair) Al Umari, "Intertextuality, Language, and Rationality in the Detective Fiction of Edgar Allan Poe and Paul Auster" (PhD diss., University of Texas at Arlington, 2006), among other works of criticism.

23   Banks, "Connection Exists," 150.

24   Banks, "Connection Exists," 150.

25   For the book, as Deleuze and Guattari explain, is an outgrowth without an obvious beginning or end, a "plateau," a "multiplicity connected to other multiplicities by superficial underground stems in such a way as to form or extend a rhizome ... Each plateau can be read starting anywhere and can be related to any other plateau." Deleuze and Guattari, *Thousand Plateaus*, 24.

26   Paul Auster, *White Spaces* (Barrytown, NY: Station Hill, 1980); here quoted as republished in Paul Auster, *Collected Poems* (Woodstock and New York: The Overlook Press, 2004), 157.

27   See, for example, Stephen Bernstein, "Auster's Sublime Closure: The Locked Room," in *Beyond the Red Notebook*, ed. Barone, 88–106; and William Lavender, "The Novel of Critical Engagement: Paul Auster's 'City of Glass'," *Contemporary Literature* 34.2 (1993): 219–39. In his attempt to identify the novel's point of view and solve its narrator/author problem, where the characters, narrators, author(s) and the writer constantly swap roles, Lavender concludes that such "[narrative] construction is

circular and seamless … The illusion is … one of infinity." See Lavender, "Novel of Critical Engagement," 223. See also John Zilcosky, "The Revenge of the Author: Paul Auster's Challenge to Theory," *Critique: Studies in Contemporary Fiction* 39.3 (1998): 195–206; Chris Tysh, "From One Mirror to Another: The Rhetoric of Disaffiliation" in 'City Of Glass' …," *The Review of Contemporary Fiction* 14.1 (1994): 46–72; Steven E. Alford, "Mirrors of Madness: Paul Auster's 'The New York Trilogy," *Critique: Studies in Contemporary Fiction* 37.1 (1995): 17–33; Madeleine Sorapure, "The Detective and the Author: 'City of Glass," in *Beyond the Red Notebook*, ed. Barone, 71–87; Brendan Martin, *Paul Auster's Postmodernity* (New York and London: Routledge, 2008); and Rubenstein, "Doubling, Intertextuality …," as more examples.

28   Dragana Nikolic, "Paul Auster's Postmodernist Fiction: Deconstructing Aristotle's 'Poetics'" (MA diss., The Queen Mary and Westfield College, University of London, 1998), published online at http://www.bluecricket.com/auster/articles/aristotle.html

29   Nikolic, "Auster's Postmodernist Fiction."

30   Paul Auster, "The Locked Room," in Auster, *New York Trilogy*, 346.

31   In fact, in Auster's oeuvre, similar multiplication of seemingly singular "stories" can also happen within a single text, such as his novel *Moon Palace*. Commenting on the life-stories of its three main characters, each of whom represent a different generation, Auster says in an interview with Larry McCaffery and Sinda Gregory: "There are three stories in the book, after all, and each one is finally the same." This interview, which started at Auster's home in Brooklyn in 1989 and continued through several phone conversations, appears in two slightly different published versions. It was first printed as "An Interview with Paul Auster" in *Mississippi Review* 20.1–2 (1991): 49–62, and a year later appeared in *Contemporary Literature* 33.1 (1992): 1–23. For the quote, see Larry McCaffery and Sinda Gregory, "An Interview with Paul Auster," in *Contemporary Literature*, 21 or *Mississippi Review*, 61.

32   Robert Briggs, "Wrong Numbers: The Endless Fiction of Auster and Deleuze and Guattari and …," *Critique: Studies in Contemporary Fiction* 44.2 (2003): 216.

33   In *City of Glass*, Quinn dreams of acquiring Stillman Sr.'s notebook because for him it "contained answers to the questions that had been accumulating in [Quinn's] mind" (Paul Auster, *City of Glass* (New York: Penguin Books, 1987), 95; or Paul Auster, "City of Glass," in Auster, *New York Trilogy*, 73). Later, at the end of the novel, it is the anonymous narrator of *City of Glass* who tries to decipher Quinn's diary. In the final book, *The Locked Room*, the notebook of the mysterious character Fanshawe is obtained by another nameless narrator (who meanwhile has become Fanshawe's "ghost" by taking over his identity and authorship of his works, and who also claims authorship of the previous two of the trilogy's books, *City of Glass* and *Ghosts*). When at the end of the book the narrator finally gets to meet and question Fanshawe, the latter responds—"[i]t's all [written] in the notebook." See Auster, "The Locked Room," *New York Trilogy*, 368.

34   I am not proposing anything new here. Briggs was one of the first critics to question the structural and ontological singularity of Auster's texts and their intricate mutual relationships, and to note the similarity with the Deleuzian rhizome. In 2010, Gary Matthew Varner wrote a thesis on Auster's rhizomatic fictions. But the first to note their resemblance with the rhizome's "pragmatics of self-difference" and the "logic of the AND" was Niall Lucy in his book *Postmodern Literary Theory: An Introduction* (1997). In the chapter introducing Deleuze and Guattari's concept of the rhizome (his primary point of interest), Lucy, like Briggs, uses Auster's *The New York Trilogy*

as an illustrative case. He notes that Auster's writing "forms a kind of radical-system or rhizome of interconnecting links and filaments to his own and other writer's texts." In this way, "none of his titles may be seen to stand alone (as a root-book), but each text carries traces of the others." Like Briggs and Banks, Lucy conducts a genealogical tracing of a few recurrent elements—in his case, characters named "Quinn," "Fanshawe," "MS Fogg" and "Zimmer"—to illustrate the "openness" and "a sort of multiplicity" of not only the identities of the characters, but also of what he calls "the undecidably coincidental or deliberate repetitions within and between his texts and those of other writers," and of entire ontological structures they construct. Naturally, he concludes that Auster's oeuvre should be approached "not through a notion of his texts as different or separate entities," but "in terms of the in-difference of the multiplicity of the text of writing." And he correctly notes that the openness of Auster's work calls for a loosening up on the part of criticism, which "must allow its findings to emerge pragmatically rather than be predetermined theoretically." Yet, one and a half decades later, his arguments remain largely unnoticed by Auster scholars and critics. See Niall Lucy, *Postmodern Literary Theory: An Introduction* (Oxford: Blackwell, 1997), 221–6.

35   I am referring here to Paul Auster's interview with Joseph Mallia, which has appeared in separate editions of *The Red Notebook* and another Auster collection of essays, *The Art of Hunger: Essays, Prefaces, Interviews,* and was originally published in the BOMB magazine as "Paul Auster Interview," *BOMB* 23 (1998): 24–7, http://www.bombsite.com/issues/23/articles/1062

36   *The Invention of Solitude* consists of two parts—"Portrait of an Invisible Man" and "The Book of Memory." The first part, written in the first-person narrative voice, contains Auster's memories and meditations on his absent father. The second, written as a third-person narrative, explores themes that Auster keeps returning to throughout his creative life—coincidence, loneliness, fate, fatherhood.

37   Among the countable red-notebook-related texts are *The New York Trilogy* (which is three stories and at the same time one textual entity); *The Red Notebook: True Stories, Prefaces and Interviews by the Author of The New York Trilogy and Mr. Vertigo*; a part which bears the title "The Red Notebook" and which itself consists of three other subparts; and so on. The different accounts of how the *City of Glass* story was set in motion by receiving a late phone call meant for a wrong addressee, in the novel itself and in Auster's memory in *The Red Notebook*, makes Briggs conclude there must be two *City of Glass* stories, multiplying the number of texts even further.

38   Mallia, "Paul Auster Interview," 26.

39   Briggs, "Wrong Numbers," 221.

40   Briggs, "Wrong Numbers," 221.

41   Briggs, "Wrong Numbers," 215.

42   Briggs, "Wrong Numbers," 221.

43   That is why biographical readings of Auster's texts fail. Looking at the author's life and body of work in order to discern the meaning of any given text can only lead to the recognition of connections established between the two realms. The fact that the book-loving protagonists of *Invisible* and *Moon Palace*, like Auster himself, have attended Columbia University does not significantly assist in the interpretative process, but only points back to the associations between Auster and his many stand-ins.

44 Varvogli, *World That Is Book*, 142; Ilana Shiloh, *Paul Auster and Postmodern Quest: On the Road to Nowhere* (New York: Peter Lang, 2002), 14 and 137.

45 Varvogli, *World That Is Book*, 142.

46 Banks, "Connection Exists," 153.

47 Deleuze and Guattari repeatedly remind the reader, "[d]on't go for the root, follow the canal ..." They direct their questions about texts not towards "what a book means, as signified or signifier," but rather "what it functions with, in connection with what other things it does or does not transmit intensities, in which other multiplicities than its own are inserted and metamorphosed ..." Deleuze and Guattari, *Thousand Plateaus*, 21 and 4.

48 Rheindorf, "Where Everything is Connected," 21.

49 Rheindorf, "Where Everything is Connected," 4.

50 One such motif that was abundantly explored in Auster criticism in the 1990s in particular was the figure of the detective and detection in shaping the narrative ontology of his early *The New York Trilogy*. For the critical essays on Auster's early "anti-detectives," see Charles Baxter, "The Bureau of Missing Persons: Notes on Paul Auster's Fiction," *The Review of Contemporary Fiction* 14.1 (1994): 40–3; Alison Russell, "Deconstructing 'The New York Trilogy': Paul Auster's Anti-Detective Fiction," *Critique: Studies in Contemporary Fiction* 31.2 (1990): 71–84; Norma Rowen, "The Detective in Search of the Lost Tongue of Adam: Paul Auster's 'City of Glass,'" *Critique: Studies in Contemporary Fiction* 32.4 (1991): 224–33; Rubenstein, "Doubling, Intertextuality ..."; Lavender, "Novel of Critical Engagement"; Barry Lewis, "Strange Case of Auster"; Jeffrey T. Nealon, "Work of the Detective, Work of the Writer: Paul Auster's 'City of Glass,'" *Modern Fiction Studies* 42.1 (1996): 91–110; and Sorapure, "Detective and the Author"; as well as later critical texts, such as Anne M. Holzapfel *"The New York Trilogy": Whodunit?: Tracking the Structure of Paul Auster's Anti-Detective Novels* (Frankfurt am Main: Peter Lang, 1996); Cameron Golden, "From Punishment to Possibility: Re-Imagining Hitchcockian Paradigms in 'The New York Trilogy,'" *Mosaic: A Journal for the Interdisciplinary Study of Literature* 37.3 (2004): 93–108; William G. Little, "Nothing to Go On: Paul Auster's 'City of Glass,'" *Contemporary Literature* 38.1 (1997): 133–63; and Dan Holmes, "Paul Auster's Deconstruction of the Traditional Hard-Boiled Detective Narrative in 'The New York Trilogy,'" *Crimeculture* (2006), http://www.crimeculture.com/Contents/Articles-Summer05/DanHolmes.html; among others.

51 Varvogli, *World That is Book*, 12.

52 Carsten (Carl) Springer, *Crises: The Works of Paul Auster* (Frankfurt am Main: Peter Lang), 2001; Mark Brown, *Paul Auster* (Manchester and New York: Manchester University Press), 2007.

53 Springer looks at the corpus of Auster's novels, plays, poems, autobiographical writings, essays and film scripts published up to 1999, which, he says, always involve searches for identity and crises experienced at different stages of life. See Auster's *The Invention of Solitude, City of Glass, Ghosts, The Book of Illusions, Oracle Night, In the Country of Last Things* as examples, and we could also add his later texts here, e.g. *The Brooklyn Follies, Travels in the Scriptorium*.

54 Shiloh, *Auster and Postmodern Quest*, 199.

55 Brown, *Paul Auster*, 5.

56 Brown, *Paul Auster*, 2.

57 As Auster says in an interview with Mark Irwin: "the degree [to which] the writer does *not* understand [the irreducible elements that a book is made of] … is the degree to which the book is allowed to become itself, to become a human and not just a literary exercise" (his emphasis). Interview with Irwin, "Memory's Escape," 43.

58 Auster himself has claimed that all his novels are actually the same book and that each new work represents an answer to its predecessor (see Auster's interview with Gérard de Cortanze, "Le monde est dans ma tête, mon corps est dans le monde," *Magazine Littéraire* 338 (Décembre 1995): 18–25. Translated by Carl-Carsten Springer as "The World Is in My Head; My Body Is in the World," http://www.stuartpilkington.co.uk/paulauster/gerarddecortanze.htm) And, as he admits in interviews elsewhere, whenever he starts a new book he wants to "reinvent [himself], to work against everything [he] made before," to "turn up and destroy all [the] previous work" and to "take a different approach" (see Auster's interview with Gabriel Esquivada, "Interview Paul Auster Writer: 'I want to reinvent myself in every new novel," *Cuba now.net*, Cuban Art and Culture, http://www.cubanow.net/pages/loader.php?sec=7&t=2&item=1077; and the interview with Jonathan Lethem, "Jonathan Lethem [Writer] Talks with Paul Auster [Writer]," *The Believer* (February 2005), http://www.believermag.com/issues/200502/?read=interview_auster). Yet, in spite of these recurring "reinventions," all that one discovers, as Auster himself has had to admit, are one's "old obsessions" and "all the maniacal repetitions of how [one] think[s]," a statement that is proven to be true by his own intratext (Lethem, "Lethem Talks with Auster"). Therefore, for critics, Auster's characters tend to be the same while appearing in "different manifestations, different permutations"; see Auster in an interview with Marc Chénetier, "Around Moon Palace. A Conversation with Paul Auster," *Revue d'Études Anglophones* 1 (1996): 5. (Chénetier also wrote a monograph on *Moon Palace*, entitled *Paul Auster as "the Wizard of Odds": Moon Palace* (1996). See Bibliography for details.)

59 Deleuze and Guattari, *Thousand Plateaus*, 22.

60 Deleuze and Guattari, *Thousand Plateaus*, 22.

61 Deleuze and Guattari, *Thousand Plateaus*, 22.

62 Deleuze and Guattari, *Thousand Plateaus*, 22–3.

63 De Landa about the Deleuzian assemblages in Manuel de Landa, *A New Philosophy of Society: Assemblage Theory and Social Complexity* (London and New York: Continuum, 2007), 11.

64 Deleuze and Guattari, *Thousand Plateaus*, 22.

65 Bruno Latour, *Reassembling the Social: An Introduction to Actor-Network-Theory* (Oxford: Oxford University Press, 2007), 12.

66 See Brian McHale's essay "Poetry as Prosthesis," in *Poetics Today* 21.1 (Spring 2000), 1–32.

67 Banks, "Connection Exists," 165. Banks never engages with Deleuze's philosophy, but her description of the characters' elastic relationships that also define them suggests a Deleuzian understanding of the dynamic assemblage. For Deleuze, and unwittingly at times for Auster himself (as in *The Invention of Solitude*), the assemblage is not a sum of its particulars, but is defined through the relationships between those. Instead of foregrounding the properties inherent in things themselves, Deleuze would rather focus on the "capacities" of things, their qualities that only become manifest once they start to interact with other elements. Although in this book we are likewise interested in exploring the dynamics of assemblages, we will depart

from this radical view to engage in the more arborescent readings of the social histories of things. See also Manuel de Landa, "Assemblages against Totalities," in *A New Philosophy of Society: Assemblage Theory and Social Complexity* (London and New York: Continuum, 2007), 10–11.

68 Banks, "Connection Exists," 165.

69 Curtis White, "The Auster Instance: A Ficto-Biography," *The Review of Contemporary Fiction* 14.1 (1994): 26.

70 De Landa discussing Anthony Giddens in de Landa, "Assemblages Against Totalities," 9–10.

71 De Landa, "Assemblages Against Totalities," 10.

72 Briggs, "Wrong Numbers," 214.

73 Briggs, "Wrong Numbers," 214.

74 Deleuze and Guattari, *Thousand Plateaus*, 25.

75 Auster's work abounds with biographical details and characters whose names resemble those of Auster and his family. In "The Book of Memory," Auster talks about the protagonist A.'s wife Dahlia (similarity with the name of Auster's first wife Lydia) and son David (spelling similar to Daniel, the name of Auster's son from the first marriage); in *City of Glass*, the private eye/writer named Paul Auster is married to Siri (the "real" Auster's wife is called Siri Hustvedt) and they have a son, Daniel; in *Leviathan*, Peter Aaron (who has the same initials as Paul Auster) marries Iris ("Siri" in reverse); in *Oracle Night*, the protagonist is a writer named John Trause (whose surname is an anagram of Auster), and so on. See Carsten (Carl) Springer's *A Paul Auster Sourcebook* (Frankfurt am Main: Peter Lang, 2001) for an extensive list.

76 Adrian Gargett, "Cruel Universe," *Spike Magazine* (online magazine/weblog), posted on November 1, 2002, http://www.spikemagazine.com/1102paulauster.php

77 See Auster's interview with McCaffery and Gregory, "Interview with Auster," *Contemporary Literature*, 3; or *Mississippi Review*, 51.

78 Another way to understand it would be via Varvogli's explanation of Auster's "deceptive realism." She notes that "to claim that [his] books come out of 'the world' and not out of other books is a very problematic statement" as it presupposes a clearly drawn distinction between "the world and the word," between lived experience and "books." She rightly mistrusts Auster as "the evidence from [his] fiction seems to contradict rather than support his statement." For her, even if characters, things and incidents in Auster's texts come from "real life," the effect is one of "deceptive realism." See Varvogli, *World That Is Book*, 6.

79 For the Auster quote, see Paul Auster, *Man in the Dark* (New York: Henry Colt and Company, 2008), 69.

80 Auster, *Man in Dark*, 69.

81 Antoine Traisnel, "Storytelling in Paul Auster's Movies" (BA diss., Université Charles de Gaulle – Lille 3, 2002), http://angellier.biblio.univ-lille3.fr/etudes_recherches/memoire_antoine_traisnel.html

82 Deleuze and Guattari, *Thousand Plateaus*, 13.

83 Banks, "Connection Exists," 151.

84 Auster, *City of Glass*, 94.

85 Auster, *City of Glass*, 112.

86 Auster, *City of Glass*, 112.

87 Igors Šuvajevs' afterword to the Latvian edition of Umberto Eco's novel *The Name*

of the Rose. See Šuvajevs, "Eko vārds," in Umberto Eko, *Rozes vārds* (Rīga: J. Rozes apgāds, 1998), 693 (my translation).

88 Šuvajevs, "Eko vārds," 693 (my translation). Here, Šuvajevs also quotes Eco from his *Semiotics and the Philosophy of Language.*

89 Šuvajevs, "Eko vārds," 693 (my translation).

90 Umberto Eco in *The Name of the Rose: Including the Author's Postscript*, transl. William Weaver (New York: Harvest Books, 1994), 526.

91 Deleuze and Guattari, *Thousand Plateaus*, 16.

92 It is only recently that Auster's critics have started to recognize the significance of his non-novelistic work, the scope of his oeuvre, and its interconnectivity. A good example is the 2011 collection of essays, edited by Stefania Ciocia and Jesús Ángel González, *The Invention of Illusions: International Perspectives on Paul Auster*, which we could also rename "Inter(disciplinary) Perspectives." See, for example, Ulrich Meurer's "Life Transmission: Paul Auster's Merging Worlds, Media and Authors" or the aforementioned essay by Banks, "Connection Exists." Auster scholars are increasingly becoming aware that not only are his multidisciplinary texts "repetitive," "uncontainable" and internally "intertextual," but that, in fact, his entire oeuvre functions as a rhizome and needs to be read as such.

93 Deleuze and Guattari, *Thousand Plateaus*, 9.

Chapter 1: Smoke that Means the Entire World

1 For the quotes given in this passage, see the following Auster texts: Auster, *City of Glass*, 7; Auster, *Invention of Solitude*, 3; Paul Auster, *The Book of Illusions* (New York: Henry Holt and Company, 2002), 1; Paul Auster, *Oracle Night* (New York: Henry Holt and Company, 2003), 1; Auster, *In the Country of Last Things*, 1. See also Paul Auster, *Leviathan* (London: Faber and Faber, 2004); and Paul Auster, *Mr. Vertigo* (London: Faber and Faber, 1994).

2 Gilles Deleuze and Félix Guattari, *Kafka: Towards a Minor Literature*, transl. Dana Polan (Minneapolis and London: University of Minnesota Press, 2003), 3.

3 Deleuze and Guattari, *Kafka*, 3.

4 Umberto Eco, *Semiotics and the Philosophy of Language* (Bloomington, IN: Indiana University Press, 1986), 81.

5 Auster in the interview with Lethem, "Lethem Talks with Auster."

6 Auster in an interview with Annette Insdorf, "The Making of Smoke," in Paul Auster, *Smoke & Blue in the Face: Two Films* (New York: Miramax Books / Hyperion, 1995), 13.

7 Auster in the interview with Insdorf, "Making of Smoke," 13.

8 Auster, *City of Glass*, 24.

9 Latour calls it "the only viable slogan" of ANT (see *Reassembling the Social*, 12, 61, 121, 179, 227, etc.).

10 I am borrowing this phrasing from Richard Corliss' article "That Old Feeling: The Great American Smoke," published in *Time* magazine, Saturday, November 22, 2003, http://www.time.com/time/arts/article/0,8599,548824,00.html

11 Umberto Eco used this phrase to refer to Humphrey Bogart's chain-smoking character of Rick Blaine in the motion picture *Casablanca*. Here, quoted in Richard Klein, *Cigarettes Are Sublime* (London: Picador, 1995), 200.

12 Klein, *Cigarettes*, 22.

13 Klein, *Cigarettes*, 26.

14 Klein, *Cigarettes*, 26–7.

15 Klein, *Cigarettes*, 26.

16 See the chapter "Zeno's Paradox," in Klein, *Cigarettes*. Orig. "La coscienza di Zeno," or literally "the conscience of Zeno," although, in some editions, the title has been translated into English as "The Confessions of Zeno." For a more recent edition with a new translation from the Italian, see Italo Svevo, *Zeno's Conscience: A Novel*, transl. William Weaver (New York: Vintage International, 2003).

17 Klein, *Cigarettes*, 91.

18 Wolfgang, Schivelbusch, "Tobacco: The Dry Inebriant," in *Tastes of Paradise: A Social History of Spices, Stimulants and Intoxicants* (New York: Vintage Books, 1993), 96. Schivelbusch notes that tobacco was an unusual source of pleasure also due to the unorthodox mode of its consumption. The term "smoking" only appeared in the course of the seventeenth century, and up until then nobody knew how to call what one did with tobacco. One spoke of "drinking smoke," while tobacco itself was referred to as a sort of dry intoxicant, or dry alcohol (Schivelbusch, "Tobacco," 97).

19 Nick Tosches, in the introduction to *Literary Las Vegas: The Best Writing about America's Most Fabulous City*, ed. Mike Tronnes (New York: Henry Holt and Company, 1995), here quoted in Corliss, "Great American Smoke."

20 Klein, *Cigarettes*, 21.

21 See Auster's interview with Irwin, "Memory's Escape," 41.

22 Paul Auster, *Leviathan*, 221.

23 Martin, *Auster's Postmodernity*, 11.

24 Paul Auster, *Moon Palace* (New York: Penguin Books, 1990), 232.

25 Auster, *City of Glass*, 160.

26 Dawn Marlan, "Emblems of Emptiness: Smoking as a Way of Life in Jean Eustache's 'La Maman et la Putain'," in *Smoke: A Global History of Smoking*, eds Sander L. Gilman and Zhou Xun (London: Reaktion Books, 2004), 256.

27 Here Auster quotes Antonin Artaud, whose poetry he has translated. See Paul Auster, "The Art of Hunger," in *The Art of Hunger: Essays, Prefaces, Interviews* (New York: Penguin Books, 2001), 9.

28 Auster, "Art of Hunger," 14 and 12.

29 Auster, "Art of Hunger," 12.

30 See also Marlan, "Emblems of Emptiness," 258.

31 As Schivelbusch points out, it is actually the smoking-induced calming of the physical body that allows the smoker to "wor[k] off those functionless, indeed dysfunctional bodily energies that had formerly been released in the physical work" and transfer them into mental activity—thinking. See Schivelbusch, "Tobacco," 111.

32 Schivelbusch, "Tobacco," 107.

33 Klein, *Cigarettes*, 9.

34 Klein, *Cigarettes*, 9.

35 Klein, *Cigarettes*, 9.

36 Auster in the conversation with McCaffery and Gregory, "Interview with Auster," *Contemporary Literature*, 18.

37 Klein, *Cigarettes*, 32.

38 Luc Sante, "Our Friend the Cigarette," in Sante, *Kill All Your Darlings: Pieces, 1990–2005*, introduced by Greil Marcus (Portland: Yeti, 2007), 93. The essay,

originally written and published untitled to accompany Sante's volume of smoking-related photographs and images, *No Smoking* (New York: Assouline, 2004), was later re-published in the retrospective collection of his essays. Because pages in *No Smoking* are unnumbered, for more convenient referencing I will be citing the 2007 edition.

39   Marlan, "Emblems of Emptiness," 260.

40   Auster, *City of Glass*, 11.

41   Auster, *City of Glass*, 63.

42   Auster, *City of Glass*, 136.

43   Auster, *City of Glass*, 24.

44   Barone, "Introduction," in *Beyond the Red Notebook*, 14.

45   Auster, *City of Glass*, 155.

46   Such a twofold interpretation of the figure of the smoking writer is not necessarily self-contradictory if one recalls the symbolic meanings of smoking as represented in seventeenth-century Dutch paintings. A pipe was often used in artist's self-portraits, where its meaning depended on how the artist (and his pipe) was positioned in the frame. As Benno Tempel explains, "When the artist is seen smoking with his back turned to an empty canvas, it stresses that he is wasting his time; when the artist is facing the canvas, the implication is that smoking brings inspiration." See Benno Tempel, "Symbol and Image: Smoking in Art since the Seventeenth Century," in *Smoke: Global History*, eds Gilman and Xun, 207.

47   Auster, *City of Glass*, 194.

48   Elizabeth Grosz discussing Henri Bergson's *Creative Evolution* (*L'Evolution créatrice*). See Grosz, "The Thing," in *The Object Reader*, eds Fiona Candlin and Raiford Guins (London and New York: Routledge, 2009), 129.

49   Richard Polt, "Typology: A Phenomenology of Early Typewriters," in The Classic Typewriter Page, http://site.xavier.edu/polt/typewriters/typology.html. (Originally presented at the Back to the Things Themselves conference, Southern Illinois University at Carbondale, March 1996.)

50   Tempel, "Symbol and Image," 210.

51   Tempel, "Symbol and Image," 210.

52   In *Smoke*, for example, Paul Benjamin tells two stories that are directly linked to tobacco and the habit of smoking. One of these stories is told in the cigar shop.

53   Klein, *Cigarettes*, 10.

54   Klein on the Sartrean cigarette, *Cigarettes*, 32.

55   Schivelbusch, "Tobacco," 105.

56   Schivelbusch, "Tobacco," 105.

57   Schivelbusch, "Tobacco," 107.

58   Here, Jean-Paul Sartre is quoted from his 1943 philosophical text *L'Être et le néant: Essai d'ontologie phénoménologique* (Paris: Gallimard, 1943), in Klein, *Cigarettes*, 37 (Klein's translation). Sartre's essay was first published in English in Hazel Barnes' translation as *Being and Nothingness: An Essay on Phenomenological Ontology* in 1956.

59   Klein, also quoting Sartre, *Cigarettes*, 38 (Klein's translation).

60   Stéphane Mallarmé, *Œuvres complètes* (Paris: Gallimard, 1945), 73; here quoted in Klein's translation in his *Cigarettes*, 64–5 (Klein's translation).

61   Corliss, "Great American Smoke."

62 Klein, *Cigarettes*, 48.

63 Paul Auster, "Smoke," in *Smoke & Blue in the Face: Two Films* (New York: Miramax Books / Hyperion, 1995), 15.

64 Auster, *Smoke & Blue*, back cover.

65 Claire appears in both the story-within-story of *The Book of Illusions*, and also in the film itself, although White in particular talks about the *mise en abyme* story from the novel.

66 Timothy Bewes, "Against the Ontology of the Present: Paul Auster's Cinematographic Fictions," in *Twentieth Century Literature* 53.3 (2007): 292.

67 Auster, "Smoke," in *Smoke & Blue*, 35.

68 Klein, *Cigarettes*, 71.

69 Pierre Louÿs, *Œuvres complètes: Contes* (Paris: Montaigne, 1930), 65–6, quoted in Klein, *Cigarettes*, 70 (Klein's translation).

70 This quote is taken from Insdorf's interview with Auster, "Making of Smoke," 15. Auster also used the name of Paul Benjamin when publishing his first novel, the hard-boiled detective *Squeeze Play*, back in 1984.

71 Paul Auster in a telephone interview conducted with Jill Owens on January 18, 2007, and published as "Author Interviews: The Book of Paul Auster," on Powells Books website, http://www.powells.com/authors/auster.html

72 Owens, "Author Interviews."

73 Auster, *Winter Journal*, 15.

74 Auster, *Winter Journal*, 15.

75 Sante, "Our Friend Cigarette," 93.

76 Klein, *Cigarettes*, 153.

77 Erich Maria Remarque, *Im Westen nichts Neues* (Cologne: Kiepenheuer un Witsch, 1990), 110–11; here quoted by Klein in his *Cigarettes*, 153 (Klein's translation).

78 Martin Heidegger, "The Thing," in *The Object Reader*, eds Fiona Candlin and Raiford Guins (London and New York: Routledge, 2009), 113–23.

79 Richard Aczel, Márton Fernezelyi, Robert Koch and Zoltan Szegedy-Maszak, "Reflections on a Table," in *Making Things Public: Atmospheres of Democracy*, eds Bruno Latour and Peter Weibel (Germany: Center for Art and Media Karslruhe and Cambridge: Massachusetts Institute of Technology, 2005), 204.

80 Auster, "Blue in the Face," in *Smoke & Blue*, 191.

81 Aczel et al., "Reflections on Table."

82 As Auster says in an interview with Carlos Graieb—"*Smoke* is, without doubt, the lightest and most optimistic thing that I've ever written." See Carlos Graieb, "Auster Creates His Universe in a Brooklyn Apartment" / "Auster cria seu universo em sobrado do Brooklyn," transl. Carl-Carsten Springer and Ricardo Miranda, and published at Paul Auster: The Definitive Website, http://www.stuartpilkington.co.uk/paulauster/carlosgraieb.htm

83 Latour, *Reassembling the Social*, 5.

84 See Donald Hall, "No Smoking," in *Playboy*, November 25, 2012, http://www.playboy.com/playground/view/no-smoking

85 Auster, *Winter Journal*, 183.

86 Grosz, "The Thing," 125.

87 Sante, *No Smoking*, back cover.

88 Sante, *No Smoking*, back cover.

89 Corliss, "Great American Smoke."

90 V.G. Kiernan, *Tobacco: A History* (London: Hutchinson Radius, 1991). Here, quoted from "Prologue: The Way We Smoke Now," in *The Faber Book of Smoking*, ed. James Walton (London: Faber and Faber, 2000), 5.

91 The words by Charles LeMaistre, former president of the American Cancer Society. He is quoted here by William G. Cahan, who in his foreword to David Krogh's *Smoking: The Artificial Passion* talks about "the shocking example[s] of the power of nicotine addiction," and the devastating effects of it that he has witnessed as a surgeon in a cancer hospital. See Cahan's "Foreword," in David Krogh, *Artificial Passion* (New York and Oxford: W.H. Freeman and Company, 1997.), ix-xi.

92 González, "Words Versus Images: Paul Auster's Films from 'Smoke' to 'The Book of Illusions,'" *Literature/Film Quarterly* 37.1 (2009), 37-8.

93 Klein, *Cigarettes*, 85-6.

94 Klein, *Cigarettes*, 137.

95 Klein, *Cigarettes*, 152.

96 Paul Auster, "Gotham Handbook," in Sophie Calle, *Double Game* (London: Violette Editions, 1999), page 2 of the typescript. When citing from the letter with instructions that Auster wrote for Calle and that has also been included in *Double Game* under the section "Gotham Handbook," I will indicate the page number that appears on the upper corner of Auster's letter in typescript. When referring to Auster's text for "Gotham Handbook," I will indicate him as author. And when referring to Calle's response texts to his instructions, I will acknowledge her authorship in the project (Calle, "Gotham Handbook"). Where available, I will also cite the original page numbers of *Double Game* (e.g., Calle, "Gotham Handbook," 246).

97 Auster, "Gotham Handbook," 2.

98 Auster, "Gotham Handbook," 2.

99 Sante, "Our Friend Cigarette," 90.

100 Klein brings to our attention here an episode in Hemingway's *For Whom the Bell Tolls* where Robert Jordan, while smoking near the bridge that he is supposed to blow up, observes his enemy smoking on the other side of the bridge, and feels slightly disheartened by his sudden recognition that he can actually relate to the smoking man. See Klein, *Cigarettes*, 149-50.

101 Klein, *Cigarettes*, 150.

102 Faustino Domingo Sarmiento *Viajes por Europa, Africa y Norte América—1845/1847* (Buenos Aires: Stockcero, 2003; first published in 1849); here quoted in *Faber Book of Smoking*, 227.

103 Jeffrey Bernard in his "Last Word," in *The Forest Guide to Smoking in London*, James Leavey (London: Quiller Press, 1996), here quoted in *Faber Book of Smoking*, 214.

104 González, "Words Versus Images," 30.

105 González, "Words Versus Images," 30.

106 Paul Auster, *Invisible* (London: Faber and Faber, 2009), 163.

107 Auster, *Winter Journal*, 183-4.

108 Sander L. Gilman and Zhou Xun, "Introduction," in *Smoke: Global History*, 23. The right to smoke for women has always been associated with the struggle for gender equality. Between the seventeenth and nineteenth centuries, rebellious women insisted on their right to smoke (and so became a subject of caricature), which was, according to Schivelbusch, "demanded as much as the right to wear trousers" (Schivelbusch, "Tobacco," 120). Throughout the history of tobacco, any sort of

oppression has often been accompanied by a restriction or ban on smoking, so that smoking itself, at least for particular social groups, becomes a symbol of resistance and rebellion and an expression of personal rights and freedom.

109 Schivelbusch, "Tobacco," 125–9.

110 Schivelbusch, "Tobacco," 129.

111 Schivelbusch also quotes historian Egon C. Corti's *A History of Smoking* to give an example from Germany's Vormärz era where smoking in public assumed an important role, while the authorities viewed it as a sign of political rebellion: "Just as someone who wore a felt hat instead of the then fashionable top hat was suspected of harboring revolutionary ideas, every smoker seen on the street was suspected of being a dangerous democrat." See Schivelbusch, "Tobacco," 129.

112 Corliss, "Great American Smoke."

113 Auster instructs Calle: "Don't just give [to beggars] one or two [cigarettes]. Give whole packs." See Auster, "Gotham Handbook," 3.

114 Auster, "Gotham Handbook," 3.

115 Klein, *Cigarettes*, 187.

116 V. G. Kiernan, *Tobacco: A History*; cited from *Faber Book of Smoking*, 5.

117 Eric Burns, *The Smoke of the Gods: A Social History of Tobacco* (Philadelphia: Temple University Press, 2006), 129.

118 Jonathan Jones, "It's About Knowing You'll Die," *The Guardian*, Monday 14, May 2007, http://www.guardian.co.uk/artanddesign/2007/may/14/art

119 Jones, "It's About Knowing You'll Die."

120 Corliss, "Great American Smoke."

121 Auster, "Art of Hunger," 20.

122 These often-quoted words have been popularly attributed to Sir Walter Raleigh.

123 Gene Borio, "The Seventeenth Century—'The Great Age of the Pipe'," in *Tobacco History Timeline*, 1993–2003, Tobacco.org, http://www.tobacco.org/resources/history/Tobacco_History17.html; Sir Walter Raleigh's smoking articles are also presented in Schivelbusch's study "Tobacco," 109, where he notes that the inscription on the inside of the tobacco case that speaks about the "those times of distress," or "most miserable time," refers to Raleigh's imprisonment in the Tower of London between 1603 and 1616.

124 Auster, *Country of Last Things*, 109–10.

125 Auster, *Man in Dark*, 73.

126 González, "Words Versus Images," 37–8.

127 Auggie to Vinnie, in Auster, "Blue in the Face," in *Smoke & Blue*, 190–1.

128 Auster, "Blue in the Face," in *Smoke & Blue*, 193.

129 Auster in the interview with Insdorf, "Making of Smoke," 15.

130 Referring to the iconic position that the cigarette has occupied in American culture, Allan M. Brandt, who in his study of tobacco marketing and legislation in the United States in the twentieth century looks at smoking from a different vantage point, muses: "It seems striking that a product of such little utility, ephemeral in its very nature, could be such an encompassing vehicle for understanding the past." A small thing such as a cigarette tells not only stories, but entire "histories." See Allan M. Brandt, "Introduction," in *The Cigarette Century: The Rise, Fall and Deadly Persistence of the Product that Defined America* (New York: Basic Books, 2007), 2–3.

131 Sante, "Our Friend Cigarette," 92–3.

132 Sante, "Our Friend Cigarette," 93.

133 Sante, "Our Friend Cigarette," 93.

134 Sante, "Our Friend Cigarette," 86.

135 Klein, *Cigarettes*, 182; also quoted in Sante, *No Smoking.*

136 Klein, *Cigarettes*, 182; also quoted in Sante, *No Smoking.*

137 Keitel in an interview with Kenneth M. Chanko, "Smoke Gets in Their Eyes," *Entertainment Weekly* 281–2, June 30, 1995, http://www.ew.com/ew/article/0,,297840,00.html

138 Martin Heidegger, *Being and Time*, transl. John Macquarrie and Edward Robinson (New York: Harper Perennial Modern Classics, 2008).

139 Auster, "Smoke," in *Smoke & Blue*, 24.

140 Auster, "Smoke," in *Smoke & Blue*, 24.

141 Gilman and Xun, "Introduction," in *Smoke: Global History*, 9.

142 Gilman and Xun, "Introduction," in *Smoke: Global History*, 17.

143 Auster, "Blue in the Face," in *Smoke & Blue*, 229–30.

144 Unlike *Blue in the Face*, however, Jarmusch's film is a compilation of shorter segments of earlier films, made over a period of 17 years.

145 Aczel, et al., "Reflections on Table," 205.

146 Aczel, et al., "Reflections on Table," 205.

147 These semi-fictional stories intervene with the film's main events, creating a typically Austeresque diegetic world which is sustained by inter- and intra-textual stories that also serve to move the plot forward. One such example is the episode in which Paul Benjamin tells Rashid the story of Bakhtin and afterwards discovers the stolen money that the boy has hidden behind a book on Bakhtin. Another one is Auggie's Christmas story that liberates Paul from his writer's block.

148 Auster, "Smoke," in *Smoke & Blue*, 69.

149 Auster, "Smoke," in *Smoke & Blue*, 75.

150 On the other hand, we could also view the hook-handed Cyrus and the eye-patched Ruby as pastiche characters that represent the urban eccentricity of the cultural melting pot that is Brooklyn. They are very traditional second-role players in Auster's works in general, typically more eccentric than the story's central (writer-) character (in this case, Paul Benjamin). If an Auster protagonist tends to appear as somewhat one-dimensional and "ordinary," then the secondary players are unarguably more lively, interesting and unusual. Just think about the marginal characters in such novels as *Moon Palace* (the old millionaire Effing), *The Brooklyn Follies* (the bookstore owner Harry Brightman), *The Music of Chance* (its two eccentric millionaires, Flower and Stone), *Book of Illusions* (the "legendary" silent film comedian Hector Mann), and, of course, *City of Glass* (the two Peter Stillman characters, and the *femme fatale* Virginia Stillman), which often contrast with Auster's traditional writer-figure.

151 Auster, "Smoke," in *Smoke & Blue*, 149.

152 Paul Auster in conversation with Larry McCaffery and Sinda Gregory, "An Interview with Auster," *Mississippi Review*, 51.

153 Auster, "Smoke," in *Smoke & Blue*, 43.

154 Paul Auster in an interview with Joe Dziemianowicz, "Lights, Camera, Cigars!" in *Cigar Aficionado* (1995). http://www.cigaraficionado.com/Cigar/CA_Archives/CA_Show_Article/0,2322,719,00.html

155 As Michael Holquist calls it in his introduction to the Bakhtin collection *Speech Genres and Other Late Essays*. Curiously, Bakhtin started smoking pages from

the end, the manuscript's conclusion, leaving a small part of the opening section (primarily on Goethe). See Holquist, "Introduction," in Mikhail Mikhaïlovich Bakhtin, *Speech Genres and Other Late Essays*, transl. Vern W. McGee, eds Michael Holquist, Caryl Emerson (Austin: University of Texas Press, 1986), xiii.

156 Auster, "Smoke," in *Smoke & Blue*, 102.

157 Gary Saul Morson, "The Baxtin Industry," *The Slavic and East European Journal* 30.1 (Spring 1986): 87.

158 See the interview with Insdorf, "Making of Smoke," 6.

159 Insdorf, "Making of Smoke," 6.

160 Insdorf, "Making of Smoke," 5–6.

161 Insdorf, "Making of Smoke," 6.

162 Insdorf. "Making of Smoke," 6.

163 As Tempel remarks in his essay, "Tobacco smoke is strikingly frequent in representations of the five senses. Besides standing for smell, it can also be a symbol of taste." See Tempel, "Symbol and Image," 208.

164 Auster in conversation with McCaffery and Gregory, "Interview with Auster," *Contemporary Literature*, 22; also in *Mississippi Review*, 57.

165 Nikolic, "Auster's Postmodernist Fiction."

166 Nikolic, also quoting from Auster's *The Art of Hunger*, in "Auster's Postmodernist Fiction."

167 Insdorf, "Making of Smoke," 6.

168 Paul Auster in an interview on *Smoke* with Chris Peachment from *The Independent*. See Chris Peachment, "Give the Man a Cigar," *The Independent*, 7 March 1996, http://www.independent.co.uk/arts-entertainment/give-the-man-a-cigar-1340694.html

169 Peachment, "Give Man a Cigar."

170 Auster, "Smoke," in *Smoke & Blue*, 44.

171 Wayne Wang in the interview with Dziemianowicz, "Lights, Camera, Cigars!"

172 Tempel, "Symbol and Image," 210.

173 Tempel, "Symbol and Image," 210.

174 Sante, "Our Friend Cigarette," 95.

175 Paul Auster in an interview with Juliet Linderman, "A Connoisseur of Clouds, a Meteorologist of Whims: The Rumpus Interview with Paul Auster," in *The Rumpus*, November 16, 2009, http://therumpus.net/2009/11/a-connoisseur-of-clouds-a-meteorologist-of-whims-the-rumpus-interview-with-paul-auster/

176 See Auster interviews with Linderman and Lethem, as well as George Dunford, "An Interview with Paul Auster," *Cordite Poetry Review*, 2 August 2008, http://cordite.org.au/interviews/paul-auster; and Michael Wood, "Paul Auster, The Art of Fiction No. 178," *The Paris Review* 167 (2003): 58–89, http://www.theparisreview.org/interviews/121/the-art-of-fiction-no-178-paul-auster; among others.

177 Paul Auster, Sam Messer, *The Story of My Typewriter* (New York: D.A.P./Distributed Art Publishers, 2002), 10.

Chapter 2: The Story of the Typewriter

1 Deleuze and Guattari, *Thousand Plateaus*, 36–7.
2 Auster, "Smoke," in *Smoke & Blue*, 28.
3 Paul Auster, "Ghosts," in Auster, *New York Trilogy*, 175.
4 Auster, "Ghosts," 219.
5 See Auster's interviews with Linderman ("Connoisseur of Clouds") and Lethem ("Lethem Talks with Auster"), in which he talks about his working habits and workspace.
6 Auster, *Winter Journal*, 106–7.
7 Friedrich A. Kittler quoting Martin Heidegger, whose essay "On the Hand and the Typewriter" (1942–3) has been included in Friedrich A. Kittler, *Gramophone, Film, Typewriter*, transl. and introduced by Geoffrey Winthrop-Young and Michael Wutz (Stanford, CA: Stanford University Press, 1999), 198–200. See also Kittler, *Gramophone, Film, Typewriter*, 183.
8 Kittler quoting Heidegger, *Gramophone, Film, Typewriter*, 183; also Heidegger's essay in *Gramophone, Film, Typewriter*, 199–200.
9 Martin A. Rice, "Amor me Jubit Mechanoscribere (Love Bids me Type)," in *Typewriter Tributes*, The Classic Typewriter Page, http://site.xavier.edu/polt/typewriters/rice.pdf, 2.
10 Kittler, *Gramophone, Film, Typewriter*, 186–7.
11 Polt, "Typology."
12 Polt, "Typology."
13 Darren Wershler-Henry, *The Iron Whim: A Fragmented History of Typewriting* (Ithaca, NY: Cornell University Press, 2007), 36–7.
14 Wershler-Henry, *Iron Whim*, 37.
15 Rice, "Amor me …," 2.
16 Paul Auster in the interview with Wood, "Art of Fiction No. 178."
17 Interview with Wood, "Art of Fiction No. 178."
18 Interview with Wood, "Art of Fiction No. 178."
19 Interview with Wood, "Art of Fiction No. 178."
20 Polt, "Typology."
21 Polt, "Typology."
22 Both in Auster and Messer, *Story of My Typewriter*, 21.
23 Rice, "Amor me …," 1.
24 Rice, "Amor me …," 2.
25 Auster and Messer, *Story of My Typewriter*, 16.
26 Paul Auster, *Winter Journal*, 106–7.
27 Auster in the interview with Wood, "Art of Fiction No. 178."
28 Rice, "Amor me …," 1.
29 Quoted from Wershler-Henry, *Iron Whim*, 43.
30 Wershler-Henry, *Iron Whim*, 44.
31 Insdorf, "Making of Smoke," 15.
32 Initially, when offered this cameo appearance in *The Music of Chance*, Paul Auster wanted to refuse and accepted the offer later rather reluctantly.
33 Wershler-Henry, *Iron Whim*, 263.
34 Paul Auster in a video interview with Austin Allen, "When Literary Games Get Personal." *Big Think*, November 5, 2009, http://bigthink.com/ideas/17290

35 See, for example, Nicholas Carr's article "Is Google Making Us Stupid?" in *Atlantic Monthly* (July/August 2008), http://www.theatlantic.com/magazine/archive/2008/07/is-google-making-us-stupid/6868/; or Sven Birkerts' *The Gutenberg Elegies: The Fate of Reading in an Electronic Age* (New York: Faber and Faber, 2006).

36 Rice, "Amor me ...," 1.

37 Rice, "Amor me ...," 1.

38 Rice, "Amor me ...," 1.

39 Rice, "Amor me ...," 1.

40 Auster in the interview with Wood, "Art of Fiction No. 178."

41 Rice, "Amor me ...," 1.

42 As Friedrich Nietzsche wrote in a letter to Peter Gast in February 1882, "*Unser Schreibzeug arbeitet mit an unseren Gedanken,*"—"Our writing tools are also working on our thoughts." Here, quoted in English in Kittler, *Gramophone, Film, Typewriter*, 200; and Wershler-Henry, *Iron Whim*, 51.

43 Polt, "Typology."

44 Kittler, *Gramophone, Film, Typewriter*, 203.

45 Wershler-Henry, *Iron Whim*, 99–100.

46 Kittler, *Gramophone, Film, Typewriter*, 229. For more on the impact of typewriting on the writer's style, see Robert Messenger's article "Typing Writers: An Endangered Species (But Not Yet Extinct)," in *The Canberra Times*, Panorama, February 14, 2009; Rino Breebart's short essay "Typewriter Love," in *Typewriter Tributes*, The Classic Typewriter Page, http://site.xavier.edu/polt/typewriters/breebaart.html; and Rice, "Amor me ..."

47 August Dvorak, *Typewriting Behavior: Psychology Applied to Teaching and Learning Typewriting* (New York: American Book Company, 1936), 74.

48 These words are actually taken from Paul Auster's description of the writings of schizophrenic Louis Wolfson in a review of his *Le Schizo et les langues* that Auster wrote for *The New York Review of Books*. It also appears in his essay "New York Babel" that has been included in *Ground Work*. See Paul Auster, "One-Man Language," *The New York Review of Books*, February 6, 1975, http://www.nybooks.com/articles/archives/1975/feb/06/one-man-language; and Paul Auster, *Ground Work: Selected Poems and Essays 1970–1979* (London and Boston: Faber and Faber, 1991). But here, to characterize Auster's style, Barry Lewis uses Auster's own words "in evidence against him." See Lewis, "Strange Case of Auster," 60.

49 Auster in the interview with Wood, "Art of Fiction No. 178."

50 Interview with Wood, "Art of Fiction No. 178."

51 Wershler-Henry, *Iron Whim*, 27.

52 Wershler-Henry, *Iron Whim*, 265.

53 Polt, "Typology."

54 Wershler-Henry, *Iron Whim*, 28.

55 Auster, *Country of Last Things*, 89.

56 Auster and Messer, *Story of My Typewriter*, 40.

57 Auster and Messer, *Story of My Typewriter*, 55.

58 Auster and Messer, *Story of My Typewriter*, 55.

59 Auster and Messer, *Story of My Typewriter*, 22–3.

60 Joshua Wolf Shenk, "The Things We Carry: Seeking Appraisal at the Antiques Roadshow," in *Harper's Magazine* (June 2001): 46–56, available online from Shenk's

personal website http://www.shenk.net/things.htm; Shenk's essay is also discussed by Wershler-Henry, *Iron Whim*, 23–4.

61 Shenk, "Things We Carry."
62 Shenk, "Things We Carry."
63 Shenk, "Things We Carry."
64 Polt, "Typology."
65 Shenk, "Things We Carry."
66 Wershler-Henry, *Iron Whim*, 23.
67 Shenk, "Things We Carry."
68 Auster, *Invention of Solitude*, 8.
69 Auster, *Book of Illusions*, 8.
70 Wershler-Henry, quoting Shenk, in *Iron Whim*, 24.
71 Wershler-Henry, *Iron Whim*, 25.
72 Wershler-Henry, *Iron Whim*, 25.
73 Rice, "Amor me …," 2.
74 Interview with McCaffery and Gregory, "Interview with Auster," *Mississippi Review*, 59.
75 Interview with McCaffery and Gregory, "Interview with Auster," *Mississippi Review*, 59.
76 Auster in the interview with Wood, "Art of Fiction No. 178."
77 Wershler-Henry, *Iron Whim*, 55.
78 Wershler-Henry, *Iron Whim*, 55.
79 Late Martin Tytell was the world's most renowned typewriter repairman. Here, he is quoted in Ian Frazier's article "Typewriter Man," in *Atlantic Monthly* 280: 5 (November 1997), 92.
80 Wershler-Henry, *Iron Whim*, 51.
81 On February 16, 1882 Nietzsche typed on his "Schreibkugel":

SCHREIBKUGEL IST EIN DING GLEICH MIR VON EISEN
UND DOCH LEICHT ZU VERDREH'N ZUMAL AUF REISEN.
GEDULD UND TAKT MUSS REICHLICH MAN BESITZEN
UND FEINE FINGERCHEN, UNS ZU BENÜTZEN.

One can find a scanned copy of the poem in its original typescript, and the poem's English translation, in Sverre Avnskog's article "Friedrich Nietzsche and His Typewriter—A Malling-Hansen Writing Ball," The International Rasmus Malling-Hansen Society, February 2, 2008, http://www.malling-hansen.org/friedrich-nietzsche-and-his-typewriter-a-malling-hansen-writing-ball.html

82 Wershler-Henry, *Iron Whim*, 51.
83 Auster and Messer, *Story of My Typewriter*, 33.
84 Auster and Messer, *Story of My Typewriter*, 32.
85 Wershler-Henry, *Iron Whim*, 51.
86 Friedrich A. Kittler, *Optical Media* (Cambridge: Polity Press, 2009), 120.
87 McHale, "Poetry as Prosthesis," 24.
88 McHale, "Poetry as Prosthesis," 24. McHale refers here to Davis Wills' work *Prosthesis* (Stanford, CA: Stanford University Press, 1995).
89 Wills, *Prosthesis*, 28; here quoted by McHale, "Poetry as Prosthesis," 24.
90 McHale, "Poetry as Prosthesis," 13.
91 Heidegger, "On Hand and Typewriter," in Kittler, *Gramophone, Film, Typewriter*, 198.

92 Heidegger, "On Hand and Typewriter," in Kittler, *Gramophone, Film, Typewriter*, 198.

93 Auster in the interview with Wood, "Art of Fiction No. 178."

94 Wershler-Henry, *Iron Whim*, 32.

95 Wershler-Henry, *Iron Whim*, 75.

96 Wershler-Henry, *Iron Whim*, 75. He refers here to Avital Ronell's *Dictations: On Haunted Writing* (Lincoln: University of Nebraska Press, 1989).

97 Wershler-Henry, *Iron Whim*, 74.

98 Auster and Messer, *Story of My Typewriter*, front flap text.

99 See Auster and Messer, *Story of My Typewriter*, 56. Auster's claims are not unlike those of William S. Burroughs, who in the introduction to his novel *Naked Lunch* writes that he has "no precise memory of writing the notes which have now been published under the title *Naked Lunch*." Whereas David Cronenberg, who later made a filmic adaptation of Burroughs' novel, attributes the authorship of the film's script to his laptop ("it was almost as if his laptop was writing the script itself," notes Wershler). See Wershler-Henry, *Iron Whim*, 119.

100 Auster and Messer, *Story of My Typewriter*, 29.

101 See Wershler-Henry in *Iron Whim*, 31–2, where he also briefly discusses the curious relationship between the writer, the painter and the typewriter.

102 See Wershler-Henry, *Iron Whim*, 101–4.

103 McHale, "Poetry as Prosthesis."

104 McHale, "Poetry as Prosthesis," 26.

105 McHale, "Poetry as Prosthesis," 26.

106 McHale, "Poetry as Prosthesis," 27.

107 Rheindorf, "Where Everything is Connected," 1.

108 Auster in an interview with Wayne Gooderham, "Paul Auster Interview," *Time Out London* [undated], http://www.timeout.com/london/books/paul-auster-interview

109 The term was first suggested by Paul Auster's friend and American filmmaker Hal Hartley, and has since been used by critics to refer to the *mise en abyme* films featured in *The Book of Illusions*. See Auster's interview with Lethem, "Lethem Talks with Auster."

110 González, "Words Versus Images," 32.

111 González, "Words Versus Images," 43. See also González's interview with Auster, "Smoke and Illusions: An Interview with Paul Auster," in *Revista de Estudios Norteamericanos* 12 (2007), 63.

112 González, "Words Versus Images," 42.

113 González, "Words Versus Images," 42–3.

114 See González, "Smoke and Illusions," 64.

115 Auster, *Invention of Solitude*, 116.

116 González, "Words Versus Images," 41.

117 González, "Words Versus Images," 41.

118 Auster in McCaffery and Gregory, "Interview with Auster," *Contemporary Literature*, 14.

119 See Brown, *Paul Auster*; Rheindorf, "Where Everything is Connected"; Stephen Fredman, "'How to Get Out of the Room that is the Book?' Paul Auster and the Consequences of Confinement." *Postmodern Culture: An Electronic Journal of Interdisciplinary Criticism* 6.3 (May 1996), http://muse.jhu.edu/journals/postmodern_culture/v006/6.3fredman.html; Alexis Plékan, "Confinement in Paul

Auster's Moon Palace and The New York Trilogy" (MA diss., University of Caen Lower Normandy, 2001); Markus Rheindorf, "Processes of Embodiment and Spatialization in the Writings of Paul Auster," *Reconstruction* 2.3 (2002), http://reconstruction.eserver.org/023/rheindorf.htm; Steven E. Alford, "Spaced-Out: Signification and Space in Paul Auster's 'The New York Trilogy'," *Contemporary Literature* 36.4 (1995): 613–32; among others.

120 Rheindorf, "Where Everything is Connected," 26.

121 Rheindorf, "Where Everything is Connected," 26.

122 Rheindorf, "Where Everything is Connected," 30; echoing Auster's *Moon Palace*, 56.

123 Fredman, "How to Get Out ..."

124 Auster, *Invention of Solitude*, 87.

125 Auster, *Book of Illusions*, 55.

126 Auster, *Book of Illusions*, 55.

127 Auster, *Book of Illusions*, 55.

128 Auster, *Book of Illusions*, 55.

129 Auster, *Book of Illusions*, 57.

130 Rheindorf, "Where Everything is Connected," 3.

131 For the sake of simplicity and consistency, we will discuss the filmic/screenplay version of the Martin Frost story, while keeping in mind that this story exists in different versions, including as an embedded narrative in *The Book of Illusions*.

132 The similarities between both stories are obvious. *Lulu on the Bridge* has been constructed the same way as the previous one. The differences lie in the nuances. The writer-character has been replaced by a jazz musician, Izzy, who after being shot in an incident in a bar loses his lung and his ability to play saxophone, and, consequently, his purpose of life. He is also lonesome and divorced. Then, unexpectedly, Izzy meets a beautiful woman, Celia, who brings him back to life, but who disappears at the end of the film. We learn that the whole story has happened in the unconscious Izzy's mind after the shooting in the bar, while an emergency car is rushing him to hospital. He dies on the way, but already as a different person. Thanks to Celia, he has experienced a kind of redemption in his life.

133 I am borrowing this metaphor from Auster, in his conversation with Larry McCaffery and Sinda Gregory, *Contemporary Literature*, 14. In 2009, González called *Lulu on the Bridge*, and especially the *mise en abyme* scenes of the Lulu film, Auster's best attempt at "opening up the process" and exposing "the plumbing of cinema," and the implications and complications of filmmaking. See González, "Words Versus Images," 39.

134 Hence also the modest critical attention given to Auster's female characters. The very few examples include González's essay "Words Versus Images"; Carlos Azevedo's article "A Portrait of the Indian Woman as Ghost Dancer: Mother Sioux in Paul Auster's 'Mr. Vertigo'," *Estudos/Studien/Studies* 1 (2001), 117–26; Stefania Ciocia's essay "A Doomed Romance? The *donna angelicata* in Paul Auster's Fiction," published in Ciocia and González's edited collection *The Invention of Illusions*; and small sub-sections in Rheindorf's MA thesis "Where Everything is Connected," and Traisnel's BA thesis "Storytelling in Auster's Movies."

135 Rheindorf, "Where Everything is Connected," 115–16.

136 Rheindorf, "Where Everything is Connected," 111.

137 Rheindorf, "Where Everything is Connected," 111.

138 Auster, *Moon Palace*, 95.

139 Paul Auster, *The Red Notebook* (London and Boston: Faber and Faber, 1991), 142.

140 For ease of reference I will be quoting from the published screenplay, not the film. See Paul Auster, *The Inner Life of Martin Frost* (London: Faber and Faber, 2007), 34.

141 Paul Auster, "Lulu on the Bridge," in *Lulu on the Bridge: A Film by Paul Auster* (New York: Henry Holt and Company, 1998), 45.

142 Auster, "Lulu on Bridge," 132.

143 In Beckett's novel, it is Mr Willoughby Kelly, the paternal grandfather of Murphy's lover Celia, who comes up with this pun: "He found it hard to think, impossible to expand the sad pun (for he had excellent French): *Celia, s'il y a, Celia, s'il ya,* throbbing steadily behind his eyes ... What had he done to her, that she did not come to see him any more?" See Samuel Beckett, *Murphy* (New York: Grove Press, 1994), 115.

144 Auster in a conversation with Rebecca Prime, "The Making of 'Lulu on the Bridge': An Interview with Paul Auster," in Auster, *Lulu on the Bridge*, 149.

145 Most of the film-within-the-film scenes were later cut out of the original film, and are only retained in the US-release version (2006) as "Deleted Scenes." The aspect of rewriting classical myths, from Eve to Lulu/Pandora, including the material from these deleted scenes, is explored by González in his essay "Words Versus Images" and by Springer in his published thesis *Crises: The Works of Paul Auster*.

146 According to Auster, "Claire isn't a traditional muse. She's an embodiment of the story Martin is writing ..." See Auster's interview with Céline Curiol, "The Making of 'The Inner Life of Martin Frost,'" in Auster, *Inner Life of Martin Frost*, 7.

147 Auster in conversation with McCaffery and Gregory, "Interview with Auster," *Mississippi Review*, 59.

148 Auster, *Country of Last Things*, 188.

149 Rheindorf, "Where Everything is Connected," 69.

150 Auster, *Inner Life of Martin Frost*, 28. Almost identical lines also appear in Auster, *Book of Illusions*, 246, where the "written film" runs for 15 pages. There are, of course, more overlaps like this, but I will not cite them all.

151 Auster, *Inner Life of Martin Frost*, 59.

152 Rheindorf, "Where Everything is Connected," 32.

153 Auster, *Inner Life of Martin Frost*, 40.

154 Auster, *Inner Life of Martin Frost*, 40–2.

155 Auster, *Inner Life of Martin Frost*, 42.

156 See Paul Auster, *The Inner Life of Martin Frost*, directed by Paul Auster (New York: New Yorker Video, 2007), DVD.

157 That is a historically grounded association—the first commercial producer of the typewriter was a company called "E. Remington and Sons" whose main business was manufacturing firearms. Kittler, who links the development of media technologies to war, even calls the typewriter "a discursive machine gun" (*Gramophone, Film, Typewriter*, 191).

158 Wershler-Henry, *Iron Whim*, 118–19.

159 Wershler-Henry, *Iron Whim*, 123.

160 Wershler-Henry, *Iron Whim*, 131.

161 Wershler-Henry, *Iron Whim*, 121.

162 McHale, "Poetry as Prosthesis," 28.

163 McHale, "Poetry as Prosthesis," 28. Charles O. Hartman experimented with

computer-assisted text generation, using computer software called Prose, to produce texts based on certain algorithms, which he afterwards edited. Hence, in a very direct sense, the project can be seen as Hartman's collaboration with a computer.

164   Auster, *Inner Life of Martin Frost*, 103.

165   Paul Auster, *Winter Journal*, 59.

Chapter 3: Doubles and Disappearances

1   Ghosts, doppelgängers, shadows and mirror-reflections seem to haunt Auster's early writings in particular (*The New York Trilogy, The Invention of Solitude*, etc.). Yet the idea as such is hardly innovative and has already been exploited by the canonical writers of nineteenth-century American literature (just think of Herman Melville's description of Narcissus in *Moby Dick*, the opening lines of Hawthorne's work *Monsieur du Miroir*, and the stories and poems of Auster's great influence, Edgar Allan Poe). As Motoyuki Shibata, who translated Auster's work from English into Japanese, points out, it is not for nothing that the protagonist of *City of Glass* has chosen as his *nom de plume* the name of William Wilson, "a famous Poe character [who is] pursued by his own double" and is thereby made insane. See Motoyuki Shibata, "On the Impossibility of Not Being a Ghost," *Ghosts Catalogue* (2003): 3–5, http://www.jonkessler.com/articles/shibata.htm.

2   Andrew J. Webber, *The Doppelgänger: Double Visions in German Literature* (Oxford: Clarendon Press; New York: Oxford University Press, 1996), 3.

3   See Jean Paul Richter's *Flower, Fruit, and Thorn Pieces ...*, commonly known as *Siebenkäs* (full bibliographical details in Bibliography.)

4   Webber, *Doppelgänger*, 3.

5   Webber, *Doppelgänger*, 3.

6   See the entry for "Doppelgänger," in *The Oxford Companion to the Body*, ed. Colin Blakemore and Shelia Jennett (Oxford and New York: Oxford University Press, 2001), 226.

7   Gordon E. Slethaug, *The Play of the Double in Postmodern American Fictions* (Carbondale and Edwardsvill: Southern Illinois University Press, 1993), 8.

8   Slethaug, *Play of the Double*, 8.

9   Lexey Anne Bartlett, "The Double Redux: Multiplying Identity in Postmodern Fiction" (PhD diss., University of Texas at Arlington, 2005).

10   Bartlett, "Double Redux," 6.

11   Webber, *Doppelgänger*, 1.

12   Friedrich A. Kittler, "Romanticism—Psychoanalysis—Film: A History of the Double," in Friedrich A Kittler, *Literature. Media. Information Systems: Essays (Critical Voices in Art, Theory, and Culture)*, ed. and introduced by John Johnston (London: Routledge, 1997).

13   Kittler, "Romanticism—Psychoanalysis—Film," 87–8.

14   Discussing the story, Bartlett writes: "the fear of an immoral or evil alter-ego that the double story used to play on has transformed into a fear that one may not know one's own self, an anxiety—but not a terror—far more in keeping with the popular spread of modem psychology." See Bartlett, "Double Redux," 24–5.

15   See Paul Auster and Jacques de Loustal, "The Day I Disappeared," in *Strange Stories*

for Strange Kids (Little Lit, Book 2), eds Art Spiegelman and Françoise Mouly (New York: RAW Junior/ HarperCollins Children's Books, 2001), 57.

16 *American Heritage Dictionary of the English Language*, 4th edn, Boston: Houghton Mifflin, 2000.

17 E. T. A. Hoffmann, "The Sand-Man," transl. J.Y. Bealby (New York: Charles Scribner's Sons, 1885). Available as part of Hoffmann's *Weird Tales. Vol. I* from Project Gutenberg, http://www.gutenberg.org/ebooks/31377

18 See Ernst Jentsch, "On the Psychology of the Uncanny" (1906), transl. Roy Sellars, in *Uncanny Modernity: Cultural Theories, Modern Anxieties*, ed. Jo Collins and John Jervis (Basingstoke: Palgrave Macmillan, 2008), 216–28. Originally published as "Zur Psychologie des Unheimlichen." *Psychiatrisch-Neurologische Wochenschrift* 8.22 (25 August 1906): 195–8 and 8.23 (1 September 1906): 203–5. For Freud's essay see Sigmund Freud, "The Uncanny," in *The Uncanny*, translated by David McLintock, with an introduction by Hugh Haughton (New York: Penguin Books, 2003). Originally published as "Das Unheimliche," *Imago* 5 (5/6) (1919): 297–324. See also Otto Rank, *Double: A Psychoanalytic Study*, translated and edited by Harry Tucker Jr. (Chapel Hill: The University of North Carolina Press, 1971). Originally published (the earliest version) as "Der Doppelgänger," *Imago* 3 (1914): 97–164.

19 Freud, quoting Jentsch, in "Uncanny," 135.

20 Freud, "Uncanny," 136.

21 Freud, "Uncanny," 138–9.

22 Freud, in notes to "Uncanny," 160.

23 Freud, in notes to "Uncanny," 160.

24 Paul Auster writes: "[i]t would be impossible to say that we are not haunted. Freud has described such experiences as 'uncanny,' or *unheimlich*—the opposite of *heimlich*, which means 'familiar,' 'native,' 'belonging to the home.' The implication ... is that we are thrust out from the protective shell of our habitual perceptions, as though we were suddenly outside ourselves, adrift in a world we do not understand. By definition, we are lost in that world ... Unhomelessness, therefore, [is] a memory of another, much earlier home of the mind." See Auster, *Invention of Solitude*, 148.

25 Auster, *City of Glass*, 25.

26 Rubenstein, "Doubling, Intertextuality ..." 246.

27 Rubenstein, "Doubling, Intertextuality ..." 250.

28 Rubenstein, "Doubling, Intertextuality ..." 246.

29 E. T. A. Hoffmann, "The Sand-Man."

30 E. T. A. Hoffmann, "The Sand-Man."

31 E. T. A. Hoffmann, "The Sand-Man."

32 E. T. A. Hoffmann, "The Sand-Man."

33 E. T. A. Hoffmann, "The Sand-Man."

34 Kittler, "Romanticism—Psychoanalysis—Film," 85.

35 Kittler, "Romanticism—Psychoanalysis—Film," 89.

36 Novalis, quoted in Kittler, "Romanticism—Psychoanalysis—Film," 90.

37 Kittler, "Romanticism—Psychoanalysis—Film," 90.

38 Jan Harris, "Cinema and Its Doubles: Kittler v. Deleuze," in *Cinema and Technology: Cultures, Theories, Practices*, ed. Bruce Bennett, Marc Furstenau and Adrian Mackenzie (Basingstoke: Palgrave Macmillan, 2008), 101.

39 Harris, "Cinema and Its Doubles," 101, also quoting John S. Titford from his essay

"Object-Subject Relationships in German Expressionist Cinema," in *Cinema Journal* 13.1 (Autumn 1973), 21.

40 Kittler, "Romanticism—Psychoanalysis—Film," 90–1.

41 See, for example, Bernstein, "Auster's Sublime Closure"; and Russell, "Deconstructing 'New York Trilogy'," 71–84; Bernd Herzogenrath, *An Art of Desire. Reading Paul Auster* (Amsterdam: Rodopi, 1999), among others.

42 See Stephen Bernstein, "The Question is the Story Itself: Postmodernism and Intertextuality in Auster's 'New York Trilogy'," in *Detecting Texts: The Metaphysical Detective Story from Poe to Postmodernism*, ed. Patricia Merivale and Susan Elizabeth Sweeney (Pennsylvania: University of Pennsylvania Press, 1999), 143.

43 Rubenstein, "Doubling, Intertextuality ..." 251.

44 Rubenstein, "Doubling, Intertextuality ..." 246.

45 Rubenstein, "Doubling, Intertextuality ..." 246.

46 Bartlett, "Double Redux," 48.

47 Bartlett quoting from Brian McHale's *Postmodernist Fiction* (New York: Methuen, 1987), 10, in Bartlett, "Double Redux," 49–50.

48 Bartlett, "Double Redux," 40.

49 See Jorge Luis Borges, "The Garden of Forking Paths," in *Labyrinths*, eds. Donald A. Yates and James E. Irby, with an invitation by William Gibson and introduction by James E. Irby (New York: A New Directions Book, 2007). First published in English translation by Donald A. Yates as "The Garden of Forking Paths," *Michigan Alumnus Quarterly Review* (Spring, 1958).

50 In *Travels in the Scriptorium*, the story's amnesiac protagonist Mr. Blank wakes up one morning to find himself locked inside of an empty room which contains only a typewriter, a manuscript and a few mementos in the form of texts and photographs. He gets visited by characters from his own fictional works, texts that the reader recognizes as Auster's earlier novels. Among the doppelgänger characters that (re)visit him are Peter Stillman Jr. (the mysterious Kaspar Hauser-like figure from *City of Glass*), who wants Mr. Blank to dress all in white; Mr. Blank's "doctor" Samuel Farr (Anna Blume's partner from *The Country of Last Things*, who also there impersonates a doctor at one point); a certain writer John Trause (the writer-antagonist from *Oracle Night*, whose name is also an anagram of "Auster"); and others. When taken together, the lives of these recurrent characters, and, consequently, their entire diegetic worlds, do not make sense as they appear contradictory—"impossible," as Banks noted earlier. This condition of unstable, fluctuating, multiple identities that coexist in an otherwise interconnected oeuvre has also interested Varner, who asks: "If identity, for characters, is ... fragile ... then could not a novel's 'identity' be equally fragile? ... Auster's short novel [*Travels in the Scriptorium*] is predicated on the idea that characters' 'lives' or 'existence' extend beyond the pages of a novel ..." See Gary Matthew Varner, "Paul Auster's Rhizomatic Fictions" (MA diss., Mississippi State University, 2010), 30–1.

51 Webber, *Doppelgänger*, 6.

52 Male and female, and heterosexuals, gays and lesbians, respectively.

53 Plato, *Symposium*, translated, with introduction and notes by Alexander Nehamas and Paul Woodruff (Indianapolis: Hackett Publishing Company, 1989), 26.

54 See André Bazin, "The Ontology of the Photographic Image," in André Bazin, *What is Cinema? Vol. 1*, essays selected and translated by Hugh Gray, foreword by Jean

Renoir, new foreword by Dudley Andrew (Berkeley and Los Angeles, and London: University of California Press, 2004).

55 See Auster in McCaffery and Gregory, "Interview with Auster," *Contemporary Literature*, 14.

56 Harris, "Cinema and Its Doubles," 98.

57 D. N. Rodowick, *Gilles Deleuze's Time Machine* (Durham and London: Duke University Press, 1997), quoted in Harris, "Cinema and Its Doubles," 98.

58 In the 4th century BC, Plato explains to us the creation of genders: "... long ago our nature was not what it is now, but very different. There were three kinds of human beings ... not two as there are now, male and female. In addition to these, there was a third, a combination of those two ..." The shape of the primeval man was "completely round, with back and sides in a circle; they had four hands each, as many legs as hands, and two faces, exactly alike, on a rounded neck. Between the two faces, which were on opposite sides, was one head with four ears. There were two sets of sexual organs, and everything else was the way you'd imagine it from what I've told you." The splitting of the primeval man into two generated what we recognize as a human body. See Plato, *Symposium*, 25.

59 Webber, *Doppelgänger*, 4.

60 Webber, *Doppelgänger*, 17.

61 Webber, *Doppelgänger*, 18, referring to a phrase coined by Austrian writer Robert Musil in his unfinished novel *Der Mann ohne Eigenschaften* (*The Man Without Qualities*), 1930–43. See Robert Musil, *The Man without Qualities* (New York: Perigee Books, 1965).

62 Webber, *Doppelgänger*, 20.

63 Webber, *Doppelgänger*, 20.

64 Webber, *Doppelgänger*, 13.

65 McHale, "Poetry as Prosthesis," 28.

66 Webber, *Doppelgänger*, 232.

67 Webber, *Doppelgänger*, 20 and 12.

68 *Double Game*, which is Calle's response to *Leviathan*, has three parts. In "Part I: The life of Maria and how it influenced the life of Sophie," Calle published the two projects that were invented by Auster for Maria's character in *Leviathan* and later reconstructed by Calle herself. "Part II: The life of Sophie and how it influenced the life of Maria" contains Calle's previously published projects that Auster used for *Leviathan*. "Part III: One of the many ways of mingling fact with fiction, or how to try to become a character out of a novel" includes "Gotham Handbook," which is a new collaboration between Auster and Calle.

69 Webber, *Doppelgänger*, 4.

70 Auster, *Leviathan*, 60.

71 Auster, *Leviathan*, 60.

72 Auster, *Leviathan*, 65.

73 Webber, *Doppelgänger*, 21–2.

74 Auster, *Leviathan*, 101–2.

75 Auster, *Leviathan*, 65–6.

76 Calle, "The Rules of the Game," in Calle, *Double Game*, pages unnumbered.

77 Calle quoted in Jeanine Griffin's "Sophie Calle and Paul Auster: Watching the Detectives," in *Creative Camera* 354 (Oct/Nov 1998), 16.

78 Maria Lind, "The Collaborative Turn," in *Taking the Matter into Common Hands: On*

Contemporary Art and Collaborative Practices, ed. Johanna Billing et al. (London: Black Dog Publishing, 2007), 26.

79 Aaron's first wife is Delia, the second—Iris, but the son's name is David; the names of Auster's two wives are Lydia and Siri, and the son is called Daniel.

80 See Arthur M. Saltzman, "Post Hoc Harmonies: Paul Auster's *Leviathan,*" in *This Mad Instead: Governing Metaphors in Contemporary American Fiction* (South Carolina: University of South Carolina Press, 2000), 64.

81 See Anna Khimasia's essay on the Auster-Calle collaboration, "Authorial Turns: Sophie Calle, Paul Auster and the Quest for Identity," *Image [&] Narrative* 19 (2007). http://www.imageandnarrative.be/inarchive/autofiction/khimasia.htm

82 See Paul Auster, "I Want to Tell You a Story," *The Observer*, November 5, 2006, http://www.guardian.co.uk/books/2006/nov/05/fiction.paulauster

83 Khimasia, "Authorial Turns."

84 Khimasia, "Authorial Turns."

85 Griffin, "Watching the Detectives," 19.

86 Webber, *Doppelgänger*, 3–4.

87 Sophie Calle, "Review of 'Suite vénitienne,'" in *Contemporary Visual Arts*, here quoted in Griffin, "Watching the Detectives," 16.

88 Auster, *City of Glass*, 8.

89 Auster, *City of Glass*, 8.

90 Calle, "Review of 'Suite vénitienne,'" quoted in Griffin, "Watching the Detectives," 16.

91 Calle, "Suite vénitienne," in *Double Game*, 84.

92 Griffin, "Watching the Detectives," 19.

93 For Baudrillard, Venice "has no equal in the inverse extreme except New York." The essay that Baudrillard wrote to accompany Calle's project was originally published as *Suite vénitienne / Please follow me*. It has been reprinted, and I will cite it as "Please Follow Me," in *The Jean Baudrillard Reader*, ed. Steve Redhead (New York: Columbia University Press, 2008). See Baudrillard, "Please Follow Me," 78.

94 Calle, "Suite vénitienne," in *Double Game*, 96.

95 Auster, *City of Glass*, 99.

96 Paul Auster, Paul Karasik and David Mazzucchelli, *City of Glass: The Graphic Novel* (New York: Picador/Henry Holt and Company, 2004), 62–4.

97 Baudrillard, "Please Follow Me," 79.

98 Griffin, "Watching the Detectives," 16.

99 See the conversation between Auster and Michel Contat, "The Manuscript in the Book: A Conversation," in *Yale French Studies* 89, Drafts (1996), transl. Alyson Waters, 180.

100 Baudrillard, "Please Follow Me," 79.

101 Auster, "Ghosts," 215–16.

102 Calle, "The Detective," in Calle, *Double Game*, 123.

103 The narrator's account of Maria's "detective" project as it appears in *Leviathan*, quoted in Calle, "The Detective," 123.

104 Calle, "The Detective," 128.

105 Calle, "Leviathan," in Calle, *Double Game*.

106 Olivier Asselin and Johanne Lamoureux, "Autofictions, or Elective identities," in *Parachute* 105 (2002), 11; see also Khimasia, "Authorial Turns."

107 Khimasia, "Authorial Turns."

108 Khimasia, "Authorial Turns."

109 Maud Lavin, "Imitation of Life" (review of "Double Game"), in *Art in America* 88.7 (July 2000), 33–4.

110 For example, to Auster's *The Chromatic Diet*, which envisages Maria eating products of a different color each day (Monday—orange, Tuesday—red, Wednesday—white, etc.), Calle adds her own meals and chooses to continue the ritual on days "that Paul Auster had given his characters the day off." On a Wednesday, when Auster had Maria eat "flounder, potatoes, cottage cheese," Calle modifies the menu, "because [she] was not satisfied with the yellow color of the potatoes," and replaces potatoes with white rice and milk. On a Monday, when the menu's color is orange, Calle adds some orange juice because "Paul Auster forgot to mention drinks." And so on. See Calle, "The Chromatic Diet," in Calle, *Double Game*, 12–13.

111 See also Khimasia, "Authorial Turns."

112 Baudrillard, "Please Follow Me," 74.

113 Olivier Renaud-Clement, a private dealer and a friend of Calle's, here quoted by Daphne Merkin, "I Think Therefore I'm Art," *T: The New York Times Style Magazine*, October 19, 2008 (The New York Edition); http://www.nytimes.com/2008/10/19/style/tmagazine/19calle.html

114 See Charlotte Schoell-Glass, "Fictions of the Art World: Art, Art History and the Art Historian in Literary Space," in *Writing and Seeing: Essays on Word and Image*, ed. Rui Carvalho Homem and Maria de Fátima Lambert (Amsterdam: Rodopi, 2006), 107–18. Cf. also Griffin, "Watching the Detectives."

115 Schoell-Glass, "Fictions of Art World," 107 and 109.

116 Schoell-Glass, "Fictions of Art World," 107.

117 Schoell-Glass, "Fictions of Art World," 116.

118 Schoell-Glass is of the same opinion—she even claims that "conceptualism" (which elsewhere she refers to as "art and art history") is the main structuring device for Auster's literary and filmic texts. Schoell-Glass, "Fictions of Art World," 107 and 112.

119 Griffin, "Watching the Detectives," 19.

120 When Calle finds the address book, she decides to reconstruct the identity of the book's owner, "to get to know this man through his friends, his acquaintances," to "discover who he was without ever meeting him and to produce a portrait of him." And she sets out to do that by calling all the people in the address book and interviewing them about the owner. See Calle, "The Address Book," in Calle, *Double Game*, 186–7.

121 Auster, *Leviathan*, 66–7.

122 Projects like *Take Care of Yourself* and *Exquisite Pain* grew from Calle's relationship breakups, while *Lourdes, Coffin, Monique* and *North Pole* are related to the death of her mother. Another untitled video project depicts her mother dying. When the traumatic experience gets staged, or captured and mediated by technology, shared and distributed among other participants, and then monotonously repeated to the point where the iterations become almost mechanical, Calle refers to the process as having therapeutic value: "… I had got over my pain … had worn out my own story through sheer repetition. The method proved radically effective." And, as she explains in an interview elsewhere—"[a]t first it was [my] therapy; then art took over." See Sophie Calle, *Exquisite Pain* (London: Thames and Hudson Ltd., 2004), 203; and Calle in an interview with Angelique Chrisafis, "He Loves Me Not," *The Guardian*, June 16, 2007, http://www.guardian.co.uk/world/2007/jun/16/artnews.art

123 Auster, *Leviathan*, 64.

124 Griffin, "Watching the Detectives," 19.

125 Baudrillard, "Please Follow Me," 76.

126 Baudrillard, "Please Follow Me," 76.

127 Calle, "The Rules of the Game."

128 Griffin, "Watching the Detectives," 19.

129 Calle says in an interview with Griffin: "I still have control of it. Many things I don't like to decide, although I keep control of it ... I feel control because I choose the rules of the game —I'm the one who has decided that I would obey my own rule." And she expresses the same thought in an interview with Christine Macel: "I like being in control and I like losing control. Obedience to a ritual is a way of making rules and then letting yourself go along with them ... That's the rule of the game, but I'm the one who chose the rule." See Calle interviewed by Griffin in "Watching the Detectives," 19; and interview with Christine Macel, "Biographical Interview with Sophie Calle," in Sophie Calle, *Sophie Calle: M'as-tu vue* (Munich, Berlin, London, New York: Prestel Publishing, 2004), 80.

130 Auster, *Leviathan*, 1.

131 Schoell-Glass, "Fictions of Art World," 116.

132 Auster, "Gotham Handbook," 3.

133 Sophie Calle, "Gotham Handbook," 246.

134 Calle, "Gotham Handbook," 246

135 Auster "Gotham Handbook," 4.

136 Auster "Gotham Handbook," 4.

137 The story first appeared in *The New York Times* Op Ed page, December 25, 1990, and was later republished separately as a collaboration between Paul Auster and an artist named Isol, *Auggie Wren's Christmas Story* (New York: Henry Holt, 2004). It has since been also republished in Auster's two collections of film scripts. Here, I quote it from Auster, "Auggie Wren's Christmas Story," in *Smoke & Blue*, 151.

138 Auster "Gotham Handbook," 4.

139 González, "Words Versus Images," 32.

140 Lind referring to Blake Stimson and Gregory Sholette's essay "Periodising Collectivism," in *Third Text: Critical Perspectives on Contemporary Art and Culture* 18 (November 2004), 573–83. A later version of the essay also appears as "Introduction: Periodizing Collectivism," in *Collectivism After Modernism: The Art of Social Imagination After 1945*, ed. Blake Stimson and Gregory Sholette (Minneapolis: University of Minnesota Press: 2007), 1–16. For Lind's reference, see her "Collaborative Turn," 18.

141 Lind, "Collaborative Turn," 27.

142 Lind, "Collaborative Turn," 16.

143 Carson, quoting from Deleuze and Guattari's *Thousand Plateaus*, in Benjamin D. Carson, "Towards a Postmodern Political Art: Deleuze, Guattari, and the Anti-Culture Book," *rhizomes* 07 (Fall 2003), http://www.rhizomes.net/issue7/carson.htm

144 Deleuze and Guattari, *Thousand Plateaus*, 17.

145 Carson, "Towards a Postmodern Political Art."

146 Paul Auster, "Introduction" to *I Thought My Father Was God and Other True Tales from NPR's National Story Project*, ed. and introduced by Paul Auster (New York: Picador, 2002), xvii.

147 Auster, *I Thought My Father Was God*, xvi.

148 Auster, *I Thought My Father Was God*, xix.

149 González, "Words Versus Images," 34.

150 Auster, "Gotham Handbook," 3.

151 In obeying Auster's instructions, Calle experiences and chronicles encounters with strangers that resonate with her own past projects. In *The Sleepers* (1979), for example, Calle invited friends and strangers to sleep in her bed continuously for eight days. In *The Bronx* (1980) she talks to strangers on the streets of South Bronx and photographs them at their favorite local spots. For the quote, see Bellis Schneewein, "You Exist Only in the Trace of the Other … (*Fiktionen mit Fantômas*)," *Corpus: Internet Magazine für Tanz, Choreografie. Performance* (11 November 2007), http://www.corpusweb.net/fiktionen-mit-fant-4.html

152 Auster knows the struggle well, as evidenced by his many texts that chronicle both such an attempt and its failure (*The Invention of Solitude*; *The Locked Room*; *Leviathan*, etc.). The following passage from *The Locked Room* sums it up best: "Every life is inexplicable … No matter how many facts are told, no matter how many details are given, the essential thing resists telling … We imagine the real story inside the words, and to do this we substitute ourselves for the person in the story, pretending that we can understand him because we understand ourselves. This is a deception. We exist for ourselves, perhaps, and at times we even have a glimmer of who we are, but in the end we can never be sure … and … we become more and more opaque to ourselves, more and more aware of our own incoherence. No one can cross the boundary into another—for the simple reason that no one can gain access to himself." See Auster, "The Locked Room," 291–2.

153 Quinn scribbles in his notebook : "And yet, what is it that Dupin says in Poe? 'An identification of the reasoner's intellect with that of his opponent.'" See Auster, *City of Glass*, 65.

154 Bruno Latour, "On Actor-Network Theory: A Few Clarifications plus More than a Few Complications," *Soziale Welt* 47.4 (1996): 369–81, also available from Latour's official website http://www.bruno-latour.fr/sites/default/files/P-67%20ACTOR-NETWORK.pdf

155 Latour, "On Actor-Network Theory."

156 That is to say, a network, or an assemblage cannot be traced and explained "from outside." And the process of tracing and explaining itself adds to the creation of the network. As Latour puts it, "One does not jump outside a network to add an explanation—a cause, a factor, a set of factors, a series of co-occurrences; one simply extends the network further. Every network surrounds itself with its own frame of reference, its own definition of growth, of referring, of framing, of explaining … There is no way to provide an explanation if the network does not extend itself." See Latour, "On Actor-Network Theory."

157 See Deleuze and Guattari, *Thousand Plateaus*, 24.

158 Latour, "On Actor-Network Theory."

Chapter 4: New York, Where All Quests Fail

1   Jesús Ángel González, "My Second Slice: How I Interviewed Paul Auster," published on González's personal page on *Issuu* digital publishing platform, January 12, 2011, http://issuu.com/jagonzal/docs/how_i_interviewed_paul_auster

2   Auster quoted from Allon Reich's "Interview with Paul Auster: Brooklyn 1988," in Brown, *Paul Auster*, 1.

3   Here are some examples: Luisa Moncada and Scala Quin, *Reading on Location: Great Books Set in Top Travel Destinations* (London: New Holland, 2011); William Corbett, *New York Literary Lights: William Corbett* (St. Paul, MN: Graywolf Press, 1998); Steven Kurutz, "Literary New York," *The New York Times*, May 14, 2006, http://travel2.nytimes.com/2006/05/14/travel/14going.html, among many others.

4   Brown, *Paul Auster*, 1.

5   Brown, *Paul Auster*, 1.

6   Phillip Lopate, ed., *Writing New York: A Literary Anthology* (New York: The Library of America/Penguin Putnam Inc., 2008), xvii.

7   Lopate, *Writing New York*, xviii–xix.

8   Paul Auster and Frieder Blickle, *Paul Auster's New York*, ed. and compiled by Thomas Überhoff, preface by Luc Sante (New York: Henry Holt and Company, 1997). [A retracted publication]

9   Luc Sante, "Preface," in Auster and Blickle, *Auster's New York*, 12–13.

10 Colson Whitehead, *The Colossus of New York: A City in Thirteen Parts* (New York: Anchor Books, 2003), 101.

11 Woody Allen, "Manhattan," in *Four Films of Woody Allen: Annie Hall, Interiors, Manhattan, Stardust Memories* (London: Faber and Faber, 2003), 181.

12 Woody Allen, "Manhattan," 182.

13 That comment by Auster was allegedly subsequently edited out of the published interview with Larry McCaffery and Sinda Gregory. Here, referred to in Brown, *Paul Auster*, 1; he quotes it from the interview manuscript, held at the New York Public Library's Berg Collection.

14 That is because New York is a multiplicity that has to be expressed through the conjunction of "AND." For the quotes see Allen, "Manhattan," 181–2.

15 Lopate, *Writing New York*, xvii.

16 Lopate, *Writing New York*, xvii.

17 Robert Moses, quoted by in Lopate, *Writing New York*, xvii.

18 Lopate, *Writing New York*, xx.

19 Quoted Lopate in *Writing New York*, xvii.

20 Allen, "Manhattan," 182.

21 Latour, "On Actor-Network Theory."

22 The phrase is borrowed from *Urban Assemblages: How Actor-Network Theory Changes Urban Studies*, ed. Ignacio Farías and Thomas Bender (London: Routledge, 2010).

23 Auster, *Moon Palace*, 122.

24 Here, quoted in Brown, *Paul Auster*, 17. It is not only Auster's early novels (*City of Glass*) that portray New York as an "inexhaustible space of endless steps." As Brown points out, in this early collection of poetry, the city is constantly represented as both an "indecipherable" and an "overwhelming" domain. See Brown, *Paul Auster*, 18.

25 Whitehead, *Colossus of New York*, 4.

26 Whitehead, *Colossus of New York*, 6.

27 Whitehead, *Colossus of New York*, 6.

28 Paul Auster, *Sunset Park* (New York, Henry Holt and Company, 2010), 132.

29 An apartment in that New York neighborhood, where one used to live 10 years ago, would carry memories of the old self as long as the building stands there, Whitehead suggests. Paul Auster, likewise, explores the memory of old, abandoned things in his memoir *The Invention of Solitude*, as well as in his recent *Sunset Park*, asking, what happens to a thing once its owner dies?

30 Whitehead, *Colossus of New York*, 6.

31 Whitehead, *Colossus of New York*, 7.

32 I owe it to Mark Brown for bringing this piece to my attention. Here, I quote the fragment from Brown, *Paul Auster*, 35–6.

33 Wojciech Kalaga, "Face/Facade: The Visual and the Ethical," *Urbanistika ir Architektūra: Town Planning and Architecture* 34:3 (2010), 121.

34 Kalaga, "Face/Facade," 122.

35 Luc Sante, "Preface," in Auster and Blickle, *Auster's New York*, 12.

36 As I later found out, this book, which was acquired as a symbolic payment from a flea market, strictly speaking cannot even be considered "a book" as its publication was retracted due to a disagreement between Auster's current and former publishers. So I will use quotation marks when referring to it as a "book." Originally, *Paul Auster's New York* first came out in German under the Rowohlt Verlag publishing house as *Mein New York*. See Paul Auster, *Mein New York*, ed. Thomas Überhoff, transl. Joachim A. Frank, Werner Schmitz (Reinbek: Rowohlt Verlag, 2000).

37 Thomas Überhoff was (and still is, at the time of writing) Auster's German editor at Rowohlt Verlag.

38 The texts included in *Paul Auster's New York* are (in the order of appearance): the nonfiction collections *Why Write?* and *The Invention of Solitude*; the novels *Ghosts*, *Moon Palace*, *Leviathan*, *The Music of Chance*, and *Mr. Vertigo*; the picture book *Auggie Wren's Christmas Story*; the collections of essays *The Art of Hunger* and *Hand to Mouth*; the novel *City of Glass*; the collection of essays, prefaces and interviews, *The Red Notebook*; and the novel *In the Country of Last Things*.

39 Sante, "Preface," in Auster and Blickle, *Auster's New York*, 13.

40 Auster and Blickle, *Auster's New York*, 16–17 /Auster, *Invention of Solitude*, 121. From now on, when citing a fragment of Auster's texts from *Paul Auster's New York*, I will also give a reference to the source in which it originally appears.

41 See Rheindorf, "Where Everything is Connected."

42 Although most of Paul Auster's characters famously use notebooks for writing, none of his texts ever mentions the particular brand of these notebooks. I found the closest detailed description of a writer's notebook in *Oracle Night*, where the protagonist talks about his discovery of a certain make of Portuguese notebooks that he becomes addicted to. As I later discovered from the archives of the Berg Collection, the notebook brand that Paul Auster prefers is not Portuguese, but the French-made Clairefontaine. See Auster, *Oracle Night*, 5–6.

43 Auster and Blickle, *Auster's New York*, 50 / Auster, *Moon Palace*, 50–1.

44 Auster and Blickle, *Auster's New York*, 47 / Auster, *City of Glass*, 8.

45 Auster and Blickle, *Auster's New York*, 47 / Auster, *City of Glass*, 9.

46 Auster and Blickle, *Auster's New York*, 87 / Auster, *Moon Palace*, 230.

47 Auster and Blickle, *Auster's New York*, 40–1 / Paul Auster, *Hand to Mouth: A Chronicle of Early Failure* (New York: Picador, 2003), 83.

48 Auster and Blickle, *Auster's New York*, 36 / Auster, *City of Glass*, 165.

49 See Paul Auster, "The Decisive Moment," in *Art of Hunger*, 42.

50 Auster and Blickle, *Auster's New York*, 72 / Auster, *City of Glass*, 183.

51 Auster and Blickle, *Auster's New York*, 65 / Auster, *Moon Palace*, 55.

52 Auster and Blickle, *Auster's New York*, 77 / Auster, *City of Glass*, 81.

53 Auster and Blickle, *Auster's New York*, 78 / Auster, *City of Glass*, 82.

54 Auster, *City of Glass*, 84.

55 Auster, *City of Glass*, 90.

56 Auster and Blickle, *Auster's New York*, 61 / Auster, *Invention of Solitude*, 102.

57 Auster and Blickle, *Auster's New York*, 61 / Auster, *Invention of Solitude*, 102.

58 Auster and Blickle, *Auster's New York*, 53 / Auster, *City of Glass*, 92.

59 Auster and Blickle, *Auster's New York*, 54 / Auster, *City of Glass*, 94.

60 Auster and Blickle, *Auster's New York*, 94–5 / Auster, *City of Glass*, 105.

61 Auster and Blickle, *Auster's New York*, 56 / Auster, *City of Glass*, 96.

62 Auster and Blickle, *Auster's New York*, 56 / Auster, *City of Glass*, 96.

63 Surely, the addition of this book has transformed the reader's sense of Auster's New York. It has now been mapped out more properly, revealing new sites and routes, and formerly unknown connections.

64 See Helene Golay, "Books: The New York Trilogy, The Brooklyn Follies & Sunset Park," in *Realcity: An Online Magazine* (online magazine/weblog), http://www.realcityonline.com/media-books-paul-auster/.

65 Auster and Blickle, *Auster's New York*, 70 / Auster, *Moon Palace*, 58.

66 Sante, "Preface," in Auster and Blickle, *Auster's New York*, 11 and 12.

67 Auster and Blickle, *Auster's New York*, 53 / Auster, *City of Glass*, 92.

68 Auster, *City of Glass*, 136.

69 Auster, *City of Glass*, 136.

70 Auster and Blickle, *Auster's New York*, 77–8 / Auster, *City of Glass*, 82.

71 Auster and Blickle, *Auster's New York*, 80 / Auster, *Moon Palace*, 16.

72 Auster and Blickle, *Auster's New York*, 80 / Auster, *Moon Palace*, 17.

73 Auster and Blickle, *Auster's New York*, 80 / Auster, *Moon Palace*, 17.

74 Auster and Blickle, *Auster's New York*, 81 / Auster, *Moon Palace*, 17.

75 Auster and Blickle, *Auster's New York*, 81 / Auster, *Invention of Solitude*, 74.

76 Auster and Blickle, *Auster's New York*, 81–2 / Auster, *Invention of Solitude*, 75.

77 To emphasize the self-awareness of the schizophrenic split that occurs to scholars, critics and "detective" biographers, and to distance himself from the latter, which represents a darker and morally more ambiguous side, Hamilton throughout the book refers to himself as "we" for he is always accompanied by his "sleuthing companion," his "sleuthing alter ego." See, e.g., Hamilton, *In Search of JD Salinger* (London, William Heinemann Ltd., 1988), 6–7.

78 Rheindorf, "Where Everything is Connected," 26–9.

79 See Auster, "Ghosts," 201–2.

80 Auster, *Invention of Solitude*, 162.

81 Auster, *Moon Palace*, 219.

82 Auster, *Moon Palace*, 217.

83 Brandon Hopkins, "Manuscript," The Chicago School of Media Theory: Theorizing

Media since 2003, Winter 2003, http://lucian.uchicago.edu/blogs/mediatheory/keywords/manuscript/

84 Auster in the interview with Contat, "Manuscript in Book," 163.

85 Interview with Contat, "Manuscript in Book," 163.

86 Hopkins, "Manuscript."

87 Of course, there is also difference between the term's original and modern meanings. While etymologically, "manuscript," a term introduced in the 1590s from Latin, denoted writing by hand with pencil or ink on some form of paper (so "a manuscript" often means a handwritten "publication" of a text, such as illuminated manuscripts, scrolls, journals, etc.), a more contemporary use of the term includes any form of writing (handwriting, typewriting, or computer-writing) that is not printed yet, but, by implication, is expected or intended to be published in print form. Hopkins separates three "stages" of the manuscript that were distinguished after the invention of the typewriter: the author would first "pen" or outline his work, then produce "a fair copy," still written by hand, which would then be followed by a "typescript" version—usually the final version of the manuscript. One can see all these stages in Auster's manuscripts—at least two holographic drafts (notebooks with outlines and notebooks with more "solid" writing) followed by a typewritten manuscript.

88 Hopkins, "Manuscript."

89 Michel Contat, best known as a collaborator, connoisseur and critic of Jean-Paul Sartre, has edited *L'Auteur et le manuscrit (Perspectives critiques)*, a collection of essays in French on manuscripts, one of his many works in this research area. Paul Auster and his first wife once translated Contat's interview with Sartre. Among the topics discussed were Sartre's manuscripts for his philosophical and literary writing. See (listed under Translations by Paul Auster) Jean-Paul Sartre and Michel Contat, "Sartre at Seventy: An Interview," *The New York Review of Books* August 7 (1975), transl. Paul Auster and Lydia Davis, http://www.nybooks.com/articles/archives/1975/aug/07/sartre-at-seventy-an-interview; for the given Contat's quote, see Auster's interview with Contat, "Manuscript in Book," 165.

90 Sidney Orr in Auster, *Oracle Night*, 5–6.

91 See Paul Auster, "Oracle Night," Drafts, Box 23, Folder 1: Blue holograph notebook "Oracle Night," Draft 1, The Paul Auster Papers 1999–2005, processed by Anne Garner, August 2008. The Paul Auster Archive, The Henry W. and Albert A. Berg Collection of English and American Literature, The New York Public Library.

92 Anne Garner, "Paul Auster Papers in the Berg," The Henry W. and Albert A. Berg Collection of English and American Literature, March 31, 2011, http://www.nypl.org/blog/2011/03/31/paul-auster-papers-berg

93 See Auster, "Oracle Night," Drafts, Box 23, Folder 1: Blue holograph notebook "Oracle Night," Draft 1, The Paul Auster Papers 1999–2005.

94 The fact that the first draft of the novel starts with the opening of the film-within-the-book, *The Inner Life of Martin Frost*, which is, after all, only a small subplot in the book's story, again recalls the rhizomatic nature of Auster's oeuvre, where one story gives birth to the other, often transcending generic and media boundaries.

95 At this point, I failed to decipher Auster's handwriting. In cases like these where Auster's handwriting appeared unintelligible to me, I have used a question mark, or the suggested possible word followed by a question mark in square brackets.

96 See Paul Auster, "Book of Illusions," Drafts, Box 1, Folder 1: Holograph notebook "The Book of Illusions. 1," Part 1 of Draft 1, The Paul Auster Papers 1999–2005, processed

by Anne Garner, August 2008. The Paul Auster Archive, The Henry W. and Albert A. Berg Collection of English and American Literature, The New York Public Library.

97   See Auster, "Book of Illusions," Drafts, Box 1, Folder 1: Holograph notebook "The Book of Illusions. 1," Part 1 of Draft 1. Paul Auster Papers 1999–2005.

98   As appears in the notebook.

99   See Paul Auster, "Book of Illusions," Drafts, Box 1, Folder 5: Holograph notebook. "The Book of Illusions. 5," Part 5 of Draft 1, The Paul Auster Papers 1999–2005, processed by Anne Garner, August 2008. The Paul Auster Archive, The Henry W. and Albert A. Berg Collection of English and American Literature, The New York Public Library.

100 See Auster, "Book of Illusions," Drafts, Box 1, Folder 1: Holograph notebook "The Book of Illusions. 1," Part 1 of Draft 1. Paul Auster Papers 1999–2005.

101 Auster in the interview with Contat, "Manuscript in Book," 170.

102 Interview with Contat, "Manuscript in Book," 169.

103 Auster in the interview with Contat, "Manuscript in Book," 170.

104 That repetitive sort of progression of writing might also be a consequence of Auster's use of his fountain pen, as Daniel Chandler suggests: the "rapid slash of the pen" can "preserve every change" that the writer makes, "even with subtle and unpremeditated degrees of unwantedness." The handwritten text "maps paths not taken in a way that enables them to be re-explored if necessary." The computer, on the other hand, tends to simply overwrite such changes—such writing is always in flux. Chandler, "Phenomenology of Writing by Hand," 68.

105 Rosamary Fernandez, "Handwriting," The Chicago School of Media Theory: Theorizing Media since 2003, http://lucian.uchicago.edu/blogs/mediatheory/keywords/handwriting/

106 Roland Barthes, *The Pleasure of the Text*, transl. Richard Miller (London: Jonathan Cape, 1976); here quoted by Daniel Chandler, "The Phenomenology of Writing by Hand," *Intelligent Tutoring Media* 3. 2/3 (May/August 1992), 69.

107 Chandler, "Phenomenology of Writing by Hand," 69. Also quoted by Fernandez, "Handwriting."

108 See Bethanne Patrick, "Interview with Paul Auster," *Goodreads*, November, 2010, http://www.goodreads.com/interviews/show/556.Paul_Auster

109 See Paul Auster, "The Story of My Typewriter," Drafts, Box 62, Folder 1: Early holograph draft, "The Story of My Typewriter," Draft 1, The Paul Auster Papers 1999–2005, processed by Anne Garner, August 2008. The Paul Auster Archive, The Henry W. and Albert A. Berg Collection of English and American Literature, The New York Public Library.

110 Contat and Auster in the interview, "Manuscript in Book," 166.

111 Auster's 1978 interview with Jabès is published, with Auster's own translation from French, in his *Art of Hunger*, 144–69. For the given quote see Auster, "Providence: A Conversation with Edmond Jabès," in *Art of Hunger*, 168.

112 Paul Auster, "Brooklyn Follies," Drafts, Miscellaneous fragments, Box 20, Folder 1: Holograph outline and early draft of "Dream Days at the Hotel Existence" [early version of The Brooklyn Follies], The Paul Auster Papers 1999–2005, processed by Anne Garner, August 2008. The Paul Auster Archive, The Henry W. and Albert A. Berg Collection of English and American Literature, The New York Public Library.

113 Auster in the interview with Contat, "Manuscript in Book," 173.

114 Interview with Contat, "Manuscript in Book," 172–3.

115 Interview with Contat, "Manuscript in Book," 173.

116 Auster in the interview with Contat, "Manuscript in Book," 161.

117 Interview with Contat, "Manuscript in Book," 163.

118 Interview with Contat, "Manuscript in Book," 165.

119 One can find a comprehensive report on the interconnectivity of Auster's prose works in a section called "On Earlier Versions" in Springer's *Auster Sourcebook*, 63–72.

120 As appears in the holograph. See Auster, "Book of Illusions," Drafts, Box 1, Folder 1: Holograph notebook "The Book of Illusions. 1," Part 1 of Draft 1, Paul Auster Papers 1999–2005.

121 See Auster, "Book of Illusions," Drafts, Box 1, Folder 1: Holograph notebook "The Book of Illusions. 1," Part 1 of Draft 1, Paul Auster Papers 1999–2005.

122 See Auster, "Brooklyn Follies," Drafts, Miscellaneous fragments, Box 20, Folder 1: Holograph outline and early draft of "Dream Days at the Hotel Existence," The Paul Auster Papers 1999–2005.

123 Auster in the interview with Contat, "Manuscript in Book," 169.

124 Auster, "Ghosts," 201–2.

125 Fredman, "How to Get Out …"

126 Auster, "The Locked Room," 368.

127 See Paul Auster, "Notebooks," Box 67, Folder 2: Holograph notebook, "Stories." The Paul Auster Papers 1999–2005, processed by Anne Garner, August 2008. The Paul Auster Archive, The Henry W. and Albert A. Berg Collection of English and American Literature, The New York Public Library.

128 This is a reference to a translation of *Chronicle of the Guayaki Indians* by Pierre Clastres that Auster has done. See Pierre Clastres, *Chronicle of the Guayaki Indians*, transl. and with a foreword by Paul Auster (New York: Zone Books, 1998).

129 See Auster, "Notebooks," Box 67, Folder 2: Holograph notebook, "Stories," The Paul Auster Papers 1999–2005.

130 Ian Hamilton, *In Search of Salinger*, 68.

131 This neat phrase comes from Farías, "Introduction: Decentring the Object of Urban Studies," in Farías and Bender, eds, *Urban Assemblages*, 3.

132 Auster, *Sunset Park*, 80.

133 Auster, *Sunset Park*, 80.

134 Auster, *Sunset Park*, 80.

135 The Green-Wood Cemetery itself later in the novel is portrayed as assembled not only of "thousands of trees and plantings," but also of dead people, their tombs and things of the past that are associated with the deceased. What we find here are tombs "of gangsters and poets, generals and industrialists, murder victims and newspaper publishers, children dead before their time, a woman who lived seventeen years beyond her hundredth birthday, and Theodore Roosevelt's wife and mother, who were buried next to each other on the same day. There is Elias Howe, inventor of the sewing machine, the Kampfe brothers, inventors of the safety razor, Henry Steinway, founder of the Steinway Piano Company, John Underwood, founder of the Underwood Typewriter Company, Henry Chadwick, inventor of the baseball scoring system, Elmer Sperry, inventor of the gyroscope." See Auster, *Sunset Park*, 135.

136 Paul Auster, *The Brooklyn Follies* (New York: Henry Holt and Company, 2006), 49–59 and 21.

137 "The Brooklyn Cigar Co." is a fictional place, constructed for the film's purposes in

vacant former post office premises on the corner of Prospect Park West and 16th Street. There are no real tobacco shops left in Brooklyn, especially since the New York City mayor passed the ban on smoking in public places in 2011 and since the 80% tax increase on tobacco products that came into force in 2010. Due to the smoking ban and the tax increase, many small tobacco companies have gone out of business. But I came across a good-looking tobacco shop in Manhattan. Every time I passed through that neighborhood, I stopped at Khalid's store, and we sat outside on the bench under a tree and shared a few cigars together. It felt like we were in an Auster movie. It felt like, by engaging in an Austeresque conversation about the role of cigarettes and by playing out an episode that could as well have originated in an Auster text, I had, in a way, compensated for the lack of tobacco shops in Brooklyn.

138 I had sent through my request for a meeting with Paul Auster weeks before I had left Auckland for New York, but it was never certain if such a meeting would take place. At the time I sent my request, Auster had been away on a tour abroad, and was supposed to return around the same time as my departure from New York.

Inconclusion

1   González, "How I Interviewed Auster."
2   Hamilton, *In Search of Salinger*, 33.
3   Hamilton, *In Search of Salinger*, 96.
4   Hamilton, *In Search of Salinger*, 66.
5   Yet, is this not how literary theory works? In her introductory guide to critical theory, Lois Tyson associates each school of thought with a pair of lenses: "Think of each theory as a new pair of eyeglasses through which certain elements of our world are brought into focus while others, of course, fade into the background … [b]ecause they are ways of seeing the world, critical theories compete with one another for dominance in educational and cultural communities. Each theory offers itself as the most (and the only) accurate means of understanding human experience." That would be, in Deleuzian understanding, the entrapment of arborescent thinking. The question, of course, is whether such entrapment is ever avoidable. See Lois Tyson, *Critical Theory Today: A User-Friendly Guide* (New York and London: Routledge, 2006), 3.
6   Auster in the interview with Joseph Mallia. See Mallia, "Paul Auster Interview," 27.
7   Auster, "Smoke," in *Smoke & Blue*, 149.
8   Auster in conversation with McCaffery and Gregory, "Interview with Auster," *Mississippi Review*, 52.
9   See Auster's interview with Contat, "Manuscript in Book," 185.

Bibliography

Primary sources

Correspondence

Auster, Paul and J. M. Coetzee. *Here and Now: Letters 2008–2011*. London: Faber and Faber and Harvill Secker, 2013.

Cross-media/collaborative projects

Auster, Paul and Frieder Blickle. *Paul Auster's New York*. Edited and compiled by Thomas Überhoff, preface by Luc Sante. New York: Henry Holt and Company, 1997. [A retracted publication] (Contains excerpts from different Paul Auster texts.)

Auster, Paul and Thomas Glenn. *The Inner Life of Martin Frost*. New York and London: Mark Batty Publisher, Thames & Hudson (distributor), 2008.

Auster, Paul and Isol. *Auggie Wren's Christmas Story*. New York: Henry Holt, 2004.

Auster, Paul and Jacques de Loustal. "The Day I Disappeared." In *Strange Stories for Strange Kids (Little Lit, Book 2)*, edited by Art Spiegelman and Françoise Mouly, 55–62. New York: RAW Junior/HarperCollins Children's Books, 2001.

Auster, Paul, Paul Karasik, and David Mazzucchelli. *City of Glass: The Graphic Novel*. New York: Picador/Henry Holt and Company, 2004. (Contains excerpts from Paul Auster's *City of Glass*.)

Auster, Paul and Sam Messer. *The Story of My Typewriter*. New York: DAP/Distributed Art Publishers, 2002.

Sophie Calle. *Double Game*. London: Violette Editions, 1999. (Includes a collaborative project between Auster and Calle, "Gotham Handbook" and fragments from Auster's *Leviathan*.)

Edited collections

Auster, Paul, ed. *The Random House Book of Twentieth-Century French Poetry*. New York: Random House, 1982.

—*I Thought My Father Was God and Other True Tales from NPR's National Story Project*. New York: Picador, 2002. (Later published as *True Tales of American Life*.)

Essays, memoirs, and autobiographies

Auster, Paul. *Ground Work: Selected Poems and Essays 1970–1979*. London and Boston: Faber and Faber, 1991.
—*The Red Notebook*. London and Boston: Faber and Faber, 1996.
—*Why Write?* New York: Burning Deck Books, 1996.
—*The Art of Hunger: Essays, Prefaces, Interviews*. New York: Penguin Books, 2001.
—*Hand to Mouth: A Chronicle of Early Failure*. New York: Picador, 2003.
—*The Invention of Solitude*. New York: Penguin Books, 2007.
—*Winter Journal*. London: Faber and Faber, 2012.

Films

Auster, Paul. *Smoke*. VHS. Directed by Wayne Wang and Paul Auster (uncredited), New York: Miramax Films, 1995.
—*Lulu on the Bridge*. DVD. Directed by Paul Auster, Santa Monica: Trimark Home Video/Lions Gate Entertainment, 1999.
—*The Inner Life of Martin Frost*. DVD. Directed by Paul Auster, New York: New Yorker Video, 2007.
Auster, Paul and Wayne Wang et al. *Blue in the Face*. VHS. Directed by Wayne Wang, Paul Auster and Harvey Wang (video segments), New York: Miramax Films, 1995.

Miscellaneous

Auster, Paul. "One-Man Language." *The New York Review of Books*, February 6, 1975, http://www.nybooks.com/articles/archives/1975/feb/06/one-man-language
Auster, Paul. *Mein New York*. (In German) Edited by Thomas Überhoff, translated by Joachim A. Frank, Werner Schmitz. Reinbek: Rowohlt Verlag, 2000.
Auster, Paul. "I Want to Tell You a Story." *The Observer*, November 5, 2006, http://www.guardian.co.uk/books/2006/nov/05/fiction.paulauster

Manuscripts and papers

Auster, Paul. The Paul Auster Papers 1963–1995. The Paul Auster Archive. The Henry W. and Albert A. Berg Collection of English and American Literature, The New York Public Library.
—The Paul Auster Papers 1999–2005. The Paul Auster Archive. The Henry W. and Albert A. Berg Collection of English and American Literature, The New York Public Library.

Novels

Auster, Paul. *City of Glass*. New York: Penguin Books, 1987.
—*The New York Trilogy*. New York: Penguin Books, 1990. (Incorporates the previously published novels *City of Glass*, *Ghosts* (1986) and *The Locked Room* (1986).
—*Moon Palace*. New York: Penguin Books, 1990.
—*The Music of Chance*. London: Faber and Faber, 1990.

—*Mr. Vertigo.* London: Faber and Faber, 1994.
—*Timbuktu.* London: Faber and Faber, 1999.
—*The Book of Illusions.* New York: Henry Holt and Company, 2002.
—*Oracle Night.* New York: Henry Holt and Company, 2003.
—*In the Country of Last Things.* New York: Penguin Books, 2004.
—*Leviathan.* London: Faber and Faber, 2004.
—*The Brooklyn Follies.* New York: Henry Holt and Company, 2006.
—*Travels in the Scriptorium,* New York: Henry Holt and Company, 2007.
—*Man in the Dark.* New York: Henry Holt and Company, 2008.
—*Invisible.* London: Faber and Faber, 2009.
—*Sunset Park.* New York: Henry Holt and Company, 2010.
Benjamin, Paul. *Squeeze Play.* London: Faber and Faber, 1992. (Written by Auster under pseudonym.)

Poetry

Auster, Paul. *Disappearances: Selected Poems.* Woodstock, NY: Overlook Press, 1988.
—*Collected Poems.* Woodstock and New York: Overlook Press, 2004. (Contains *White Spaces.*)

Prose poetry

Auster, Paul. *White Spaces.* Barrytown, NY: Station Hill, 1980.

Screenplays

Auster, Paul. *The Music of Chance.* London: Faber and Faber, 1991.
—*Smoke & Blue in the Face: Two Films.* New York: Miramax Books/Hyperion, 1995. (Includes "Auggie Wren's Christmas Story.")
—*Lulu on the Bridge: A Film by Paul Auster.* New York: Henry Holt and Company, 1998.
—*The Inner Life of Martin Frost.* London: Faber and Faber, 2007.

Translations by Paul Auster

Clastres, Pierre. *Chronicle of the Guayaki Indians.* New York: Zone Books, 1998.
Mallarmé, Stéphane. *A Tomb for Anatole.* San Francisco: North Point Press, 1983.
Sartre, Jean-Paul. *Life/Situations: Essays Written and Spoken.* New York: Pantheon, 1977 (with Lydia Davis).
Sartre, Jean-Paul and Michel Contat. "Sartre at Seventy: An Interview." *The New York Review of Books* August 7 (1975). http://www.nybooks.com/articles/archives/1975/aug/07/sartre-at-seventy-an-interview) (together with Lydia Davis).

Secondary sources

Books and chapters

Aczel, Richard, Márton Fernezelyi, Robert Koch and Zoltán Szegedy-Maszák. "Reflections on a Table." In *Making Things Public: Atmospheres of Democracy*. Edited by Bruno Latour and Peter Weibel. Germany: Center for Art and Media Karslruhe and Cambridge: Massachusetts Institute of Technology, 2005.

Adler, Michael H. *The Writing Machine: A History of the Typewriter*. London: George Allen & Unwin Ltd., 1973.

Allen, Woody. *Four Films of Woody Allen: Annie Hall, Interiors, Manhattan, Stardust Memories*. London: Faber and Faber, 2003.

Bakhtin, Mikhail Mikhaĭlovich. *Speech Genres and Other Late Essays*. Translated by Vern W. McGee, edited by Michael Holquist and Caryl Emerson. Austin: University of Texas Press, 1986.

Bangs, John K. *The Enchanted Typewriter*. New York: Harper & Brothers, 1899. Available from Project Gutenberg, http://www.gutenberg.org/ebooks/3162

Banks, Michelle. "The Connection Exists: Hermeneutics and Authority in Paul Auster's Fictional Worlds." In *The Invention of Illusions: International Perspectives on Paul Auster*, edited by Stefania Ciocia and Jesús Ángel González, 149–71. Newcastle upon Tyne: Cambridge Scholars Publishing, 2011.

Barone, Dennis, ed. *Beyond the Red Notebook: Essays on Paul Auster*. Philadelphia: University of Pennsylvania Press, 1995.

Barthes, Roland. *The Pleasure of the Text*. Translated by Richard Miller. London: Jonathan Cape, 1976.

—*Image, Music, Text*. Translated by Stephen Heath. New York: Hill and Wang, 1977.

Baudrillard, Jean. *The System of Objects*. Translated by James Benedict. New York: Verso, 2006.

—"Please Follow Me." In *The Jean Baudrillard Reader*. Edited by Steve Redhead. New York: Columbia University Press, 2008.

Bazin, André. *What is Cinema? Volume 1*. Essays selected and translated by Hugh Gray, foreword by Jean Renoir, new foreword by Dudley Andrew. Berkeley and Los Angeles, and London: University of California Press, 2004.

Beckett, Samuel. *Murphy*. New York: Grove Press, 1994.

Bergson, Henri. *Creative Evolution*. Translated by Arthur Mitchell. Introduced by Pete A. Y. Gunter. New York: Barnes and Noble Books, 2005. (Originally published in French as *L'Évolution créatrice* in 1907; first published in English in 1911.)

Bernstein, Stephen. "Auster's Sublime Closure: The Locked Room." In *Beyond the Red Notebook: Essays on Paul Auster*, edited by Dennis Barone, 88–106. Philadelphia: University of Pennsylvania Press, 1995.

— "The Question is the Story Itself: Postmodernism and Intertextuality in Auster's 'New York Trilogy.'" In *Detecting Texts: The Metaphysical Detective Story from Poe to Postmodernism*, edited by Patricia Merivale and Susan Elizabeth Sweeney, 134–53. Pennsylvania: University of Pennsylvania Press, 1999.

Birkerts, Sven. *The Gutenberg Elegies: The Fate of Reading in an Electronic Age*. New York: Faber and Faber, 2006.

Blakemore, Colin and Shelia Jenett, eds. *The Oxford Companion to the Body*. Oxford and New York: Oxford University Press, 2001.

Borges, Jorge Luis. "The Garden of Forking Paths." In *Labyrinths*, edited by Donald A. Yates and James E. Irby, with an invitation by William Gibson and introduction by James E. Irby, 19–29. New York: A New Directions Book, 2007. First published in English translation by Donald A. Yates as "The Garden of Forking Paths." *Michigan Alumnus Quarterly Review* (Spring, 1958).

Brandt, Allan M. *The Cigarette Century: The Rise, Fall and Deadly Persistence of the Product that Defined America*. New York: Basic Books, 2007.

Brown, Mark. *Paul Auster*. Manchester and New York: Manchester University Press, 2007.

Burns, Eric. *The Smoke of the Gods: A Social History of Tobacco*. Philadelphia: Temple University Press, 2006.

Calle, Sophie. *Suite vénitienne*/Jean Baudrillard. *Please Follow Me*. Translated by Dany Barash and Danny Hatfield. Seattle: Bay Press, 1988.

—*Exquisite Pain*. London: Thames and Hudson, 2004.

—*Sophie Calle: M'as-tu vue*. Munich, Berlin, London, New York: Prestel Publishing, 2004.

Candlin, Fiona and Raiford Guins, eds. *The Object Reader*. London and New York: Routledge, 2009.

Chénetier, Marc. *Paul Auster as "the Wizard of Odds": Moon Palace*. Paris: Didier Érudition, 1996.

Ciocia, Stefania and Jesús Ángel González, eds. *The Invention of Illusions: International Perspectives on Paul Auster*. Newcastle upon Tyne: Cambridge Scholars Publishing, 2011.

Conrad, Joseph. "The Secret Sharer." First published in *Harper's Magazine* (August; September, 1910). Later published as part of the short-story collection *Twixt Land and Sea*. London: J. M. Dent and Sons, 1912. Available from Project Gutenberg, www.gutenberg.org/ebooks/220

Contat, Michel, ed. *L'auteur et le manuscrit (Perspectives critiques)*. Paris: Presses Universitaires de France, 1991.

Corbett, William. *New York Literary Lights: William Corbett*. St. Paul, MN: Graywolf Press, 1998.

Corti, Egon C. *A History of Smoking*. London: George Harrap, 1931.

de Landa, Manuel. *A New Philosophy of Society: Assemblage Theory and Social Complexity*. London and New York: Continuum, 2007.

Deleuze, Gilles and Félix Guattari. *Kafka: Towards a Minor Literature*. Translated by Dana Polan. Minneapolis and London: University of Minnesota Press, 2003.

—*A Thousand Plateaus: Capitalism and Schizophrenia*. Translated by Brian Massumi. London: Continuum International Publishing Group, 2004.

Dvorak, August. *Typewriting Behavior: Psychology Applied to Teaching and Learning Typewriting*. New York: American Book Company, 1936.

Eco, Umberto. *Semiotics and the Philosophy of Language*. Bloomington, IN: Indiana University Press, 1986.

—*The Name of the Rose: Including the Author's Postscript*. Translated by William Weaver. New York: Harvest Books, 1994.

Farías, Ignacio and Thomas Bender, eds. *Urban Assemblages: How Actor-Network Theory Changes Urban Studies*. London: Routledge, 2010.

Foucault, Michel. *The Archaeology of Knowledge & The Discourse on Language*. New York: Vintage, 1982.

Freud, Sigmund. "The Uncanny." In *The Uncanny*. Translated by David McLintock, and introduced by Hugh Haughton. New York: Penguin Books, 2003. Originally published as "Das Unheimliche." *Imago* 5 (5/6) (1919): 297–324.

Gilman, Sander L. and Zhou Xun, eds. *Smoke: A Global History of Smoking*. London: Reaktion Books, 2004.

Grosz, Elizabeth. "The Thing." In *The Object Reader*, edited by Fiona Candlin and Raiford Guins, 124–38. London and New York: Routledge, 2009.

Hamilton, Ian. *In Search of J. D. Salinger*. London: William Heinemann Ltd, 1988.

Harris, Jan. "Cinema and Its Doubles: Kittler v. Deleuze." In *Cinema and Technology: Cultures, Theories, Practices*, edited by Bruce Bennett, Marc Furstenau and Adrian Mackenzie, 88–104. Basingstoke: Palgrave Macmillan, 2008.

Heidegger, Martin. "Martin Heidegger on the Hand and the Typewriter (1942–43)." In Friedrich A. Kittler ("Typewriter"), *Gramophone, Film, Typewriter*. Translated and introduced by Geoffrey Winthrop-Young and Michael Wutz, 198–200. Stanford: Stanford University Press, 1999.

—*Being and Time*. Translated by John Macquarrie and Edward Robinson. New York: Harper Perennial Modern Classics, 2008.

—"The Thing." In *The Object Reader*. Edited by Fiona Candlin and Raiford Guins, 113–23. London and New York: Routledge, 2009.

Heinze, Rüdiger. *Ethics of Literary Forms in Contemporary American Literature*. Münster: LIT Verlag, 2005.

Herzogenrath, Bernd. *An Art of Desire. Reading Paul Auster*. Amsterdam: Rodopi, 1999.

Hoffmann, E. T. A. "The Sand-Man." Translated by J. Y. Bealby. New York: Charles Scribner's Sons, 1885. Available as part of Hoffmann's *Weird Tales. Vol. I* from Project Gutenberg, http://www.gutenberg.org/ebooks/31377

Holquist, Michael. "Introduction." In Mikhail Mikhaïlovich Bakhtin, *Speech Genres and Other Late Essays*. Translated by Vern W. McGee, edited by Michael Holquist, Caryl Emerson, ix–xxiii. Austin: University of Texas Press, 1986.

Holzapfel, Anne M. *"The New York Trilogy": Whodunit?: Tracking the Structure of Paul Auster's Anti-Detective Novels*. Frankfurt am Main: Peter Lang, 1996.

Hutchisson, James M., ed. *Conversations with Paul Auster*. Jackson: University Press of Mississippi, 2013.

Jentsch, Ernst. "On the Psychology of the Uncanny," translated by Roy Sellars. In *Uncanny Modernity: Cultural Theories, Modern Anxieties*, 216–28. Edited by Jo Collins and John Jervis. Basingstoke: Palgrave Macmillan, 2008. Originally published as "Zur Psychologie des Unheimlichen." *Psychiatrisch-Neurologische Wochenschrift* 8.22 (25 August 1906): 195–8 and 8.23 (1 September 1906): 203–5.

Kiernan, V. G. *Tobacco: A History*. London: Hutchinson Radius, 1991.

Kittler, Friedrich A. "Romanticism—Psychoanalysis—Film: A History of the Double." In Friedrich A. Kittler, *Literature. Media. Information Systems: Essays (Critical Voices in Art, Theory, and Culture)*, edited and introduced by John Johnston, 85–100. London: Routledge, 1997.

—*Gramophone, Film, Typewriter*. Translated and introduced by Geoffrey Winthrop-Young and Michael Wutz. Stanford: Stanford University Press, 1999.

—*Optical Media*. Cambridge: Polity Press, 2009.

Klein, Richard. *Cigarettes Are Sublime*. London: Picador, 1995.

Krementz, Jill. *The Writer's Desk*. New York: Random House, 1996.

Kress, Gunther. *Literacy in the New Media Age (Literacies)*. New York: Routledge, 2003.

Kress, Gunther and Theo van Leeuwen. *Reading Images: The Grammar of Visual Design.* New York: Routledge, 2006.

Krogh, David. *Smoking: The Artificial Passion.* New York and Oxford: W. H. Freeman and Company, 1997.

Latour, Bruno. *Reassembling the Social: An Introduction to Actor-Network-Theory.* Oxford: Oxford University Press, 2007.

Latour, Bruno and Peter Weibel, eds. *Making Things Public: Atmospheres of Democracy.* Germany: Center for Art and Media Karslruhe and Cambridge: Massachusetts Institute of Technology, 2005.

Leavey, James, ed. *The Forest Guide to Smoking in London.* London: Quiller Press, 1996.

Lind, Maria. "The Collaborative Turn." In *Taking the Matter into Common Hands: On Contemporary Art and Collaborative Practices.* Edited by Johanna Billing et al., 15–31. London: Black Dog Publishing, 2007.

Lopate, Phillip, ed. *Writing New York: A Literary Anthology.* New York: The Library of America/Penguin Putnam Inc., 2008.

Louÿs, Pierre. *Œuvres complètes: Contes.* Paris: Montaigne, 1930.

Lucy, Niall. *Postmodern Literary Theory: An Introduction.* Oxford: Blackwell, 1997.

Mallarmé, Stéphane. *Œuvres complètes.* Paris: Gallimard, 1945.

Marlan, Dawn. "Emblems of Emptiness: Smoking as a Way of Life in Jean Eustache's 'La Maman et la Putain.'" In *Smoke: A Global History of Smoking,* edited by Sander L. Gilman and Zhou Xun, 256–64. London: Reaktion Books, 2004.

Martin, Brendan. *Paul Auster's Postmodernity.* New York and London: Routledge, 2008.

McHale, Brian. *Postmodernist Fiction.* New York: Methuen, 1987.

Meurer, Ulrich. "Life Transmission: Paul Auster's Merging Worlds, Media and Authors." In *The Invention of Illusions: International Perspectives on Paul Auster,* edited by Stefania Ciocia and Jesús Ángel González, 173–92. Newcastle upon Tyne: Cambridge Scholars Publishing, 2011.

Moncada, Luisa and Scala Quin. *Reading on Location: Great Books Set in Top Travel Destinations.* London: New Holland, 2011.

Moretti, Franco. *Graphs, Maps, Trees.* London and New York: Verso, 2005.

Musil, Robert. *The Man without Qualities.* New York: Perigee Books, 1965.

Peacock, James. *Understanding Paul Auster.* Columbia: University of South Carolina Press, 2010.

Plato. *Symposium.* Translated, with introduction and notes by Alexander Nehamas and Paul Woodruff. Indianapolis: Hackett Publishing Company, 1989.

Rank, Otto. *Double: A Psychoanalytic Study.* Translated and edited by Harry Tucker Jr. Chapel Hill: The University of North Carolina Press, 1971. Originally published (the earliest version) as "Der Doppelgänger." *Imago* 3 (1914): 97–164.

Remarque, Erich Maria. *Im Westen nichts Neues.* Cologne: Kiepenheuer und Witsch, 1990.

Richter, Jean Paul Friedrich. *Flower, Fruit, and Thorn Pieces; or The Wedded Life, Death, and Marriage of Firmian Stanislaus Siebenkæs, Parish Advocate in the Burgh of Kuhschnappel (A Genuine Thorn Piece)* [Commonly known as *Siebenkäs*]. Translated from German by Alexander Ewing. London: George Bell and Sons, 1897. Available from Open Library, https://openlibrary.org/books/OL14008204M/ Flower_fruit_and_thorn_pieces_or

Rodowick, D. N. *Gilles Deleuze's Time Machine.* Durham and London: Duke University Press, 1997.

Ronell, Avital. *Dictations: On Haunted Writing.* Lincoln: University of Nebraska Press, 1989.

Saltzman, Arthur M. "Post Hoc Harmonies: Paul Auster's *Leviathan.*" In *This Mad Instead: Governing Metaphors in Contemporary American Fiction*, 63–73. South Carolina: University of South Carolina Press, 2000.

Sante, Luc. *No Smoking.* New York: Assouline, 2004.

—*Kill All Your Darlings: Pieces, 1990–2005.* Introduced by Greil Marcus. Portland: Yeti, 2007. (Includes the essay "Our Friend the Cigarette.")

Sarmiento, Faustino Domingo. *Viajes por Europa, Africa y Norte América—1845/1847.* Buenos Aires: Stockcero, 2003. (First published in 1849.)

Sartre, Jean-Paul. *L'Être et le néant.* Paris: Gallimard, 1943.

—*Being And Nothingness: An Essay in Phenomenological Ontology.* Translated by Hazel Barnes. New York: Citadel, 2001. (First published in English in 1956.)

Schivelbusch, Wolfgang. "Tobacco: The Dry Inebriant." In *Tastes of Paradise: A Social History of Spices, Stimulants and Intoxicants*, 96–146. New York: Vintage Books, 1993.

Schoell-Glass, Charlotte. "Fictions of the Art World: Art, Art History and the Art Historian in Literary Space." In *Writing and Seeing: Essays on Word and Image*, edited by Rui Carvalho Homem and Maria de Fátima Lambert, 107–18. Amsterdam: Rodopi, 2006.

Shiloh, Ilana. *Paul Auster and Postmodern Quest: On the Road to Nowhere.* New York: Peter Lang, 2002.

Slethaug, Gordon E. *The Play of the Double in Postmodern American Fictions.* Carbondale and Edwardsville: Southern Illinois University Press, 1993.

Sontag, Susan. "A Note on Novels and Films." In *Against Interpretation*, 242–8. New York: Picador, 2001.

Sorapure, Madeleine. "The Detective and the Author: 'City of Glass.'" In *Beyond the Red Notebook: Essays on Paul Auster*, edited by Dennis Barone, 71–87. Philadelphia: University of Pennsylvania Press, 1995.

Springer, Carsten (Carl). *A Paul Auster Sourcebook.* Frankfurt am Main: Peter Lang, 2001.

—*Crises: The Works of Paul Auster.* Frankfurt am Main: Peter Lang, 2001.

Šuvajevs, Igors. "Eko vārds." In Eko, Umberto, *Rozes vārds*, 683–94. Translated by Dace Meiere. Riga: J. Rozes apgāds, 1998.

Svevo, Italo. *La coscienza di Zeno.* Milan: Arnoldo Mondadori, 1988.

—*Zeno's Conscience: A Novel.* Translated by William Weaver. New York: Vintage International, 2003.

Tempel, Benno. "Symbol and Image: Smoking in Art since the Seventeenth Century." In *Smoke: A Global History of Smoking*, edited by Sander L. Gilman and Zhou Xun, 206–17. London: Reaktion Books, 2004.

Tronnes, Mike, ed. *Literary Las Vegas: The Best Writing about America's Most Fabulous City.* New York: Henry Holt and Company, 1995.

Tyson, Lois. *Critical Theory Today: A User-Friendly Guide.* New York and London: Routledge, 2006.

Varvogli, Aliki. *The World That Is the Book.* Liverpool: Liverpool University Press, 2001.

Walton, James, ed. *The Faber Book of Smoking.* London: Faber and Faber, 2000.

Webber, Andrew J. *The Doppelgänger: Double Visions in German Literature.* Oxford: Clarendon Press and New York: Oxford University Press, 1996.

Wershler-Henry, Darren. *The Iron Whim: A Fragmented History of Typewriting.* Ithaca, NY: Cornell University Press, 2007.

Whitehead, Colson. *The Colossus of New York: A City in Thirteen Parts*. New York: Anchor Books, 2003.

Wills, David. *Prosthesis*. Stanford, CA: Stanford University Press, 1995.

Journal articles

Alford, Steven E. "Mirrors of Madness: Paul Auster's 'The New York Trilogy.'" *Critique: Studies in Contemporary Fiction* 37.1 (1995): 17–33.

—"Spaced-Out: Signification and Space in Paul Auster's 'The New York Trilogy.'" *Contemporary Literature* 36.4 (1995): 613–32.

Asselin, Olivier and Johanne Lamoureux. "Autofictions, or Elective Identities." *Parachute* 105 (2002): 11–18.

Azevedo, Carlos. "A Portrait of the Indian Woman as Ghost Dancer: Mother Sioux in Paul Auster's 'Mr. Vertigo.'" *Estudos/Studien/Studies* 1 (2001): 117–26.

Baxter, Charles. "The Bureau of Missing Persons: Notes on Paul Auster's Fiction." *The Review of Contemporary Fiction* 14.1 (1994): 40–3.

Bewes, Timothy. "Against the Ontology of the Present: Paul Auster's Cinematographic Fictions." *Twentieth Century Literature* 53.3 (2007): 273–97.

Birkerts, Sven. "Reality, Fiction and 'In the Country of Last Things.'" *The Review of Contemporary Fiction* 14.1 (1994): 66–9.

Briggs, Robert. "Wrong Numbers: The Endless Fiction of Auster and Deleuze and Guattari and …" *Critique: Studies in Contemporary Fiction* 44.2 (2003): 213–24.

Carson, Benjamin D. "Towards a Postmodern Political Art: Deleuze, Guattari, and the Anti-Culture Book." *Rhizomes: Cultural Studies in Emerging Knowledge* 07 (Fall 2003), http://www.rhizomes.net/issue7/carson.htm

Chandler, Daniel. "The Phenomenology of Writing by Hand." *Intelligent Tutoring Media* 3. 2/3 (May/August 1992): 65–74.

Fredman, Stephen. "'How to Get Out of the Room that is the Book?' Paul Auster and the Consequences of Confinement." *Postmodern Culture: An Electronic Journal of Interdisciplinary Criticism* 6.3 (May 1996), http://muse.jhu.edu/journals/postmodern_culture/v006/6.3fredman.html

Golden, Cameron. "From Punishment to Possibility: Re-Imagining Hitchcockian Paradigms in 'The New York Trilogy.'" *Mosaic: A Journal for the Interdisciplinary Study of Literature* 37.3 (2004): 93–108.

González, Jesús Á. "Words Versus Images: Paul Auster's Films from 'Smoke' to 'The Book of Illusions.'" *Literature/Film Quarterly* 37.1 (2009): 28–48.

Griffin, Jeanine. "Sophie Calle and Paul Auster: Watching the Detectives." *Creative Camera* 354 (Oct/Nov 1998): 16–19.

Kalaga, Wojciech. "Face/Facade: The Visual and the Ethical." *Urbanistika ir Architektūra: Town Planning and Architecture* 34:3 (2010): 120–27.

Khimasia, Anna. "Authorial Turns: Sophie Calle, Paul Auster and the Quest for Identity." *Image [&] Narrative* 19 (2007), http://www.imageandnarrative.be/inarchive/autofiction/khimasia.htm

Latour, Bruno. "On Actor-Network Theory: A Few Clarifications plus More than a Few Complications," *Soziale Welt* 47.4 (1996): 369–81. Available also from http://www.bruno-latour.fr/sites/default/files/P-67%20ACTOR-NETWORK.pdf

Lavender, William. "The Novel of Critical Engagement: Paul Auster's 'City of Glass.'" *Contemporary Literature* 34.2 (1993): 219–39.

Lavin, Maud. "Imitation of Life" (review of "Double Game"), *Art in America* 88.7 (July 2000): 33–4.

Lewis, Barry. "The Strange Case of Paul Auster." *The Review of Contemporary Fiction* 14.1 (1994): 53–61.

Little, William G. "Nothing to Go On: Paul Auster's 'City of Glass.'" *Contemporary Literature* 38.1 (1997): 133–63.

McHale, Brian. "Poetry as Prosthesis." *Poetics Today* 21.1 (Spring 2000): 1–32.

Morson, Gary Saul. "The Baxtin Industry." *The Slavic and East European Journal* 30.1 (Spring 1986): 81–90.

Nealon, Jeffrey T. "Work of the Detective, Work of the Writer: Paul Auster's 'City of Glass.'" *Modern Fiction Studies* 42.1 (1996): 91–110.

Orr, Stanley. "Postmodernism, Noir, and the Usual Suspects." *Literature/Film Quarterly* 27.1 (1999): 65–73.

Peacock, James. "Carrying the Burden of Representation: Paul Auster's 'The Book of Illusions.'" *Journal of American Studies* 40.1 (April 2006): 53–69.

Rheindorf, Markus. "Processes of Embodiment and Spatialization in the Writings of Paul Auster." *Reconstruction* 2.3 (2002), http://reconstruction.eserver.org/023/rheindorf. htm

Rowen, Norma. "The Detective in Search of the Lost Tongue of Adam: Paul Auster's 'City of Glass.'" *Critique: Studies in Contemporary Fiction* 32.4 (Summer 1991): 224–34.

Rubenstein, Roberta. "Doubling, Intertextuality, and the Postmodern Uncanny: Paul Auster's 'New York Trilogy.'" *Lit: Literature Interpretation Theory* 9.3 (1998): 245–62.

Russell, Alison. "Deconstructing 'The New York Trilogy': Paul Auster's Anti-Detective Fiction." *Critique: Studies in Contemporary Fiction* 31.2 (Winter 1990): 71–84.

Titford, John S. "Object-Subject Relationships in German Expressionist Cinema." *Cinema Journal* 13.1 (Autumn 1973): 17–24.

Tysh, Chris. "From One Mirror to Another: The Rhetoric of Disaffiliation in 'City of Glass.'" *The Review of Contemporary Fiction* 14.1 (1994): 46–72.

White, Curtis. "The Auster Instance: A Ficto-Biography." *The Review of Contemporary Fiction* 14.1 (1994): 26–9.

Zilcosky, John. "The Revenge of the Author: Paul Auster's Challenge to Theory." *Critique: Studies in Contemporary Fiction* 39.3 (1998): 195–206.

Theses and dissertations

Al Umari, Kifah (Moh'd Khair). "Intertextuality, Language, and Rationality in the Detective Fiction of Edgar Allan Poe and Paul Auster." PhD diss., University of Texas at Arlington, 2006.

Bartlett, Lexey Anne. "The Double Redux: Multiplying Identity in Postmodern Fiction." PhD diss., University of Texas at Arlington, 2005.

Nikolic, Dragana. "Paul Auster's Postmodernist Fiction: Deconstructing Aristotle's 'Poetics.'" MA diss., The Queen Mary and Westfield College, University of London, 1998, available online at http://www.bluecricket.com/auster/articles/aristotle.html

Plékan, Alexis. "Confinement in Paul Auster's Moon Palace and The New York Trilogy." MA diss., University of Caen Lower Normandy, 2001.

Rheindorf, Markus. "'Where Everything is Connected to Everything Else': Interior and Exterior Landscape in the Poetry, Essays, and fiction of Paul Auster." MA diss., University of Vienna, 2001.

Traisnel, Antoine. "Storytelling in Paul Auster's Movies". BA diss., Université Charles de Gaulle – Lille 3, 2002, http://angellier.biblio.univ-lille3.fr/etudes_recherches/memoire_antoine_traisnel.html

Varner, Gary Matthew. "Paul Auster's Rhizomatic Fictions." MA diss., Mississippi State University, 2010.

Interviews

Allen, Austin. "When Literary Games Get Personal." *Big Think*, November 5, 2009, http://bigthink.com/ideas/17290

Chénetier, Marc. "Around Moon Palace. A Conversation with Paul Auster." *Revue d'Études Anglophones* 1 (1996): 5-35.

Chrisafis, Angelique. "He Loves Me Not" (an interview with Sophie Calle). *The Guardian*, June 16, 2007, http://www.guardian.co.uk/world/2007/jun/16/artnews.art

Contat, Michel. "The Manuscript in the Book: A Conversation." *Yale French Studies* 89, Drafts (1996): 160-87. Translated by Alyson Waters.

Curiol, Céline. "The Making of 'The Inner Life of Martin Frost.'" In Paul Auster, *The Inner Life of Martin Frost*. London: Faber and Faber, 2007.

de Cortanze, Gérard. "Le monde est dans ma tête, mon corps est dans le monde." *Magazine Littéraire* 338 (Décembre 1995): 18-25. Translated by Carl-Carsten Springer as "The World Is in My Head; My Body Is in the World," http://www.stuartpilkington.co.uk/paulauster/gerarddecortanze.htm

Dunford, George. "An Interview with Paul Auster." *Cordite Poetry Review*, 2 August 2008, http://cordite.org.au/interviews/paul-auster

Dziemianowicz, Joe. "Lights, Camera, Cigars!" *Cigar Aficionado* (Summer 1995), http://www.cigaraficionado.com/Cigar/CA_Archives/CA_Show_Article/0,2322,719,00.html

Esquivada, Gabriel. "Interview: Paul Auster Writer." *Cuba now.net*, Cuban Art and Culture (2000), http://www.cubanow.net/articles/interview-paul-auster-writer

Frazer, Ian. "Typewriter Man." (Interview with Martin Tytell) *Atlantic Monthly* 280:5 November (1997): 81-92.

González, Jesús Ángel. "Smoke and Illusions: An Interview with Paul Auster." *Revista de Estudios Norteamericanos* 12 (2007): 57-67, http://www.institucional.us.es/revistas/revistas/estudios/pdf/12/09%20Gonzalez%20definitivo.pdf

—"'Happy Accidents': An Interview with Paul Auster." *Literature/Film Quarterly* 37.1 (2009): 18-27, http://portaleducativo.educantabria.es/binary/877/LFQHappy%20Accidents.pdf

Gooderham, Wayne. "Paul Auster Interview." *Time Out London* [undated], http://www.timeout.com/london/books/paul-auster-interview

Graieb, Carlos. "Auster Creates His Universe in a Brooklyn Apartment"/"Auster cria seu universo em sobrado do Brooklyn," trans. Carl-Carsten Springer and Ricardo

Miranda. Paul Auster: The Definitive Website, http://www.stuartpilkington.co.uk/
paulauster/carlosgraieb.htm

Insdorf, Annette. "The Making of 'Smoke.'" In Paul Auster, *Smoke & Blue in the Face: Two
Films*, 3–16. New York: Miramax Books/Hyperion, 1995.

Irwin, Mark. "Memory's Escape: Inventing the Music of Chance—A Conversation
with Paul Auster." *Denver Quarterly* 28:3 (Winter 1994): 111–22. Republished in
Conversations with Paul Auster, ed. James M. Hutchisson (Jackson: University Press of
Mississippi, 2013).

Lethem, Jonathan. "Jonathan Lethem [Writer] Talks with Paul Auster
[Writer]." *The Believer* (February 2005), http://www.believermag.com/
issues/200502/?read=interview_auster

Linderman, Juliet. "A Connoisseur of Clouds, a Meteorologist of Whims: The Rumpus
Interview with Paul Auster." *The Rumpus*, November 16, 2009, http://therumpus.
net/2009/11/a-connoisseur-of-clouds-a-meteorologist-of-whims-the-rumpus-
interview-with-paul-auster/

Macel, Christine. "Biographical Interview with Sophie Calle." In Sophie Calle, *Sophie
Calle: Did You See Me?* Munich, Berlin, London, New York: Prestel Publishing, 2004.

Mallia, Joseph. "Paul Auster Interview." *BOMB* 23 (1998): 24–7, http://www.bombsite.
com/issues/23/articles/1062

McCaffery, Larry and Sinda Gregory. "An Interview with Paul Auster." *Mississippi Review*
20.1–2 (1991): 49–62.

—"An Interview with Paul Auster." *Contemporary Literature* 33.1 (1992): 1–23.

Owens, Jill. "Author Interviews: The Book of Paul Auster." *Powell's Books*,
http://www.powells.com/authors/auster.html

Patrick, Bethanne. "Interview with Paul Auster." *Goodreads*, November, 2010,
http://www.goodreads.com/interviews/show/556.Paul_Auster

Peachment, Chris. "Give the Man a Cigar." *The Independent*, March 7, 1996,
http://www.independent.co.uk/arts-entertainment/give-the-man-a-cigar-1340694.html

Prime, Rebecca. "The Making of 'Lulu on the Bridge': An Interview with Paul Auster." In
Paul Auster, *Lulu on the Bridge*, 141–68. New York: Henry Holt and Company, 1998.

Reich, Allon. "Interview with Paul Auster: Brooklyn 1988." *Keepsake* 9. London: The
Menard Press, 1988.

Wood, Michael. "Paul Auster, The Art of Fiction No 178." *The Paris Review*,
167 (2003): 58–89. http://www.theparisreview.org/interviews/121/
the-art-of-fiction-no-178-paul-auster

Magazine articles

Carr, Nicholas. "Is Google Making Us Stupid?" *Atlantic Monthly* July/
August (2008), http://www.theatlantic.com/magazine/archive/2008/07/
is-google-making-us-stupid/6868/

Chanko, Kenneth M. "*Smoke* Gets in Their Eyes." *Entertainment Weekly*, June 30, 1995,
http://www.ew.com/ew/article/0,,297840,00.html

Corliss, Richard. "That Old Feeling: The Great American Smoke," *Time*, Saturday,
November 22, 2003, http://www.time.com/time/arts/article/0,8599,548824,00.html

Hall, Donald. "No Smoking." *Playboy*, November 25 (2012), http://www.playboy.com/
playground/view/no-smoking

Merkin, Daphne. "I Think Therefore I'm Art." *T: The New York Times Style Magazine*, October 19, 2008 (The New York Edition), http://www.nytimes.com/2008/10/19/style/tmagazine/19calle.html

Shenk, Joshua Wolf. "The Things We Carry: Seeking Appraisal at the Antiques Roadshow." *Harper's Magazine* (June 2001): 46–56. Also available online from http://www.shenk.net/things.htm

Springer, Carsten (Carl). "Paul Auster and the Crisis of the Individual." *The Definite Website*. http://www.stuartpilkington.co.uk/paulauster/carlcarstenspringer1.htm

Newspaper publications

Jones, Jonathan. "It's About Knowing You'll Die." *The Guardian*, Monday 14 May 2007, http://www.guardian.co.uk/artanddesign/2007/may/14/art

Kurutz, Steven. "Literary New York." *The New York Times*, May 14, 2006, http://travel2.nytimes.com/2006/05/14/travel/14going.html

Messenger, Robert. "Typing Writers: An Endangered Species (But Not Yet Extinct)." *The Canberra Times*, Panorama, February 14, 2009.

Website and blog entries

Avnskog, Sverre. "Friedrich Nietzsche and His Typewriter—A Malling-Hansen Writing Ball," The International Rasmus Malling-Hansen Society, February 2, 2008, http://www.malling-hansen.org/friedrich-nietzsche-and-his-typewriter-a-malling-hansen-writing-ball.html

Borio, Gene. "The Seventeenth Century—'The Great Age of the Pipe'," in *Tobacco History Timeline*, 1993–2003. Tobacco.org, http://www.tobacco.org/resources/history/Tobacco_History17.html

Breebart, Rino. "Typewriter Love." *Typewriter Tributes*, The Classic Typewriter Page, http://site.xavier.edu/polt/typewriters/breebaart.html

Fernandez, Rosamary. "Handwriting," The Chicago School of Media Theory: Theorizing Media since 2003, http://lucian.uchicago.edu/blogs/mediatheory/keywords/handwriting/

Gargett, Adrian. "Cruel Universe." *Spike Magazine* (online magazine/weblog), posted on November 1, 2002, http://www.spikemagazine.com/1102paulauster.php

Garner, Anne. "Paul Auster Papers in the Berg." The Henry W. and Albert A. Berg Collection of English and American Literature, March 31, 2011, http://www.nypl.org/blog/2011/03/31/paul-auster-papers-berg

Golay, Helene. "Books: The New York Trilogy, The Brooklyn Follies & Sunset Park," *Realcity: An Online Magazine* (online magazine/weblog), http://www.realcityonline.com/media-books-paul-auster/

González, Jesús Ángel. "My Second Slice: How I Interviewed Paul Auster," published on González's personal page on *Issuu* digital publishing platform, January 12, 2011, http://issuu.com/jagonzal/docs/how_i_interviewed_paul_auster

Holmes, Dan. "Paul Auster's Deconstruction of the Traditional Hard-Boiled Detective Narrative in 'The New York Trilogy'." *Crimeculture* (2006), http://www.crimeculture.com/Contents/Articles-Summer05/DanHolmes.html

Hopkins, Brandon. "Manuscript." The Chicago School of Media Theory: Theorizing Media since 2003, Winter 2003, http://lucian.uchicago.edu/blogs/mediatheory/keywords/manuscript/

Kincaid, Paul. "'Travels in the Scriptorium' by Paul Auster." Review of *Travels in the Scriptorium*, by Paul Auster. *Strange Horizons*, December 19, 2006, http://www.strangehorizons.com/reviews/2006/12/travels_in_the_.shtml

Polt, Richard. "Typology: A Phenomenology of Early Typewriters." The Classical Typewriter Page, http://site.xavier.edu/polt/typewriters/typology.html (Originally presented at the Back to the Things Themselves conference, Southern Illinois University at Carbondale, March 1996.)

Rice, Martin A. "Amor me Jubit Mechanoscribere (Love Bids me Type)." *Typewriter Tributes*, The Classic Typewriter Page, http://site.xavier.edu/polt/typewriters/rice.pdf

Schneewein, Bellis. "You Exist Only in the Trace of the Other … (*Fiktionen mit Fantômas*)." *Corpus: Internet Magazine für Tanz, Choreografie. Performance*, 11 November 2007, http://www.corpusweb.net/fiktionen-mit-fant-4.html

Shibata, Motoyuki. "On the Impossibility of Not Being a Ghost." *Ghosts Catalogue* (2003): 3–5, http://www.jonkessler.com/articles/shibata.htm

Dictionary and encyclopedia entries

American Heritage Dictionary of the English Language, 4th edn. Boston: Houghton Mifflin, 2000.

Copyright Permissions

Chapter 3: Doubles and Disappearances

Index

Printed in Great Britain
by Amazon